WALKING WITH BHAGAT SINGH SOON AFTER INDEPENDENCE

Oh, What a heart then ceased to throb!
(N.A. Nekrasov, *In Memory of Dobrolyubov*)

Walking With Bhagat Singh

Soon After Independence

Amar Kant Jttu

AAKAR

Walking With Bhagat Singh Soon After Independence
Amar Kant Jttu

First Published 2019
Reprinted 2020

ISBN 978-93-5002-618-2 (Hb)

Published by
AAKAR BOOKS
28 E Pocket IV, Mayur Vihar Phase I
Delhi 110 091 India
aakarbooks@gmail.com

Laser Typeset at
Arpit Printographers, Delhi

Printed at
Sapra Brothers, Noida

Dedicated
to the Revolutionaries
Fighting for the Establishment
of Scientific Socialism in the World.

————*————

Also
to the Memory
of
Our Noble 'Maaji' who was foundly and lovingly
called 'Bebe' and Who Till the Last Breath
of 96 Years of Her Precious Life
Showered Her Love and Affection
on Her Children and
Her Near and Dear Ones
and
My Father Who Died at the Young Age of 23 Years
(Almost at Bhagat Singh's Age)
Repeating "Please Take Care of My Son" on His Lips
and
My Grandfather Who Brought Me Up,
Educated and Settled Me in Life

Content

Glorious Deeds of Revolutionaries: The Salt of History

Except those who are devoid of a largeness of the heart, palpably insensitive to the grandeur of human character and disdain the slightest association with actions connected with militant revolutionary upsurge, every other genuine lover of an independent status of his country should proclaim to the world that theirs are the

Deeds which should not pass away,
And names that must not wither away.

It might be confidently said about them that "the human race owes something to these men of noble minds and brave hearts," and if their calumniators in the plane of non-violence have denied all recognition to them in the sphere of political history of our country, these despised martyrs "have contributed to the glorious virtues without which wealth and power tend to turn men into brutes. Amidst much that is sordid and mean, their examples stand like that of the Romans and Greeks of old who courted ruin in the service of the cause which they held dear. The deeds of such men are the salt of history and as long as man appreciates high aspiration and endeavour to realise it, their remembrance shall remain a precious heritage of our race".

[*The Great Indians* by R. Williams]

It is accepted by all fair-minded persons that the individual acts of the intrepid fighters have served as flashes of lightning in the pitch darkness of serfdom spread over a period of roughly ten centuries. The footprints that these martyrs have left on the sands of time and which are being studiously obliterated, would serve the future historians of India as material for portraying the picture, however incomplete, the sacrifices made by a band of young men unmindful of name, fame and earthly gains—consecrating their lives at the altar of the motherland.

[*The Roll of Honour* by Kali Charan Ghosh]

Bhagat Singh's Behest to the Revolutionaries

"They should make shanties in the slums and mud-huts in the villages, their new hearths and homes, teaching the poor children during the daytime and explaining, in the evening, to the workers and the peasants and their women what the State based on Scientific Socialism would be and how it would eradicate their poverty."

"The War Shall Continue"

Let us declare that the state of war does exist and shall exist so long as the Indian toiling masses and the natural resources are being exploited by a handful of parasites. They may be purely British capitalist or mixed British and Indian or even purely Indian. They may be carrying on their insidious exploitation through mixed or even on purely Indian bureaucratic apparatus. All these things make no difference. No matter, if your government tries and succeeds in winning over the leaders of the upper strata of Indian society through petty concessions and compromises and, thereby, cause a temporary demoralisation in the main body of the forces. No matter, if once again the vanguard of the Indian Movement, the Revolutionary Party, finds itself deserted in the thick of the war. No matter, if the leaders to whom personally, we are much indebted for the sympathy and feelings they expressed for us, but,nevertheless, we cannot overlook the fact that they did become so callous as to ignore and not to make a mention in the peace negotiations of even the homeless, friendless and penniless female workers who are alleged to belong to the vanguard and whom the leaders consider to be enemies of their utopian non-violent cult which has already become a thing of the past; the heroines who had ungrudgingly sacrificed or offered for sacrifice their sons, husbands, brothers and all that were nearest and dearest to them, including themselves, whom your government has declared to be outlaws. No matter, if your agents stoop so low as to fabricate baseless calumnies against their spotless characters to damage their and their Party's reputation. The war shall continue.

It may assume different shapes at different times. It may become now open, now hidden, now purely agitational, now a fierce life and death struggle. The choice, of course, whether bloody or comparatively peaceful, which way it should adopt, rests with you. Choose which ever you like. But that war shall be incessantly waged without taking into consideration the petty and the meaningless ethical ideologies. It shall be waged ever with new vigour, greater audacity and unflinching determination till a Socialist Republic is established and the present social order is completely replaced by a new social order, based on social prosperity and thus every sort of exploitation is put an end to and humanity is ushered into the era of genuine and permanent peace. In the very near future the final battle shall be fought and final settlement arrived at.

[An extract from a letter written to the Governor of Punjab by Bhagat Singh just a day before his execution. In the said letter, Bhagat Singh had stated that since the Special Tribunal had awarded him and his two colleagues, death sentences for waging war against King George of England and therefore they were war criminals. He requested the Governor not to execute them on the gallows but instead order his military to shoot them by a firing squad.]

—Bhagat Singh

Acknowledgements

Hundreds of books, articles, poems and songs have been authored on Bhagat Singh and many more would be penned. Every author of these publications had attempted to illuminate his valorous deeds and his scholarly and revolutionary writings in a fresh light. Here is one more entitled *Walking With Bhagat Singh Soon After Independence*. There is yet no end to it and many more will come in future. The best opus on him, however, is still awaited. In America, there have been historians such as Howard Zinn and Eduardo Galeano who have written history books such as *The People's History of the United States* and *Open Veins of Latin America* from the point of view of the oppressed and the exploited. India, it is hoped, would also have her Howard Zinn and Eduardo Galeano who will write in their history books on the struggles of the tribals (who were amongst the aboriginals of India) as well as highlighting the roles played by the Ghadrites and the revolutionaries spearheaded by Bhagat Singh and by the Indian National Army, the Quit India Movement, the Naval Ratings Rebellion in 1946 and which ultimately forced the British imperialists to quit India.

The distinguished intellectuals and authors who, through their books, have inspired me to write this book and to whom I feel grateful, are Suniti Kumar Ghosh, [His *India and Raj* and other works]; R.P. Dutt [His *India Today* and other works]; Mohinder Singh Pannu [His *Partners of British Rule—Liberators or Collaborators*]; Ashok Mitra [His *A Prattler's Tale, Calcutta Diary, The Hoodlum Years* and other works]. I may add that Ashok Mitra, a distinguished Marxist intellectual, who was the Finance Minister in the First Left Front Government in West Bengal, was my teacher, teaching us Economics

Theory as well as my guide with regard to a thesis paper during my postgraduation in 1951-52 at Lucknow University.

There are innumerable books on Bhagat Singh. I could lay my hand on only a few of them. These books have helped me in completing this work for which I am indebted to the authors of those books. Some of these distinguished authors are Shiv Varma, Manmath Nath Gupta, Hans Raj Rehbar, Jitendra Nath Sanyal, Satyam, Prof. Chaman Lal, Prof. Irfan Habib, Prof. K.C. Yadav, Kuldip Nayar, Omesh Saigal, A.G. Noorani, M.M. Juneja, Kama Maclean, V.N. Dutta, Chander Pal Singh and others.

Amongst the publications, I would proudly mention and to whose editors and writers I am indebted to, are *Frontier*, a weekly published from Kolkata, whose founder Editor was Samar Sen and the present Editor is Timir Basu, providing always an excellent analysis of most of the national and international developments affecting the common man. I would add the name of P.J. James of *Red Star* whose writings have influenced me. There are other journals and which have, in one way or the other, played a role in shaping my views and this book, some of which are being mentioned. These are *Analytical Monthly Review, Economic and Political Weekly, Mainstream, Proletarian Era, Red Star, Liberation, Mazdoor Ekta Lehar,* fortnightly, *New Age* weekly and *People's Democracy* weekly. Amongst the daily newspapers, I owe my gratitude to *The Tribune, The Indian Express, The Hindustan Times, The Times of India* and *The Hindu,* which have kept me regularly in touch with the developments in India and the rest of the world.

I express my gratitude to the members of the staff of R.H. Stafford Library, Central Park Place, Woodbury, Minnesota, USA; members of the staff of the Nehru Memorial Museum and Library, and National Archives, New Delhi for providing to me every assistance in collecting the information on Bhagat Singh and other revolutionaries, required by me.

At the R.H. Stafford Library, I was able to consult some of the books which it would have been difficult for me to obtain in India. Some of those books are listed here:

1. *Chavas: The Organisation of the Working Class* by Owen Jones
2. Quotes by Ellen Wilkinson
3. *The Transfer of Power Series of India* [TOPI], a few of the 12 volumes that related to the period from 1942 to 1950
4. The British Documents on the End of Empire Project [BDEEP] for the period 1945-51
5. *Britain's Declining Empire—The Road to Decolonisation 1918-1968* by Ronald Hyam
6. *Decolonisation and the British Empire, 1775-1997 by* D. George Boyce
7. *A Revolution is Not a Dinner Party: A Feast of Images of the Maoist Transformation of China* by Richard H. Solomon
8. *Mao's Revolution and the Chinese Political Culture* by Richard H. Solomon
9. *The China Factor in America's Foreign Relations* by Richard H. Solomon
10. *Power, Politics and the People: Studies in British Imperialism and Indian Nationalism* by Sabyasachi Bhattacharya
11. *The Roll of Honour: Anecdotes of Indian Martyrs* by Kali Charan Ghosh
12. *The Indian Ideology* by Perry Anderson
13. *A Quest For Gandhi* by Reginald Reynolds
14. *The Enemy* by Felix Greene
15. *As It Happened* by C.R. Attlee
16. *Viscount Halifax* by Alan Campbell Johnson

At the Nehru Memorial Museum and Library, New Delhi, I was able to go through and take notes of the press reports relating to the various revolutionary actions such as the Saunders' murder, Delhi Assembly Bomb Explosion, Sessions Court Trial, Lahore Conspiracy Case Trial including the statements of Bhagat Singh and other revolutionaries ranging from 1928 to 1931 from the micro-filmed copies of *The Tribune, The Hindustan Times, The Civil and Military Gazette* which otherwise would have been almost impossible to obtain elsewhere. Similarly at the National Archives, New Delhi,

I was able to see and take notes of important documents, relating to HSRA and the Lahore Conspiracy Case Trial.

I owe my profound gratitude to Dr. Shalley K. Gupta for sparing his precious time by helping me in revising, editing and proof-reading of the book. Comrade B. Srinivasa Rao deserves my thanks for giving useful suggestions on the subject-matter of the book.

I am grateful to my wife, Mrs. Sumitra Kant who looked after my health, medical aid and food like a mother. I have been diligently supported by her and my children—Neeraj, Shalley, Manu (himself a writer and a poet) and Suveen, and daughters-in-law Gita, Anvita, Shubha and grandchildren—Nikhil, Shivani, Nishant, Mahima, Malvika, Ishana, Irina and Suhani whose love, affection and presence have always been a source of strength motivating me in my day-to-day activities.

I am thankful to Rajveer Thakur, Rakesh Kumar and Komaljeet Kaur—who, pursuing their studies in the University, spared time for typing and thus getting the manuscript completed.

Last but not the least, I owe Mr. K.K. Saxena and the learned staff of his renowned publication venture, Aakar Books, my gratitude which I cannot express fully in words, for publishing this book, written by an author who had no previous book to his credit.

There used to be the Soviet Union of Lenin and Stalin when people in India were able to get books on Marxism-Leninism at prices as low as 8 annas (half a rupee) to Rs. 2 but that time has long since gone. Now, fortunately, Aakar Books run by Mr. K.K. Saxena have come in and books on Marxism-Leninism authored by American and British writers which in their countries were priced as high as $15 to $30, are made available through their efforts at rates as low as Rs. 200 to Rs. 400 in India. I express my gratitude to them and hope my sentiments for them will be shared by all book-lovers.

Prefaces

SHAHEED-E-AZAM BHAGAT SINGH

Shalley K. Gupta, PhD

Why is it that in every struggle of the youth in India, it is Shaheed-e-Azam Bhagat Singh who continues to inspire? If it was Che Guevera in America and France, it was Bhagat Singh in India. Surely, Bhagat Singh was not the only martyr who laid down his life at the altar of freedom. There were others, before and after him who were equally great and who had the noblest thoughts when they smilingly laid down their lives. Their sacrifice was no less great. But then what separates him from his other comrades? Does the answer lie in his philosophy and political ideology?

Today the very government, which praises him to the sky; erects monuments and statues in his memory—in short, does everything possible to divorce Bhagat Singh, the revolutionary, from his ideas and ideology; is the government which did not and would not blink an eyelid to murder the youth of a free India who are fighting for the ideals which were so dear to Bhagat Singh. Today all sorts of reactionaries, communalists and obscurants are wrongly and dishonestly trying to use for their own politics the name and fame of Bhagat Singh and his comrades like Chandra Shekhar Azad. Their views on religion, the nature of Indian society, Socialism, etc. have been distorted and simplified to suit their purposes. It has been a sinister and deliberate policy of our rulers and their collaborators to put him and his comrades on a high pedestal to be ritually honoured but not to be followed. But as Bhagat Singh once said, "You can kill individuals, but not the ideas. Great Empires crumbled, but the ideas survived". It becomes our duty to view Bhagat Singh in the correct perspective as one of the greatest freedom fighters, revolutionary,

Socialist and Marxist thinker of India. His statements in the courts, various pamphlets and leaflets, the manifestos of the Hindustan Socialist Republican Association (HSRA) and Naujawan Bharat Sabha, *The Philosphy of the Bomb, An Address to the Young Political Workers, Why I Am An Atheist*, his statements before the Sessions Court and the Lahore High Court Bench, his Prison Notebooks and other articles clearly project him as a great ideologue who was well-conversed with contemporary Marxist thought.

Very early in his political career, Bhagat Singh had formed a definite view about independence, Socialism, etc. which differed from the Congress leaders not only in the use of methods but the very concept of independence. Even in 1928, he feared a compromise between the Congress and British imperialism. "Along with the advent of the 20th century, the British bureaucracy had adopted quite a new policy towards India. They are drawing our bourgeoisie and petite bourgeoisie into their fold by adopting the policy of concessions. Their cause is being made common. The progressive investment of British capital in India will inevitably lead to that end. In the very near future we will find that this class and its great leaders (the Congress leadership) have thrown their lots with the foreign rulers. Some round table conference or any other such body will end in a compromise between the two. They will not help the masses any more", wrote Bhagat Singh. And again, "The Congress seeks to gain some power by getting the businessmen and capitalists to exercise pressure on England. But this way does not lie the salvation for the millions of workers and peasants of India ... the peasants have to liberate themselves not only from the foreign yoke but also from the yoke of landlords and capitalists. This is not the goal of the Congress. It cannot be said to be standing for complete revolution. Get some concessions for India's wealthy class through economic pressure on government, that is what the Congress wants".

On the other hand, the HSRA had a clear-cut programme of their actions and a clear understanding of the nature of the revolution. Bhagat Singh said, "The Revolutionaries believe that the deliverance of their country will come through revolution. The revolution, they are constantly working and hoping for, will not only express itself in the form of an armed conflict between the foreign government and its supporters and the people, it will also usher in a new social order. The revolution will ring the death knell of capitalism and class distinctions and privileges. It will bring joy and prosperity to the starving millions who are seething today under the terrible yoke of both foreign and Indian exploitation. It will bring the nation into its own. It will give birth to a new state, a new social order. Above all, it will establish the dictatorship of the proletariat and will forever banish social parasites from the seat of political power".

Bhagat Singh was often accused of being a terrorist. Gandhiji in particular attacked the HSRA for being a terrorist organisation in his article, *The Cult of the Bomb*. Their reply to this accusation was a counter article, *The Philosophy of the Bomb*. It says, "Terrorism is a phase, a necessary inevitable phase in the revolution. Terrorism is not the complete revolution and the revolution is not complete without terrorism. It shatters the spell of superiority of the ruling class and raises the status of the subject race in the eyes of the world, because it is the most convincing proof of a nation's hunger for freedom. Here in India, as in other countries in the past, terrorism will develop into the revolution and revolution into independence... social, political, economic". His interpretation of the concept of non-violence so dear to our Gandhians is worth noting:

> What generally goes by the name of non-violence, is in reality the theory of soul-force, used for achieving personal and national rights through self-suffering. When a revolutionary believes certain things to be right, he asks for them, pleads for them, argues for them, wills to attain them with all the soul force at his command. He stands the greatest amount of suffering for their sake; is always prepared to make the highest sacrifice for their attainment and also backs his efforts with all the physical force he is capable of. So he adds physical force to the soul force. You may coin what other word you like to describe his methods but you cannot call it violence, because that would constitute an outrage on the dictionary meaning of that word.

"Force when aggressively used is violence and therefore morally unjustified. But when it is used in furtherance of a legitimate cause, it has its moral justification. Elimination of force at all costs is utopian, and the new movement which has arisen in the country and of which we have given a warning is inspired by the ideals which guided Guru Gobind Singh and Shivaji; Kamal Pasha and Reza Khan; Washington and Garibaldi; Lafayette and Lenin.

There was a firm theoretical foundation and a deep political conviction in everything that the HSRA did. While alive, they were hounded and vilified by both British imperialists and their Indian collaborators. But they were undaunted in their mission. In court Bhagat Singh said:

> We are neither perpetrators of dastardly acts and therefore a disgrace to the country as the pseudo socialist Dewan Chaman Lal is reported to have described us; nor were we 'lunatics' as *The Tribune* would have it believed. We humbly claim to be no more than serious students of history and conditions of our country and human aspirations and we despise hypocrisy. Our practical protest was against the institution which since its birth has eminently displayed not only its worthlessness but its far-reaching power for mischief. The more we have pondered, the more deeply we have been convinced that it exists only to demonstrate to the world the Indian humiliation and its helplessness; and it symbolises the overriding domination of an irresponsible and autocratic rule.

Unlike earlier revolutionaries and his other contemporaries, Bhagat Singh was an atheist. In his article, *Why I Am An Atheist* written in prison a few days before his death sentence he said: "Belief in God softens the hardships, can even make them pleasant. In God, 'Man' can find very strong consolation and support. Without this, 'Man' has to depend on himself. To stand on one's own legs amid storms and hurricanes is not a child's play. At such testing moments, vanity, if any, evaporates and man cannot dare to defy the general beliefs. If he does, then we must conclude that he has got certain other strengths than mere vanity. When 'Man' tries to stand on his own legs and becomes a realist, the need for God, this artificial crutch, this imaginary saviour comes to an end. Anyone who stands for progress has to criticise, disbelieve and challenge every item of the old faith ... the first thing for him is to shatter the whole down and clear a space for the erection of a new philosophy ...criticism and independent thinking are the two indispensable qualities of a revolutionary".

It is often propagated by certain people that revolutionaries are murderers and they have no value for human life; that their actions cause a great harm to the country and its cause. But was it proper for Gandhiji in his fits of 'non-violence' to withdraw the Non-Co-operation Movement at its heat; a deed which caused incalculable loss to the freedom movement. Gandhiji and the Congress leadership had no compunctions to reach a compromise for their narrow political gains by signing the so-called Gandhi-Irwin Pact-virtually over the dead bodies of Bhagat Singh, Rajguru and Sukhdev. Gandhiji called for their early execution so that their death and the resulting demonstrations would not cause any hindrance to the Karachi Congress Session. A letter that Gandhiji wrote to the Viceroy is quite revealing. It says, "If the boys should be hanged, they had better be hanged before the Karachi Congress Session, not after it". And they were hanged on March 23, 1931. Gandhiji even refused to cooperate in the matter of raising a memorial to them. He wrote as follows to the Memorial Committee, Lahore:

> Your reasoning does not appeal to me. A memorial erected in honour of anybody would undoubtedly mean that the memorialists would copy the deeds of those in whose memory they erect a memorial. It is also an invitation to posterity to copy such deeds. I am, therefore, unable to identify myself in any way with the memorial.

While the whole of India mourned their death and huge demonstrations and processions were taken out against the hangings, the Karachi Congress Session had only this to say and that too very grudgingly and in a very formally worded tone:

> "This Congress, while disassociating itself from and disapproving of political violence in any shape or form, places on record its admiration of the bravery and sacrifice of the late Bhagat Singh and his comrades, Sukhdev and Rajguru; and mourns with families the loss of their lives." This resolution, drafted by Mahatma Gandhi, was moved by the outgoing Congress President, Pt. Jawaharlal Nehru while Sardar Vallabhbhai Patel, the newly-elected President, was presiding over the Session. There was not a word in the Congress resolution condemning the British rulers for their barbarous acts.

Within four months, the Karachi Congress resolution praising Bhagat Singh and his comrades for their bravery and sacrifice was called a "Mistake" by Mahatma Gandhi in his speech at the Bombay meeting held on August 6, 1931, under the presidentship of Sardar Vallabhbhai Patel. Earlier the resolution was unanimously approved by the Congress Working Committee members including Pt. Jawaharlal Nehru *(The History of the Indian National Congress,* Vol. 1, p. 69)

The Free Press Journal of Bombay said, "The Working Committee is open to impeachment on the charge of surrender and betrayal".

The immense popularity that Bhagat Singh enjoyed can be seen from the fact that a public meeting was attended by more than 10,000 people in Lahore to mourn their death at a time when the government had strictly banned all such gatherings. According to a government report it was, 'the largest gathering that had attended any political meeting for some considerable time past'.

Even Dr. P. Sitaramayya (the official historian of the Congress) wrote in the *History of the Indian National Congress,* it is no exaggeration to say that at the moment Bhagat Singh's name was as widely known all over India and was as popular as Gandhiji.

Bhagat Singh died at the tender age of 23, an age in which most of us are blissfully unaware of the suffering and the miseries in our society. In this crisis-ridden period for our country, we must review our priorities and justify our faith in the youth. For, was it not Bhagat Singh who said, "The young can bear the most inhuman tortures smilingly and face death without hesitation because the whole history of human progress is written with the blood of young men and women."

The three most popular icons, namely, Bhagat Singh, Mahatma Gandhi and Pandit Jawaharlal Nehru have been assessed from the perspective of the revolutionaries in general and Bhagat Singh in particular. The assessment in this book, from an angle so far overlooked, provides a new vision to judge the roles played by the three most popular icons in the freedom struggle. It is a well researched work about Bhagat Singh's ideology.

BHAGAT SINGH AND HIS PHILOSOPHY

Neeraj K. Gupta, PhD

This is a much studied and investigated work on Bhagat Singh. Numerous books have been written on him. It would seem that everything that can be written about him must have been written. But this book gives a new perspective on his life, times and his ideology.

Of all the martyrs, who gave their lives for the freedom of India, Bhagat Singh occupies a special place. He was just 23 years old when his life was taken away. In such a short time period, his work, actions and writings have left a legacy that has forever made him the icon of youth. If Bhagat Singh had been alive today, he would be 110 years old. But he remains forever a young person in the eyes of Indian youth. One often wonders what gave him that special status. After all there were thousands of other young men who sacrificed their lives. This book attempts to answer this question in a new way.

When we talk of Bhagat Singh, we need to look at his personality from many aspects. He was a revolutionary. His name and fame spread far and wide. The powerful British Empire was scared of him. The Indian leaders of those times took note of him and were forced to comment on him. One can sense admiration but at the same time they criticised him. Mahatma Gandhi and Pt. Jawaharlal Nehru called him and his revolutionary colleagues terrorists, while Pt. Nehru also thought of them having a fascist mentality.

The British Empire labelled him as a terrorist. Many of the Indian leaders and the authors of the books on him also called him a terrorist and referred to his actions as terrorism. How does one distinguish between a terrorist and a revolutionary or a freedom fighter? Throughout history freedom movements had to resort to violent means to achieve justice. The Americans had their civil war, the Russians had their revolution, the Chinese had to resort to violence to get rid of the British and then the Americans, and Vietnamese had to fight long wars to achieve independence from the French and then from the Americans. But the actions of Bhagat Singh were described as terrorism by not only the British but also by the Indian leaders. Gandhiji propounded the philosophy of non-violence. But he had no qualms in encouraging Indians to join the British army to fight in the First World War.

By definition a terrorist is one who creates terror in the minds of someone, and so do the violent means adopted by freedom fighters. The difference really is in who feels the terror. A freedom fighter attempts to create terror in the minds of oppressors. The ordinary citizens do not feel the terror. That is a very important distinction. In today's world when many countries face terrorism, this distinction is important. The people we call terrorists today have created terror in the minds of ordinary people. In fact the oppressors are relatively safe in their secure environment. It is only the common people who face the brunt of terrorists' actions today. But Bhagat Singh's actions did not create terror in the minds of ordinary citizens. In fact even the ordinary British people living in India did not feel the terror. So it would be unfair to call him a terrorist. Bhagat Singh killed John Saunders, a British police officer, to avenge the death of Lala Lajpat Rai. He had thrown a bomb in the Assembly. But none of these actions can be called terrorist actions. The bombs thrown in the Assembly were not directed at the people sitting in the Assembly. As Bhagat Singh said, "it was meant to create a noise and not kill..."

If we look at the long list of martyrs of the Indian freedom struggle, there were so many others who had taken to violent means, but cannot be called terrorists. Madan Lal Dhingra killed William Hutt Curzon Wyllie and this act was considered the first act of the Indian freedom movement in the 20th century. He defended himself in the British Court. Even Sir Winston Churchill admired his statement of defence made in the court. But Mahatma Gandhi criticised his actions. Udham Singh took revenge for the Jallianwala Bagh Massacre by killing Michael O'Dwyer in England. Even though he could escape in the chaos created by his killing, he chose not to run or kill innocent civilians. His actions were again condemned by Mahatma Gandhi. The sacrifice of these young men was no less than that of Bhagat Singh, but somehow the name of Bhagat Singh stands like a shining star by itself. This book captures this aspect of Bhagat Singh.

Bhagat Singh did not just sacrifice his life for the cause of freedom. He also had an ideology believing in Marxism and a vision for India after freedom. He was a unique intellectual and his writings had logic and an ideological base. Even while he was waiting for his execution, he was reading books and writing notes. He firmly believed that a free India needs to follow the Marxist ideology. A few hours before his execution he was reading Lenin's *The State and Revolution*. This level of commitment at such a young age and standing on the gallows waiting for his execution was rare. He was not only willing to sacrifice his life for the freedom of his country but he gave the movement an ideological base. His goal was socialist revolution leading to a social order based on the dictatorship of the proletariat. In his pamphlet *An Address to the Young Political Workers* written on February 2, 1931, just a few weeks before his execution, he asked 'the professional revolutionaries' to inculcate class polities and educate the masses on socialist theory. One can just wonder what a giant intellectual he would have been, if he had survived. That is what makes him unique.

The British had put to death thousands of young men who fought for freedom in India. Bhagat Singh, again, aroused special fear in them. The book gives extensive quotes about the role played by Mahatma Gandhi and Pandit Jawaharlal Nehru. They were against the revolution as well as the revolutionaries. Many of the anecdotes are not well known. The written history of India for masses has sanitised the role of its "mainstream" leaders. But this book documents the role of the leaders of those times very well. The anecdotes provide an interesting read and also provide a window to the thought process of Indian leaders of those times. One can only wonder if Bhagat Singh could have been saved by the appeals of Gandhi or Nehru. But one thing is clear. The public sentiment throughout India was in Bhagat

Singh's favour. The emotions were high. The British were scared, so scared that they did not dare to wait for the morning to hang him, as was the normal practice. The martyrs, Bhagat Singh, Sukhdev and Rajguru, were hanged on the evening of March 23, 1931, in secret and the bodies were not handed over to the relatives, again contrary to the normal practice. Such was the terror in the British minds.

BHAGAT SINGH WAS A TORCHBEARER OF SCIENTIFIC SOCIALISM

Dr. Vitull K. Gupta

"Bhagat Singh", even after more than 85 years of martyrdom, remains a legend and a cult figure, for a youth in his 20s. Qualities like heroism, sacrifice, political clarity and ability to catch the imagination of people were really remarkable and contributed in making him a legend occupying a unique position among all Indian revolutionaries.

The media has thankfully been glorifying, propagating, spreading, publishing ideas, thoughts and little-known facts about Bhagat Singh who emerged as a symbol of the most radical nationalist movement against imperialism and colonialism. The government efforts to remember him however, are just symbolic.

Bhagat Singh was a great thinker who understood the power of ideas that made him an undisputed ideologically Marxist leader with tremendous courage. If all Indians, especially, politically-minded ones focus, propagate and spread revolutionary ideas of freedom fighters like Bhagat Singh, the very first victims of the revolutionary movement will be the neo-colonial political class and bureaucrats who exploit the common people for their own selfish motives. For the fear of public onslaught, rulers ensure that historical figures, freedom fighters, martyrs, and revolutionaries are neglected and look like sorry remnants of the past rather than vibrant torchbearers of a socialist future.

BHAGAT SINGH: A THINKER, A PHILOSOPHER, A THEORIST OF REVOLUTIONARY POLICIES

Arvind Garg
[A New York-based photo-artist and writer]

The book had opened my eyes to something I had been completely blind about before reading it. I had never thought of Bhagat Singh as more than a brave and patriotic revolutionary who sacrificed his life in an attempt to shock and strike a blow to the foreign rulers with the mostly symbolic act of throwing a bomb in the Assembly, and for which he happily paid with his life. What the book reveals is not only a man of action but also a thinker, philosopher and a theorist of revolutionary politics. I am simply amazed at the scope of his intellectual reach, his vast readings, his capacity for reasoning and clear thinking as well as the clarity of his thought, which he is able to practise without even a thin veil of sentimentality or romanticisim. And I enjoyed his language and his style which is very conversational as opposed to didactic or authoritative. It feels as if he is sitting in front of the reader and making his point totally rationally rather than relying on the much-abused forces of faith and superstition.

The extent of research that seems to have gone into the making of this book, both from primary sources like historical documents and secondary sources like critical commentary by different historians, is indeed impressive. There are original quotations specific to the case being made at any given stage, from correspondence between Indian nationalists and the British rulers of India, as well as the revolutionaries led by Bhagat Singh that greatly help a reader's understanding of the complexities of a long-drawn struggle for independence.

It is an important and much needed addition to the literature of not only Indian history but world history, especially, 20th century history in which Marxism played a role.

Introduction

Let Us Walk with Bhagat Singh on His Path of Scientific Socialism.

The master's tools will never be used to dismantle the master's house.
–A proverb

The world is what it is, men who are nothing, who allow themselves to become nothing, have no place in it. –V.S. Naipaul

Merciless criticism and independent thinking are the two necessary traits of revolutionary thinking. –Bhagat Singh

If dissent is not allowed, then the pressure cooker will burst.
–Supreme Court of India

The book *Walking With Bhagat Singh Soon After Independence* is an effort to make a critical appraisal of India's three most popular icons, namely, Shaheed-e–Azam Bhagat Singh, Mahatma Gandhi and Pt. Jawaharlal Nehru from the prism of the revolutionaries spearheaded by Bhagat Singh.

It highlights Bhagat Singh's ideology and explains that he was a true Marxist. It enlightens how his striking notices after Saunders' murder and after the bomb explosions in the Assembly and stirring statements in the Sessions Court and before the Lahore High Court Bench and other writings electrified his countrymen with revolutionary political consciousness that brought 'Long Live the Revolution' and 'Down with Imperialism' on the lips of everyone.

The book describes how the revolutionary wave was skilfully blunted by Mahatma Gandhi and Pt. Jawaharlal Nehru. Injustice was done to Bhagat Singh and the Indian people by those who refused to consider him a Marxist. It was a tragedy that many communists considered Pt. Nehru and not Bhagat Singh, a Marxist. They, it seemed, had been following Bernsteinism and Kautaskyism more than Marxism. Everyone of those, contesting Bhagat Singh's credentials as a Marxist, presumed himself to be an authority on Marxism.

The book further aims at exposing the failure of a concoction of Keynesianism and state capitalism masked as Democratic Socialism to better the lot of have-nots.

Another objective is to emphasise the indispensability of Scientific Socialism envisaged by Bhagat Singh as the only remedy to ameliorate the plight of the oppressed and the exploited human beings. This could be brought about through a Socialist Revolution and the establishment of a Socialist State based on Marxism as visualised and conceived by Bhagat Singh.

Innumerable books have been written on each of these three icons, appraising their roles in the country's freedom struggle but the critical part of the same had been generally in moderation. Any piercingly critical analysis was generally frowned upon and was considered to be akin to showing disrespect to the great personalities. "We give too much importance to hero-worship. If a person is considered great, no negative views are tolerated. The same thing happened with my criticism of Rabindranath Tagore", said Mr. Girish Karnad, an eminent actor-director-playwright, in an idea exchange session with *Loksatta* in Pune, published in the *Sunday Express* of September 8, 2013. The situation in the Western countries was different where one could see their leading personalities in the various fields of life critically appraised vigorously and rigorously.

Mahatma Gandhi, Pt. Jawaharlal Nehru, Subhas Chandra Bose, Rabindranath Tagore, Dr. Baba Saheb B.R. Ambedkar and other icons were not divine and above criticism. They did not consider themselves to be so and would never have wished to be contemplated as such. Criticism of an icon or a popular leader showed his relevance and popularity, and the greater the criticism the more relevant and popular he was in the political life of the country as well as in her history. The tendency to turn the icons into mythical figures, as if they were above human fallibility, was a mistake and injustice to them as well as to the people.

Mahatma Gandhi and Pt. Jawaharlal Nehru were geniuses and so was Bhagat Singh.While the genius of the first two icons had been superabundantly glorified, there was an element of restraint and frugality in Bhagat Singh's case, for his genius had not been recognised commensurately. He was praised to the sky for his bravery and for smilingly embracing the guillotine sacrificing his life. His writings delineating his ideology which were as relevant, rather more relevant, today, as those were 85 years ago, were often ignored and distorted. In his pamphlet, *An Address to the Young Political Workers* written on February 2, 1931, just a few weeks before his hanging, he had outlined some very definite and indubitable guidelines about how to prepare for the socialist revolution.

It is probably for the first time that Pt. Jawaharlal's political life vis-à-vis Bhagat Singh is being critically reviewed. Mahatma Gandhi's political philosophy and politics had been analysed earlier also by, amongst others, Suniti Kumar Ghosh, Rajani Palme Dutt and Mohinder Singh Pannu, but not through the prism of Bhagat Singh that is being done in this book, probably, for the first time. In this context, the role and purpose of the 'Satyagraha' movements led by Mahatma Gandhi and approved and joined by the rest of the Congress Party leadership including Pt. Jawaharlal Nehru have also been appraised.

During the years of the First World War, when the British rulers needed the enlistment of Indians in the British armed forces to fight for them in Europe, Mahatma Gandhi took it as his mission to campaign for the recruitment of poor Indians in the British Army. He would tell them:

> There can be no partnership between the brave and the effeminate. We are regarded as cowardly people. If we need to become free from

> this reproach, we should learn the use of arms. *[CWMG,* Vol. 14, pp. 430-440]

After the British had won the First World War, they faced the grave internal danger from the Ghadrites and the revolutionaries in India. Mahatma Gandhi was again in the vanguard to save the British imperialist rulers. He excavated the strategem of *Satyagraha/ Ahimsa* (non-violence). *Satyagraha* postulates the conquest of the adversary by suffering in one's own person and not the remotest idea of injuring the other and that is *Satyagraha*, as defined by Mahatma Gandhi. Physical force is forbidden.

Mahatma Gandhi's main purpose for launching the 'Satyagraha' movements was to divert people from the Socialist path to the non-violence. And in this task, the British rulers acted as his allies. They played their undeclared roles most appropriately.

"*Satyagraha* is the only way", it seems to me, "to stop terrorism". (read revolutionary ideology) Mahatmaji would state. *[CWMG,* Vol.15, p. 107]

The official historian of the Congress, Dr. Pattabhi Sitaramayya pointed out: "It is really to subdue violence (read Scientific Socialist ideology) that this movement was inaugurated". [*The History of the Indian National Congress*, p. 402]

The freedom struggle was a war for the revolutionaries not only against the British rulers but also against the foreign capital as well as against the Indian capital. They stood for revolution by means of organised armed rebellion, in order to liberate their beloved motherland from the foreign rulers as well as from the exploitation by the Indian capitalist class.

By fostering *Satyagraha* (non-violence), both Mahatma Gandhi and Pt. Jawaharlal Nehru were successfully able to thwart the efforts of Bhagat Singh and his revolutionary colleagues to bring about a Socialist Revolution.

This collection of writings on and related to Bhagat Singh, Mahatma Gandhi and Pt. Jawaharlal Nehru appraises their different paths to gain India's freedom and the emancipation of workers, peasants and other sections of poor Indian people. Each of the three icons has been assessed citing what the concerned icon had said, written, practised or not practised and accordingly has been quoted. While the roles of Mahatma Gandhi and Pt. Jawaharlal Nehru towards the revolutionaries had been adversarial, these remained reconciliatory towards the British imperialist rulers that had ultimately led to the friendly transfer of power to the Congress Party leadership in 1947 and perpetuated a cosy relationship with not only Great Britain as foreboded by Bhagat Singh but also with other colonial and imperialist powers such as the USA, France, Germany, Japan, etc., which are now called *'strategic partners'* or *'natural friends'*. The Head of the State visiting these former colonial countries gets red-carpet treatment by them as they enter into deals to sell various types of war weapons worth billions of dollars to the country of the visiting dignitary. The print and electronic media in the home country highlights the red carpet reception cementing the unity of the Indian capital with the global capital and projecting the Indian state as one of the global powers.

There are Prefaces by Dr. Shalley K. Gupta, Dr. Neeraj K. Gupta, Dr. Vitull K. Gupta and Arvind Garg, a New York-based photo-artist and writer preceded by an introduction, and acknowledgements. The first chapter entitled *Tracking Down Bhagat Singh and Pt. Jawaharlal Nehru* explores the role played by Pt. Jawaharlal Nehru in relation to the actions and statements of Bhagat Singh and exposes his hypocricy and crocodile tears. Efforts were also made to play down Bhagat Singh's ideological contribution and in this respect, his [Pt. Nehru] own statements and actions have been cited.

There are two more chapters on Pt. Jawaharlal Nehru. One chapter titled *How Britain Had to Transfer Power to India in 1947?* explains the compulsion under which Great Britain had to suddenly hand over power to the Indian leadership of the Congress Party and the Muslim League. Citing the well-known economist, J.M. Keynes' advice to the newly elected Prime Minister C.R. Attlee as well as the views of the other British statesmen as disclosed in the *Transfer of Power Series of India [TOPI],* it has been made clear that Great Britain had to relinquish power to her trusted and collaborative leaders of the Congress and Muslim League. It was to save India from the threat of revolution. The other reason was the paucity of Great Britain's manpower and bankruptcy of her financial resources and not due to 'Satyagraha' and civil disobedience movements. It is a myth to say that these movements of the Congress won India's freedom. The British imperialists had rather appreciated the value of the beneficial role, Mahatma Gandhi had played through these movements in saving the British Empire in India from bloodshed [Read Revolution].

"Gandhi was the best policeman the British had in India", declared the then Member of the British Parliament, Ellen Wilkinson, after her official visit to India in 1932.

In another chapter captioned *'After the Transfer of Power',* the failure of Pt. Nehru's modest three Five Year Plans to solve the food problem had been brought out. In this chapter quoting Mr. J.F. Kennedy, the then Senator and a future President of the USA's speech, delivered at the Conference on India and the United States at Washington DC on May 4, 1959, expressing his concern over China's gigantic progress in all spheres within 10 years of her Socialist Liberation under the leadership of Mao Tse Tung, India's poor performance within the same period had been brought to light.

In a lengthy chapter entitled *The Indian National Congress, Gandhiji and Revolutionaries,* Mahatma Gandhi's role, with a missionary zeal, in helping and saving the British rulers from their enemies in Europe during the First World War and after the war from the Ghadrites and the revolutionaries has been elucidated meticulously. Further, Mahatmji's views on some of the national issues have been expounded. He was a supporter of the propertied classes, the zamindari system (landlordism) and capitalism; and was opposed to workers' strikes; supported the caste system, though opposed untouchability; urged the women to act like Sita and Draupadi.

In late 1931, Mahatma Gandhi accepted an invitation to visit Mussolini in Rome while the Mahatma was returning from London after attending a Round Table Conference. Reportedly, the two men—the vain Italian fascist and the modest, unassuming Indian ascetic—got along extremely well and admired each other. Gandhiji reviewed a black-shirted fascist youth honour-guard during his visit.

Mahatmaji had words of praise for Hitler and his quotes on him are included in the chapter. He had, in his writings, used words about the Africans which were considered derogatory by them (Africans) and that had led to the removal of his statue from the campus of one of the universities in Ghana (Africa).

Was Gandhiji Duty–Bound To Save Bhagat Singh?, this question has been clarified, stating that requiring Mahatmaji to save Bhagat Singh and his two colleagues from the gallows was not justified. Both Gandhiji and Bhagat Singh held diametrically opposite views on various social, economic and political issues and that those were poles apart from each other.

Mahatmaji, therefore, only played to the galleries by speaking to Lord Irwin about Bhagat Singh during his meetings with him (Lord Irwin). He had to do that because the Karachi Session of the Congress and the execution of Bhagat Singh and his two colleagues occurred almost simultaneously on dates closer to each other. In this connection, Mahatma Gandhi and Lord Irwin have been quoted in detail.

Citing what Bhagat Singh had repeatedly stated showing his firm faith both in Class Struggle and in the Dictatorship of the Proletariat as per the Touch-Stone given by V.I. Lenin in his *The State and Revolution*, Bhagat Singh is brought out to be a true, committed and devoted Marxist in the chapter captioned *Bhagat Singh Was A True Marxist.* There is a separate chapter entitled *Salient Features of Bhagat Singh's Ideology*.

Bhagat Singh, it may be added, was not dogmatic as Karl Marx, Friedrich Engels and V.I. Lenin had repeatedly stressed that the Science and Philosophy of Marxism was not a dogma which cannot be varied. Convinced of the truth of its essence, V.I. Lenin had stated that, "Marxism was a theory giving only general guiding ideas, which can be applied differently in England, for instance, than in France, differently in France than in Germany, differently in Germany than in Russia." Many of the Marxists in India and elsewhere often quoted it like a dogma, thereby, committing blunders leading to irreparable damages to the cause of revolution and Marxism.

Unfortunately, many of the authors of the books and articles on Bhagat Singh did not think of him as an ideologue. Efforts were on to obliterate his ideology. They praised only his patriotism and admired his bravery and sacrifice. But there are other authors such as Harpal Brar, Hans Raj Rehbar, Omesh Saigal, Satyam, Manmath Gupta who had unreservedly thought of him as a true Marxist. They, as well as his critics, have been quoted in the chapter, *Bhagat Singh Was a True Marxist* in the book.

Each of Bhagat Singh's major and minor writings such as the *Manifestoes of the Hindustan Socialist Republican Association* and *The Naujawan Bharat Sabha, The Statement in the Sessions Court, Statement Before the Lahore High Court Bench, The Philosophy of the Bomb*, his pamphlets captioned, *An Address to the Young Political Workers, Why I Am An Atheist? We Claim to be Shot Dead: Letter to Governor, Punjab,* in short, every writing, spoke of his Marxist approach and knowledge concerning the issues facing the country and raised on various occasions during his lifetime.

This book had been planned to include many other writings of Bhagat Singh such as *Introduction to Dreamland, Blood Sprinkled on the Day of Holi (The Sacrifices of Babbar Akalis), Religion and National Politics; Students and Politics; Communal Problem and its Solution*; *The Problem of Untouchability; The Kuka Rebellion: The First Battle of Freedom in Punjab; The Peasant Agitation, Punjab, 1907; Universal Brotherhood: Indian Perspective,* his four write-ups on *Anarchism* and *Russian Nihilists.* These had been deleted in the final draft of the manuscript of this book, as they would have made the book bulky and unwieldy.

Bhagat Singh's petition to the Home Member, Government of India in which he had reiterated impressively and forcefully, the demands of the hunger strikers, that needs to be studied by all jail officials and politicians, also could not be included.

Bhagat Singh's two letters regarding the line of defence in Hari

Kishan's case (Hari Kishan had fired at the Governor of Punjab while he was coming out of the University Hall, Lahore after delivering the convocation address on December 23, 1930) have been deleted. These, in addition to his statements before the Sessions Court and before the Lahore High Court Bench, respectively, show him to be a legal luminary, superior to the likes of Mr. Asaf Ali. The Manifesto of the Naujawan Bharat Sabha has been deleted as most of the points in it have been covered in the other writings of Bhagat Singh. There was a chapter on indicators of development, in which it had been clarified that there were two types of developments. One was development that mainly promoted the benefits to the elites and their embedded intellectuals. There was, however, another type of development that was for the emancipation of the have-nots. This too could not be included.

In his article on 'Communal Problem and Its Solution', Bhagat Singh had offered the concept of 'Inculcation of Class Consciousness' among the people as the solution of communal, caste, etc. problems. All the poor people in the world, he had added, were, irrespective of their religion, caste, region, race or nation, had the same rights. It is in their interest that they forgot their distinctions by acquiring secular democratic values and culture in the process of their struggle to take over power from the capitalist rulers.

Bhagat Singh felt pained to see people believing in superstitions, engaged in the debates relating to God and Soul and crying desperately to reach the Almighty and Heaven. That was in the first quarter of the 20st century. The situation has not changed at all. The only change is that during Bhagat Singh's times in the last century, the people believing in superstitions were mostly illiterate or semi-literate. Now, in the 21st century, almost a century after what Bhagat Singh had written, the superstitious Indians are mostly highly educated—Members of Civil Services, PhDs, postgraduates and doctors having studied science at some stage of their educational career. Many of them are often seen standing on the roads in front of temples, a hundred metres away from the stone and cloth idols of the gods, with their newly purchased shining cars and the priest chanting scriptures and invoking blessings, pasting vermilion on the bonnet of the car. His widely published pamphlet captioned *Why I Am An Atheist?* needs to be read repeatedly. Bhagat Singh's writings are highly-educative and amazingly were written while he was just 22 years old. Most of the issues on which these articles had been written by Bhagat Singh continue to be as controversial and making news headlines as they were doing a century ago. *Students and Politics* is one such issue. Bhagat Singh had strongly pleaded for the students to be well aware of the problems facing their country. The other chapters are equally relevant to understand and evaluate the three icons, who have been extensively quoted and also showing that nothing has been tampered with. This is to authenticate the relevance of the points and issues discussed which it is hoped the readers would appreciate.

Bhagat Singh's ideology was Scientific Socialism and what later on came to be known as Marxism-Leninism-Maoism. His aim was to liberate India from the foreign yoke and from the native capital through a revolution and set up a new social order based on Scientific Socialism. The need of the hour is to raise once again Bhagat Singh's war cries of *Long Live the Revolution, Down with Imperialism* and *Workers of the World Unite.*

—Amar Kant Jttu

1

Tracking Down Bhagat Singh and Pt. Jawaharlal Nehru

Shaheed-e-Azam Bhagat Singh, as he is often and rightly called, had a short life of slightly more than 23 years, having been born on September 28, 1907 and, martyred on March 23, 1931. He has been honoured with the title of *Shaheed-e-Azam* (the greatest martyr). It happened without any award ceremony at a Convocation Hall or 'Bhawan' and there is no *Sannad* or a degree. His grateful countrymen did so spontaneously and quietly residing in their villages, towns and cities alike with humility and pride.

Nevertheless, he is generally called and written simply as *Bhagat Singh*. Whenever he is called or written so, thereby, depriving him of his title, we feel something missing and there is a feeling of guilt of showing him disrespect. Yet he continues to be often called and endearingly written shorn of his title. But when we do so, in our consciousness, subconsciousness and even in our unconscious mind, he, for ever, is etched as 'Shaheed-e-Azam'. It is an extraordinary and unique honorific, superior to and higher than any *Nobel Prize* and *Bharat Ratna*.

He was born in a revolutionary family, in which the spirit of sacrifice ran in their blood and bones. It was natural for Bhagat Singh to imbibe the same while he was still in his teens. While he was still in his early youth, his life was cut short by the cruel-hearted British imperialists and, thus, his political career too could not be long. In this short but meaningful life, every day of his few years was full of valour and daring actions confronting the vicious British rulers in various ways.

Bhagat Singh soon acquired the stature of an all-time iconic revolutionary, inspiring young and old of every generation. He was praised for his courage and bravery by one and all. Mahatma Gandhi felt privileged to listen to his story of patriotism calling his courage reckless and his daring unequalled. So did Pt. Jawaharlal Nehru, Pt. Madan Mohan Malaviya, Sardar Vallabhbhai Patel and many others, soon after he and his two comrades were executed by the inhuman colonial rulers. Here, a thought comes to one's mind and also a question.

How and why is it Bhagat Singh alone has been highlighted with so much praise and admiration, while there have been hundreds and thousands of others who had kissed the gallows as bravely and courageously as him for the cause of the country's emancipation?

Pt. Jawaharlal Nehru was amazed at his popularity and wondered how a mere chit of a boy had become a guide to others and why, he asked, with a tinge of regret, even the creed of non-violence had to pay the highest tribute to Bhagat Singh. The reason, Pt. Nehru went on, at the AICC Session at Karachi held at the end of March 1931, was, his sacrifice and bravery had reached the upper limit.

But so was the sacrifice and bravery of Chandra Shekhar Azad, a legend and inspiration to his countrymen with a reward on his head running into tens of thousands and gallows frowning at him throughout his revolutionary life. And yet a terror, sending shivers down the spine of the police officials having killed a number of them and injuring many others through bomb explosions and the Viceroy miraculously escaping travelling in a train in December 1929. Betrayed by a traitor, Azad was killed in a prolonged shooting encounter with the police.

And there have been numerous others whose bravery and sacrifice was no less than that of Bhagat Singh and Chandra Shekhar Azad. *Roll of Honour: Anecdotes of Indian Martyrs*, a book in two volumes by Kali Charan Ghosh from Calcutta, gives an account, of all those valiant freedom fighters, who sacrificing their lives without a sigh, challenged the vicious British imperialists, right from the conquest of Bengal by the English in 1757.

Pt. Jawaharlal Nehru had attributed the popularity of Bhagat Singh to the "upper limit" of his sacrifice. How had he determined the "upper limit"? There is no measure to do so and it is difficult to quantify the "upper limit". But if there is any such "upper limit", then one would find many heroes such as Gopi Nath Saha, Birsa Munda, etc. reaching the "upper limit" through the sacrifice of their lives at the altar of freedom. Pt. Nehru, who was not only a freedom fighter, politician, statesman and the first Prime Minister of India, was also an historian having authored works like *Glimpses of World History* and *The Discovery of India* as well as his own *An Autobiography.* He was not expected to have missed the glimpses of the role played by the Indian revolutionaries in their country's freedom struggle, ultimately, forcing the British imperialists to think of the impossibility of continuing to rule India after the Second World War, but these *Glimpses* found little space in his a thousand-page great history book.

Whatever the "upper limit", the sacrifice and bravery could not be the only reason of Bhagat Singh's popularity. Getting popularity and praise was not his or other revolutionaries' aim. How casually, calmly and lightly, the impending execution of their death sentences was being taken by them while at the same time feeling deeply concerned at the plight of so many other political prisoners rotting in jails, is apparent from the following extract of a letter of 'Maha-atma' Sukhdev written to Mahatma Gandhi a few days before they were executed.

> Since your compromise, (Gandhi-Irwin Pact signed on March 6, 1931) you have called off your movement and consequently all your prisoners have been released. But what about the revolutionary prisoners? Dozens of Ghadr Party prisoners imprisoned since 1915 are still rotting in jails in spite of having undergone the full terms. Scores of Martial Law prisoners are buried in those living tombs. And so are dozens of Babbar Akali prisoners. Deogarh, Kakori, Machhua Bazaar and Lahore Conspiracy Case, 1915 prisoners are among those numerous still locked behind bars. More than half a dozen conspiracy trials are going on at Lahore, Chittagong, Bombay, Calcutta and elsewhere. Dozens of revolutionaries are absconding and amongst them are many

> females. More than half a dozen prisoners are actually waiting for their execution. What about all these people? The three Lahore Conspiracy Case condemned prisoners who have luckily come into prominence and who have acquired enormous public sympathy, do not form the bulk of the revolutionary Party. Their fate is not the only consideration before the Party. As a matter of fact, their executions (and Sukhdev was one of the three to be executed) are expected to do greater good than the commutation of their sentences.

In a first tribute to the three martyrs, immediately after their execution when he said, "now all is over", Pt. Jawaharlal Nehru began saying, "I have remained absolutely silent during their last days, lest a word of mine may injure the prospect of commutation."

One would ask, "why he remained silent? And how his word demanding commutation of their death sentences would have injured the prospect of commutation? As the President of the All India Congress Party, popularly also called the *Rashtrapati* (President of the country), was it not his duty to make all-out efforts to save those precious lives while thousands of petitions signed by lakhs of people demanding commutation of death sentences were being sent to Lord Irwin, the Viceroy ? He should have been the first not only to sign such a petition but also think of other steps, including the launching of a civil disobedience movement, demanding commutation of their life-sentences. Pandit Jawaharlal Nehru, as the then President of the All India Congress Committee, could have asked Lord Irwin, the Viceroy, for a meeting with him, for the purpose of requesting him for commuting the death sentences of the three patriots. He could have also requested Mahatma Gandhi to launch a civil disobedience movement for the commutation of their death sentences.

Then in the same short tribute,and in a feeble attempt to redeem himself for his inaction, Pt. Nehru says, "when England speaks to us and talks of settlement, there will be the corpse of Bhagat Singh between us lest we forget."And forget he did, this resolve of his,when within a week, he, as the main speaker at the AICC Session at Karachi, endorsed rather strongly, the Settlement, called the Gandhi-Irwin Pact, ensuring its approval by the Congress delegates, thereby, exposing his own duplicity and his false tears.

Mahatma Gandhi and Pt. Jawaharlal Nehru must have known about the several stirring posters such as, "Beware ye Bureaucracy, J.P. Saunders is dead, Lala Lajpat Rai is avenged". "Long Live the Revolution" and "Down with Imperialism", pasted on the walls all over Lahore just after Saunders' killing in 1928. 'Red Leaflet'–"It Takes A Loud Voice to Make the Deaf Hear", thrown along with the two bombs in the Central Legislative Assembly on April 8, 1929 by Bhagat Singh and B.K. Dutt, must have been read by them. Further, their thrilling statements, given in the Courts extensively reported with banner headlines on the front pages in the media and read with rapt attention by the people, besides numerous other documents must have been viewed by Mahatma Gandhi and Pt. Jawaharlal Nehru.These "actions" articulating their ideology and their aims on every available occasion, were meant to arouse the revolutionary socialist political consciousness of the people. To run away after the murder of Saunders or to escape after throwing the bombs in the Central Assembly was not their plot as clarified by Sukhdev in his well-known half-written letter. Their aim in all these "actions" was to enlighten the public and that the Saunders' murder as well as bombs in the Assembly were "political actions" and were the result of the government's policies and for which it (government) was responsible. Mahatma Gandhi and Pt. Jawaharlal Nehru must have understood the significance of their "actions" as well as the inherent threat to the Congress posed by the ideology expressed by Bhagat Singh.

The valiant revolutionary fighters, who sacrificed their lives with the cry of *"Long Live the Revolution"* and *"Down with Imperialism"* on their lips, had made the lives of the British and Indian bureaucrats serving British imperialism vulnerable and unsafe. They have been dubbed "terrorists" and "anarchists" akin to some sort of criminals. Should Bhagat Singh's daring act of avenging Lala Lajpat Rai's death be dubbed merely an act of terrorism? Calling it an act of terrorism, as Pt. Jawaharlal Nehru did, meant it to be some damnable act, although the 'act' had vindicated the honour of the nation as acknowledged by Pt. Nehru himself.

Who can forget notices bearing the headlines:

'The Hindustan Socialist Republican Army', "Beware ye Tyrants, Beware"!

"Beware ye Bureaucracy, Beware", "Saunders is Dead, Lala Lajpat Rai is Avenged", Long Live the Revolution", "Down with Imperialism".

These bulletins received wide publicity all over the country through six column headlines on the front pages of many newspapers and spread by word of mouth throughout the country.

Soon after the first revolutionary action, another one followed on April 8, 1929. Every patriot Indian remembers the famous 'Red Leaflet' bearing the headline: 'The Hindustan Socialist Republican Army' and beginning with... "LOUD EXPLOSION NECESSARY TO MAKE THE DEAF HEAR" thrown in the Central Legislative Assembly Hall after dropping the two harmless bombs. The '*action*' in the Central Legislative Assembly Hall was followed by the historic statement in the Court of the Sessions Judge, New Delhi on June 6, 1929 that Pt. Jawaharlal Nehru, as the General Secretary of the Congress Party, had thought appropriate to publish in his *The Congress Bulletin* acknowledging it to have received wide appreciation from the Congress rank and file. A letter of Pt. Nehru addressed to Mahatma Gandhi on July 13, 1929 reveals their attitude towards Bhagat Singh and his comrades. Disapproving of its publication, Mahatma Gandhi appears to have reproached Pt. Nehru for doing so. In his letter the relevant extract of which is being reproduced, Pt. Nehru apologised.

> I am sorry you disapproved of my giving Bhagat Singh and Dutt's statement in the *Congress Bulletin*. I was myself a little doubtful as to whether I should give it but when I found that there was very general appreciation of it among Congress circles, I decided to give extracts. It was difficult, however, to pick and choose and gradually most of it went in. But I agree with you that it was somewhat out of place. I think you are mistaken in thinking that the statement was the work of their counsel. My information is that the counsel had nothing or practically nothing to do with it. He might have touched up the punctuation. I think the statement was undoubtedly a genuine thing...

How was it out of place to be published in *The Congress Bulletin*? Pt. Jawaharlal Nehru should have stood by it. The Congress leadership including Mahatma Gandhi should have felt proud of his statement and rather should have owned it. It was "a practical protest against the institution of the Central Legislative Assembly" [The so-called Indian Parliament]. There should have been no reason to disagree with what had been stated by Bhagat Singh and B.K. Dutt in their statement before the Sessions Court. The rank and file of the Congress had amply shown their agreement with the views expressed in the same. Pt. Nehru himself seemed to have appreciated the statement and that's why he published it in *The Congress Bulletin*. Mahatmaji too should have approved the same. The Congress Party meant its rank and file, not just its leaders. *The Congress Bulletin* represented not only the Party's ideology, programme and its activities but also the sentiments, opinions, thoughts, reactions, ideas, impressions of the people in general and Congress men in particular.

One witnesses Bhagat Singh's phenomenal brilliance in another statement before the Lahore High Court Bench wherein he, like a legal luminary, emphasised the importance of 'motive' arguing that the 'motive of action' should be the main consideration while judging the offence of an accused.

His letter to the Punjab Governor, his last writing in which he had declared that "the state of war does exist between the Indian nation and the British nation and shall exist so long as the Indian toiling masses...are being exploited by a handful of parasites—who may be purely British capitalists or mixed British and Indian or even purely Indian."

There are, of course, numerous other writings of Bhagat Singh equally important such as "An Address to the Young Political Workers"; "Why I Am An Atheist?"; His Party's [The Hindustan Socialist Republican Association] Manifesto; "The Philosophy of the Bomb", authored by Bhagat Singh and typed, got printed, published and issued by the Party's Propaganda Secretary, Bhagwati Charan Vohra in response to Gandhiji's "The Cult of the Bomb".

Many of Bhagat Singh's writings were issued under the name

of Kartar Singh and Bal Raj, fictitious names to mislead the British authorities and to prevent the documents falling into their hands.

A passage by Pt. Jawaharlal Nehru in his *An Autobiography* [pp. 261-262] gives a glimpse of how poorly he thought of the revolutionaries. He called them terrorists having definitely the fascist mentality.

"I remember a curious incident about that time (February 1931) which gave me an insight into the mind of the terrorist group (The Hindustan Socialist Republican Association of which Chandra Shekhar Azad and Bhagat Singh were the prominent members) in India. This took place after my discharge from prison either a little before father's death or a few days after. (Pt. Motilal Nehru died on February 6, 1931). A stranger came to see me at our house and I was told that he was Chandra Shekhar Azad. I had never seen him before but I had heard of him ten years earlier when he had non-cooperated from school and gone to prison during the N.C.O. (Non-Cooperation) Movement in 1921. A boy of 15 years of age or so then, he had been flogged in prison for some breach of jail discipline. Later he had drifted towards the terrorists (revolutionaries) and became one of their prominent men in North India. (Chandra Shekhar Azad was the Commander-in-Chief of The Hindustan Socialist Republican Army). All this I had heard vaguely and I had taken no interest in these rumours. I was surprised, therefore, to see him. He had been induced to visit me because of the general expectation (owing to our release) that some negotiations between the Government and the Congress were likely. He wanted to know if in case of a settlement, his group of people would have any peace. Would they still be considered and treated as outlaws, hunted out from place to place with a price on their heads and the prospect of the gallows ever before them? Or was there a possibility of their being allowed to pursue peaceful vocation? He told me that as far as he was concerned as well as many of his associates, they were convinced now that purely terrorist methods were futile and did no good. He was not, however, prepared to believe that India would gain her freedom wholly by peaceful methods. He thought that some time in the future, a violent conflict might take place, but this would not be terrorism. He ruled out terrorism as such so far as the question of Indian freedom was concerned. But then, he added, what was he to do when no chance was given to him to settle down, as he was being hounded all the time? Many of the terrorist acts that had occurred recently, according to him, were purely in self-defence".

"I was glad to learn from Azad, and I had confirmation of this subsequently, that the belief in terrorism was dying down. As a group notion, indeed, it had practically gone, and individual and sporadic cases were probably due to some special reason—act of reprisal or individual aberration, and not a general idea. This did not mean, of course, that the old terrorists or their new associates had become converts to non-violence, or admirers of British rule. But they did not think in terms of terrorism as they used to. Many of them, it seemed to me, have definitely the fascist mentality."

"I tried to explain to Chandra Shekhar Azad what my philosophy of political action was and tried to convert him to my view-point. But I had no answer to his basic question: what was he to do now? Nothing was likely to happen that would bring him or his like any relief or peace. All I could suggest was that he should use his influence to prevent the occurrence of terrorist acts in the future for these could only injure the larger cause as well as his own group".

"Two or three weeks later, while the Gandhi-Irwin talks were going on, I heard at Delhi that Chandra Shekhar Azad had been shot down and killed by the police in Allahabad. He was recognised in the day-time in a park and was surrounded by a large force of police. He tried to defend himself from behind a tree; there was quite a shooting-match and he injured one or two policemen before he was shot down".

Pt. Nehru dubbed the revolutionaries not only as terrorists but also thought of them having a fascist mentality and, thereby, did a great injustice to the country's martyrs and revolutionary freedom fighters. Revolutionaries' actions were repeatedly called terrorist acts which according to him were countered by the creed of non-violence as stated below:

"Terrorism, in spite of occasional recrudescence, has no longer any real appeal for the youth of India", asserted Pt. Nehru. He, then, flattered himself by proudly declaring in 1936 in his *An Autobiography*:

> Fifteen years' stress on non-violence has changed the whole background in India and made the masses much more indifferent to, and even hostile to, the idea of terrorism as a method of political action.

But did Pt. Nehru realise that this "indifference of the masses and their hostility to the idea of terrorism" as a result of his and Gandhiji's preaching of non-violence, as claimed by him, had the effect of strengthening and perpetuating the British rule?

Pt. Nehru had slighted the contributory role, terrorism played in bringing about revolution. Bhagat Singh had stated:

> Terrorism instills fear in the oppressors. It brings hopes of revenge and redemption to the hearts of the oppressed masses. It gives courage and self-confidence to the wavering. It shatters the spell of the superiority of the ruling class.

Pt. Jawaharlal Nehru had analysed the phenomenon of Bhagat Singh and his popularity in more than two pages (174-176) of his autobiography, published in 1936, well, more than five years after his (Bhagat Singh) and his two comrades, Sukhdev and Raj Guru's execution. After giving a deep thought, he reached a conclusion as follows:

> He [Bhagat Singh] did not become popular because of his act of terrorism, but because he seemed to vindicate, for the moment, the honour of Lala Lajpat Rai, and through him of the nation. He became a symbol, the act was forgotten, the symbol remained, and within a few months, each town and village of the Punjab, and to a lesser extent in the rest of northern India, resounded with his name. Innumerable songs grew up about him, and the popularity that the man achieved, was something amazing.

It goes to Bhagat Singh's credit that Pt. Jawaharlal Nehru, an eminent leader of the Congress Party, had to think it necessary to discuss Bhagat Singh phenomenon in his autobiography. Pt. Nehru, must have felt compelled to do so. Bhagat Singh's popularity was proving to be too *"amazing"*, bewildering and uncomfortable to the bourgeois nationalist leadership of the country and it had to be downplayed and he did try. But could he do so?

Dr. Shalley K. Gupta had made some pertinent observations as follows:

> Pt. Jawaharlal Nehru always appeared, and it was most probably deliberate, to fluctuate between the two extremes of political ideology, the role of revolutionary action vs non-violence and the future economic basis of a free India. This was to wean away the young men's mind from thinking of joining the revolurionaries by creating an impression that he [Pt. Nehru] too is a revolutionary and, thereby, prompting them to follow him. He did his best to underplay Bhagat Singh and his Party's revolutionary role and his true Marxist ideology. Even the epic hunger-strike lasting more than 110 days by Bhagat Singh and his comrades and the country-wide upsurge against the British rule was shrewdly obliterated by Pt. Nehru in evaluating the revolutionaries.

Should Bhagat Singh's daring act of avenging Lala Lajpat Rai's death and vindicating the nation's honour be dubbed an act of terrorism? Calling it an act of terrorism, as Pt. Jawaharlal Nehru did, meant it to be some damnable act. Was it not a just and revolutionary act? Again no Indian has forgotten this justified and valorous act. May be Pt. Nehru did.

Had this been the only reason of Bhagat Singh's popularity, then Sardar Udham Singh should have been equally, if not more, popular than Bhagat Singh. He had killed Sir Michael O'Dwyer, then Lt. Governor of Punjab, responsible for the diabolical crime of butchering hundreds of innocent young and old, women and children, in the blood-bath at Jallianwala Bagh in 1919 at Amritsar. Sardar Udham Singh too had vindicated the honour of the nation as well as of those who got butchered by Sir Michael O' Dwyer and that he did even 20 years after the massacre. There were others such as Madan Lal Dhingra who vindicated the honour of the nation. But they are almost like footnotes in the history of the country.

Pt. Jawaharlal Nehru, while discussing the Bhagat Singh

phenomenon in his *Autobiography*, neither took into consideration his (Bhagat Singh) and his Party—"The Hindustan Socialist Republican Army's" other revolutionary actions nor their revolutionary writings issued in the form of notices, leaflets, statements, articles, booklets, letters, etc.

Pt. Jawaharlal Nehru did not see or did not wish to see the revolutionary movement in India and saw only terrorism and terrorists in various parts of the country. He swept aside all the daring "actions" and writings of Bhagat Singh and his Party's Revolutionary Army. He remembered only the murder of Saunders, that too, as it avenged the death of Lala Lajpat Rai and vindicatd his and the nation's honour, but regretfully, at the same time, labelled it '*an act of terrorism*'.

Did Mahatma Gandhi or Pt. Jawaharlal Nehru or any member of their own Congress Party dare to think of avenging Lala Lajpat Rai's death and vindicate his and the nation's honour through the creed of non-violence or otherwise? Lala Lajpat Rai was one of the tallest leaders not only of the country but was of the Congress Party also. Only the revolutionaries, such as Shaheed-e-Azam Bhagat Singh, Udham Singh, Madan Lal Dhingra and many others, had thought of doing so putting their lives at stake and displaying a rare courage to vindicate the honour of the nation. The Congress leadership should have felt proud of them.

The revolutionaries had made a unique impact on the masses. People were overawed by their courage, fearless patriotic spirit and sacrifice of their lives and showered admiration on their marvellous actions. They thought of them as 'revolutionary freedom-fighters' and not 'terrorists' as Pt. Nehru and some other historians had designated them.

Can any patriotic Indian forget Sukhdev's brilliant letter to Mahatma Gandhi written just a few days before his execution. This letter was written in the context of his [Gandhiji] compromise with the British Indian Government known as the '*Gandhi-Irwin Pact*'. Under this compromise, Gandhiji's civil-disobedience movement prisoners were released, Sukhdev, in his letter, a part of which is already reproduced in the earlier pages in this chapter, reminds Mahatmaji of the fate of the Ghadr Party, Babbar Akali and various revolutionary conspiracy cases prisoners rotting in jails. But Gandhiji did not speak to Lord Irwin, the Viceroy about them. Nor did Pt. Jawaharlal Nehu, the then Congress President ever plead their case.

The epic hunger-strike lasting more than 110 days by Bhagat Singh and his comrades and the mass revolutionary movement resulting in a country-wide revolutionary upsurge against the British rule created by them while locked behind the prison walls, was shrewdly obliterated by Pt. Nehru in evaluating the revolutionaries in more than 600 pages of his *An Autobiography*. Pt. Nehru observes, "and within a few months each town and village of the Punjab and to a lesser extent in the rest of northern India, resounded with his [Bhagat Singh] name."

It was not "to a lesser extent in the rest of the northern India" as asserted by Pt. Nehru. Bhagat Singh's name, fame, daring acts and the news of how smilingly he and his comrades kissed the gallows spread in no time throughout the nooks and corners of India and "was as widely known all over India and was as popular as Gandhiji." Articles, editorials, poems, in newspapers such as *The Hindu. The Deccan Chronicle* of South India, *Amrit Bazar Patrika* of Bengal, *Free Press Journal* of Bombay and in many other newspapers in all parts of the country, began to be published.

Pritam Singh, Professor at Oxford Brookes University, UK, in his research found that in states as different as Assam and Andhra Pradesh, there were folk songs and rural craft works celebrating Bhagat Singh's bravery.

Mr. Periyar E.V. Ramasami, then well-known and popular literary personality in the South, wrote an important article/editorial in *KUDIARASU*, on March 29, 1931. His long editorial/article began stating, "There is no one who has not condoled the death of Mr. Bhagat Singh by hanging. There is none who has not condemned the British Government of India for hanging Bhagat Singh. Besides, we now see several people known as patriots and national heroes scolding Mr. Gandhi for the happening of this event". Mr. Periyar's article has been included and published in almost every book on Bhagat Singh. *The Modern Rationalist* thought it appropriate to publish it again in its issue as recently as in November 2006. Reports and articles on Bhagat Singh's execution were published as far as in *Daily Worker* in New York, USA and Berlin in Europe.

And it was Bhagat Singh and his The Hindustan Socialist Republican Army and not the Congress Party led by Mahatma Gandhi and Pt. Jawaharlal Nehru who made this people's "anger", "indignation" and "national humiliation", a serious and a major issue and in practice, an act of "terrorism" on the Indian people to be avenged with "counter-terrorism" on the British imperialist rulers. They, the Congress Party and its leadership, including Mahatma Gandhi and Pt. Jawaharlal Nehru, on the other hand, condemned the revolutionaries calling them 'lunatics' and 'madmen'.

This new revolutionary development highly unnerved not only the British rulers but also the bourgeois nationalist leadership of the country. The people, however, were secretly very happy. The action and notices of the revolutionaries were etched in the eyes and minds of people and never forgotten. It was a master-stroke by the leadership of revolutionists that reverberated among the young and the old of the Indian nation.This could not be cherished by the Indian bourgeois nationalist leadership. Another claim proudly flaunted forth was: "Fifteen years stress on non-violence has changed the whole background in India and made the masses much more indifferent to, and even hostile to the idea of terrorism as a method of political action." This is Pt. Nehru in his *Autobiography.*

One sees contrary "glimpses" of Pt. Nehru's views, in his *Glimpses of World History:*

"To the tiger of imperialism, there will only be the fiercest opposition and today our country has to deal with that ferocious animal. It may be possible to tame the wild tiger of the forest and to charm away its native ferocity, but there is no such possibility of taming capitalism and imperialism when they combine and swoop down on an unhappy land". And India is one of such unhappy lands in the world where not the tigers of the forest but tigers of capitalism and imperialism have been and are still swooping down in the 21st century since 1757.

Could these tigers be tamed with non-cooperation and civil disobedience movements and Mahatma Gandhi and Pt. Nehru's "non-violence"? They, in the actions of the revolutionaries, saw the potentialities of the growth of a new phenomenon of revolution against the British rule. This new development started weighing heavily on the minds of the collaborationist leadership of the country as this could affect the interests of the Indian bourgeoisie and their political leadership, the Congress, adversely.

Pt. Nehru, therefore, thought of writing about Bhagat Singh in detail eulogising him individually and that too on the basis of avenging Lala Lajpat Rai's death and for his bravery in sacrificing his life, excluding him from all the other revolutionary actions as well as his writings. He even ignored the formation of the Hindustan Socialist Republican Association, a real revolutionary socialist Party articulating the Marxist ideology. This was Pt. Nehru's masterful stroke.

Many of the writers of history books have toed the ideology of social democracy sanitised, sanctioned and followed by mainstream nationalist leaders including, especially, Pt. Jawaharlal Nehru. The role of the valiant revolutionary fighters, who, by sacrificing their own lives, had made the lives of the British and Indian bureaucrats, serving British imperialism, vulnerable and unsafe, was usually either undervalued or deprecated, calling them terrorists. The significance of the formation of organisations such as the Naujawan Bharat Sabha, the Hindustan Socialist Republican Association and the Hindustan Socialist Republican Army was ignored. Their manifestoes had never found any space in their history books. Terrorism was condemned in its totality without acknowledging its promotional role in inculcating revolutionary fervour and in bringing about revolution. In recent years as Bhagat Singh's popularity has grown all over the country, his *moorat* [statue] has been installed within the premises of the Parliament Complex in New Delhi. The *moorat*, however, is a feeble substitute for understanding and following his true ideology. The ideology and political views of Bhagat Singh were outlined in his numerous writings and statements which were never mentioned by Pt. Nehru. The historians, while eulogising Bhagat Singh's bravery and sacrifice of his life, also ended up eulogising and glorifying Pt. Nehru and Mahatma Gandhi.

The author of *Glimpses of World History* would write about Karl Marx and Lenin devoting about nine chapters on Marxism and the Soviet Union and about hundreds of kings, queens, social reformers, philosophers and religious men but not about the countless lion-hearted revolutionaries, the Anushilan Samiti, the Ghadr Party, the Hindustan Republican Association and Bhagat Singh's the Hindustan Socialist Republican Association and their dauntless actions which shook the foundations of the British Empire and due to which, the British Prime Minister C.R. Attlee had to transfer, on a platter, power to Pt. Jawaharlal Nehru, the President of the Indian National Congress Party, in his internationally acclaimed book of more than a thousand pages.

2

Bhagat Singh's Baptism in Marxism

During the non-cooperation movement in 1921, Mahatma Gandhi had given a call to the young men to shun all government and government-aided educational institutions and these included the DAV institutions. Bhagat Singh left the DAV High School in Lahore and joined the National College which was established by Lala Lajpat Rai, Bhai Parmanand and others. Such national institutions were established in other parts of the country as well to facilitate the education of young men who had boycotted the government institutions. At the National College, Bhagat Singh met some of his future colleagues of the Hindustan Socialist Republican Association and the Lahore Conspiracy Case. They included Bhagwati Charan Vohra, Sukhdev and Yashpal. Amongst the teachers were Acharya Jugal Kishore who taught Political Science, Bhai Parmanand taught Modern European History and Professor Jayachandra Vidyalankar taught Ancient Indian History. For a while, Ghulam Hussain, formerly in Islamia College of Peshawar, taught Socialism. In the beginning, Lala Lajpat Rai used to come and teach the students. All of them helped their students to develop an interest in the studies of Socialism. One of the teachers in the College was Chhabildas, who had become the Principal of the College after the retirement of Acharya Jugal Kishore. He played a prominent role not only as a teacher but also in inculcating awareness about Socialism and the Soviet Union, amongst the students and, later on, amongst the general public, by writing small pamphlets mostly in Urdu—the prevailing language in those times. These pamphlets were printed in large numbers, and made available to the public at a price of two pice only.

Bhagat Singh was one of the favourite students of Professor Jayachandra Vidyalankar who taught History. He helped Bhagat Singh in establishing contacts with many revolutionaries when, later on, he left for Kanpur. At the National College, Bhagat Singh got the opportunity to study books on Marxism and other subjects written by well-known Marxist and other thinkers and writers such as Karl Marx, Friedrich Engels, Lenin, Maxim Gorki, Rousseau, Plato, Aristotle, Fyodor Dostoevsky, Thomas Paine and so many others. One can have an idea of his wide reach of subjects and authors from his 'Jail Notebook' and in this endeavour, he was greatly helped by Raja Ram Shastri, the then Librarian of Dwarka Das Library. Raja Ram Shastri would collect books on History, Politics, Economics as well as revolutionary literature, magazines and journals from all over the country which were not easily available. He himself had developed an interest in Socialism and read books by Karl Marx, Lenin and other thinkers. In this task, he was fully supported by Lala Lajpat Rai, Lala Jagan Nath and Lala Feroze Chand who had given him a free hand to buy books of his choice. He would purchase books from the leading booksellers of Lahore such as Rama Krishna and Sons.

Dwarka Das Library and its Librarian Raja Ram Shastri, it can be said, played a leading role in getting Bhagat Singh, Bhagwati Charan Vohra, Sukhdev and many others educated in the Philosophy of Marxism. Raja Ram Shastri remained associated with the Library till 1930. The Library remained the major source of books to Bhagat Singh and other revolutionaries while they remained behind bars. It would make available all books listed by the revolutionaries in their letters to their friends, visitors or family members and for that, the Library management would not shirk buying from the market the books requested by the revolutionaries. Dwarka Das Library and the National College served as the nursery and gurukul of the Socialist ideology for the revolutionaries, and these two institutions having served almost like the 'Marxist Universities' for Bhagat Singh, Sukhdev, Bhagwati Charan Vohra and other revolutionaries, occupy an important place in the Revolutionary History of India.

Dwarka Das Library is, at present, functioning at Lala Lajpat Rai Bhawan, Chandigarh after it had been brought from Lahore in 1947. The management of Bhawan under Babu Onkar Chand, a devoted follower of Lala Lajpat Rai, still tries to procure and stock most of the books on Marxism-Leninism as it used to do during the Bhagat Singh years and its Lahore days.

In a recorded interview available in the Nehru Memorial Library and Museum, Teen Murti Bhawan, New Delhi, Shastriji reflected on his life in the historic Library. An extract of this interview is reproduced here.

"The golden opportunity which I got in working in this Library was truly a turning point in my life. During my student days at Kashi Vidyapeeth, I was much impressed by the political revolution of France, and I had selected this very topic for my course research project. Since till 1926, I had never been exposed to socialist ideology and was not aware of the Russian Revolution, the question of my being under its influence did not arise. Thus, I continued to be imbued with nationalism and patriotism as my articles of faith. When I reached Lahore, I got employed in the Library. I got a chance to study books by Marx, Lenin and others including about the Russian Revolution and I became a socialist, being highly impressed by this kind of literature. There were very many good books collected by Lala Lajpat Rai in the Library. Besides, under the guidance of Lala Jagan Nath and Lala Feroze Chand, I began purchasing books from Rama Krishna & Sons.

"All around the Library, there were colleges. As the Library was a rich repository of books for the radical-minded youth, many students used to visit its reading room daily. I was always seeking an opportunity to suggest to young men to read Socialist literature. It did not take long for me to notice that this Library was frequented both by revolutionary party youth as also by CID men. I started keeping a sharp eye on the readers to identify such students who had a radical outlook, who could be won over to Socialism by providing them revolutionary literature. It was from this urge that I became acquainted with young men like Bhagat Singh, Sukhdev,

Yashpal, Bhagwati Charan Vohra, Hans Raj Vohra, Dhanwantri, Ram Krishan, Ehsan Elahi, Durga Das Khanna and others. Out of all those, Bhagat Singh, Sukhdev and Bhagwati Charan Vohra were closer to me.

Bhagat Singh was known to be a voracious reader of books and it was said that he always carried books in his pockets whether he was at Lahore, Kanpur or elsewhere as well as while travelling, but it is not possible now to know exactly which books and authors he read. A fairly good idea, however, can be gained from his 'Jail notebook' and his various articles written when he was associated with 'Kiriti' magazine and the list of books he mentioned to be supplied to him in the letters written to his friends and family members and also the books presented in Court as evidence by the Prosecution.

The names of these books with the names of their authors throw a light giving us an idea of the intellectual growth of Bhagat Singh and what a giant of an incredible intellect Bhagat Singh was by the time of his death at the age of 23. The lists are long and interesting and these also serve as a useful guide for study to everyone. Some of the names of books and authors, read by Bhagat Singh, from his diary are mentioned below:

1. *Capital* by Karl Marx; 2. *The Origin of the Family, Property and the State* by Friedrich Engels; 3. *Where is Britain Going?* by Leon Trotsky; 4. *A World History for the Workers* by Alfred Barton; 5. *Rights of Man* by Tom Paine; 6. *The Cry for Justice* by Upton Sinclair; 7. *From Marx to Lenin* by Morris Hillquit; 8. *The Iron Heel* by Jack London; 9. *Wastes of Capitalism* by Theodor Hertzka; 10. *Children of the Dead End* by Patrick MacGill; 11. *Poverty and Riches* by Scott Nearing; 12. *The Lessons of October* by Leon Trotsky; 13. *Les Miserables* by Victor Hugo; 14. *Crime and Punishment* by Fyodor Dostoevsky; 15. *The House of the Dead* by Fyodor Dostoevsky; 16. *The New Spirit* by B.C. Pal; 17. *Indian Unrest* by Valentine Chirol; 18. *Tracticus Politicus* by Spinoza; 19. *Citizen and Man* by Emile; 20. *Essays in Application* by Henry Van Dyke; 21. *Militarism*; 22. *Why Men Fight*; 23. *Soviets at Work*; 24. *Collapse of the Second International*; 25. *Left Wing Communism*; 26. *Mutual Aid*; 27. *Fields, Factories and*

Workshops; 28. *Civil War in France*; 29. *Land Revolution in Russia*; 30. *Theory of Historical Materialism.*

By the time Bhagat Singh left the National College and went to Kanpur, in 1924, he had become well-accquainted with Marxism, and had made up his mind to devote his life for the emancipation of his compatriots from the foreign yoke. With an introduction from his Professor Jayachandra Vidyalankar for Ganesh Shankar Vidyarthi, a prominent public figure and sympathiser of the revolutionaries, he met him at his office who welcomed him warmly and provided suitable accommodation. Vidyarthi had been bringing out a weekly-*Pratap* and Bhagat Singh joined it as Balwant, an assumed name. Before seeing Vidyarthi, Bhagat Singh had also met Manmath Nath Gupta in the Vartman office with a short note from Sachindra Nath Sanyal who too had accorded him a warm welcome and offered all assistance.

Vidyarthi's office used to be an *adda* (meeting place) of the revolutionaries where Bhagat Singh met B.K. Dutt, B.K. Sinha, Shiv Varma, Chandra Shekhar Azad and others and held discussions on political issues including the goings on in the Congress and the state of the revolutionary movement.

3

The Naujawan Bharat Sabha

The time, Bhagat Singh and his colleagues spent in the National College, Lahore, as students of Professor Jayachandra Vidyalankar, Acharya Jugal Kishore, Bhai Parmanand, Principal Chhabildas and others as well as at Dwaraka Das Library with its Librarian Raja Ram Shastri, was the most formative and creative period of their lives. Marxism, the Russian Revolution, achievements of the Soviet Union and, of course, the question of India's liberation from the British colonial yoke, were amongst the most important subjects discussed under the guidance of the learned and radical-minded teachers, at these institutions.

Mahatma Gandhi had withdrawn his non-cooperation movement and the promise of "Swaraj within one year" had been forgotten. People and, especially, the youth had lost their faith in Mahatma Gandhiji's leadership and his concepts of non-violence and non-cooperation. Their minds were turning to the earlier revolutionary views of 'freedom by all means' and 'at all costs.'

Bhagat Singh

Bhagwati Charan Vohra

It was at this juncture (1926) that Bhagat Singh and his colleagues—Bhagwati Charan Vohra, Sukhdev and others thought of taking practical measures by setting up Naujawan Bharat Sabha as a first step to prepare the masses, especially the youth, for revolution. In this task, they were assisted by Dr. Saifuddin Kitchlew, Dr. Satyapal, Ram Krishan, Ram Chand, Kedar Nath Sehgal, Principal Chhabildas, Ehsan Elahi and others. Ram Krishan, Bhagat Singh and Bhagwati Charan Vohra were made the President, General Secretary and Propaganda Secretary respectively. Ram Chand was made the Vice-President. The motto of the Sabha was, "Revolution By the Masses and For the Masses."

Its objectives were:

(a) The infusion of the spirit of patriotism into the hearts of the youth.
(b) The establishment of an independent republic of labourers and peasants.
(c) The infusion of the spirit of patriotism into the hearts of the youth.
(d) The advancement of the social and economic movements free from communal sentiments.

With direct appeal to the youth, the Sabha had caught their imagination. Within a short time, the Sabha included the establishment of Socialism as a part of its objectives. This was done through a resolution passed at its Provincial Conference held on April 13 and 14, 1928 at Jallianwala Bagh in Amritsar. It stated as its objective:

> "The achievement of a completely independent sovereign socialist republic of peasants and workers", reiterating, "by all possible means including through armed revolution as its goal."

At the Conferenc, Dr. Satya Pal moved a resolution to be sent to the All India Congress Committee to change the creed of non-violence for the attainment of 'Swaraj' to that of "by all possible means." The rsolution was passed by an overwhelming majority.

An important and a significant decision taken at the Conference was substitution of the Tricolour Flag by the Red Flag. Another resolution passed was on religion as one's personal matter separate from politics.

Inter-community dinners were often held in which Hindus, Muslims and Sikhs participated and where secular and socialist ideas were propagated. The concept and philosophy of socialism explained was that of 'Scientific Socialism' as propounded by Karl Marx and not 'Fabian Socialism' of various hues such as 'Democratic Socialism' which were referred to as 'Socialism' and those expounding it called themselves "socialists." The Indian National Congress too, at one of its sessions under the Presidentship of Pt. Jawaharlal Nehru, had adopted it, calling it 'Democratic Socialism', as one of its objects. According to such Fabian socialists, Socialism could be brought about by gradually reforming and transferring the capitalist system through adult franchise and voting in the bourgeois parliamentary system. Scientific Socialism, that is the rule of the proletariat [workers and peasants], would never be allowed to be set up by a bourgeois state, a state ruled by the capitalists as the capitalist rulers would suppress and arrest the proletariat leadership under the laws such as the law of sedition dubbing them as the enemies of the state. The proletariat revolutionaries were similarly used to be arrested and executed by the Czarist regime in Russia before 1917 as well as in other capitalist states in the past and as is now done in the present times.

Bhagwati Charan Vohra, the Propaganda Secretary of the Naujawan Bharat Sabha issued the Manifesto of the Sabha drafted by Bhagat Singh in which the real characteristic of the so-called nationalist leadership comprising the National Congress, the Muslim League, the Liberal Party and such other bodies in the provinces, was exposed as being the representatives of the various groups of the bourgeoisie and big landlords. The Manifesto of the Sabha went on:

> Our leaders are fighting amongst themselves to decide what will be the share of each community in the hoped for achievements. Simply to conceal their cowardice and lack of spirit of sacrifice, they are creating false issues and screening the real ones. These arm-chair politicians have their eyes set on the handful of bones that may be thrown to them, as they hope for, by the mighty British rulers.

The Naujawan Bharat Sabha was a semi-secret organisation with an open and secret programme for preparing the youth for the armed revolution. Bhagat Singh, Sukhdev and Bhagwati Charan Vohra kept an eye on the young men active in the programmes of the Sabha who could be recruited for the revolutionary work.

The Sabha held meetings and seminars at different places. On some occasions, they would invite prominent revolutionaries from other provinces to address such seminars who would apprise the youth of their own experiences. Mrs. Suhasini Nambiar was invited at the All India Naujawan Bharat Sabha Conference at Lahore in December 1929. At another Conference, the Sabha invited Dr. Bhupendra Nath Dutta from Bengal. Dr. Dutta, brother of Maharishi Aurobindo Ghosh was the Editor of *Yugantar*. One of his editorials in his paper reads:

> "Whether it is well to submit to being assaulted like so many heads of cattle or sheep or whether it is better for self-defence to wield 'lathis' in return for lathis [sticks]."

His brother, Maharishi Aurobindo Ghosh at the time [in the first decade of the 20th century] had written: "Tyrants have tried but have they ever succeeded in repressing the natural love of freedom in man? Repression has grown in strength. Crushed under the heel of the tyrant, it has assumed myriad forms and in successive incarnations, gained strength and inspiration from repeated failures and endless sufferings. It has risen finally to overthrow its oppressor for good. This is the teaching of history; this is the message of humanity..."

"But like the scriptural adder, tyrannies have eyes but they see not; have ears bur they hear not; and the universal teaching of history and the eternal message of humanity are both lost on them." Relating such extracts from his paper and narrating the phenomenal and stupendous actions of the revolutionaries of his earlier times, Dr. Dutta would sharpen the political consciousness of the young men to an unprecedented level.

An All India Naujawan Bharat Sabha Conference was held on December 29, 1929 at Lahore at which in her presidential address, Mrs. Suhasini Nambiar, an eminent socialist youth leader from the

South, clarified the role of the various classes of people in India's independence movement.

She explained that the class of people comprising the capitalists, zamindars [feudal landlords] and a section of the wavering and vacillating intellectuals and professionals represented by the Congress were out for a compromise with British imperialism. They would be satisfied with the Dominion Status, though they might sometimes raise their voices for independence. The interests of the masses comprising the working class, peasantry and the middle class, could be only safeguarded when India gets not only the complete independence but it is also a socialist state ruled by the proletariat and the middle class. Explaining further, she stated that, Lord Irwin was not yet prepared to grant even the Dominion Status and that the Congress leadership would be satisfied with what had already been announced or at the most with some more powers.

Here we must remember that political struggle or opposition is only the resultant of a clash of economic interests. This situation will not change even if there is only political independence and unless India is a socialist state.

The anti-imperialist youth of India, she exhorted, must correctly realise the role they have to play in the struggle. They must know that every industrial strike, every economic dispute between the landlord and the tenant, is definitely a struggle against imperialism and for the overthrow of all exploiters. To be able to carry on successfully the fight against imperialism, the members of the Sabha must form study circles to study the Science of Socialism and working class struggle. They have to carry on organisational work both in the industrial and rural areas. (The speech was extensively reported in *The Tribune*, Lahore in its issue dated January 1,1930. The above is an edited version.)

The Naujawan Bharat Sabha was in the forefront of the huge demonstration led by Lala Lajpat Rai against the Simon Commission at Lahore.

Along with the Naujawan Bharat Sabha, Bhagat Singh had promoted students' unions in educational institutes. These also served as recruiting centres for revolutionary work. The Sabha had started a newspaper called *Naujawan* with the objective of developing Marxist understanding and revolutionary consciousness among the youth.

The files of the home-political branch of the British Government maintained by the National Archives of India contained many details about the programme and activities of the Naujawan Bharat Sabha as well as of the students' unions in the colleges. These activities had unnerved the government so much that it warned the management of the institutions to stop their grant and even recognition if they failed to curb the revolutionary activities.The teachers who preached revolutionary and 'Boleshevik' ideas were threatened with removal from service while the doors of government employment were shut for those youth who participated in the revolutionary activities.

The Sabha spearheaded the campaign in support of the demands of the hunger-strikers of the Lahore Conspiracy Case prisoners led by Bhagat Singh. Later on, the members and activists of the Sabha were in the first line of battle for the commutation of the death sentence on Bhagat Singh, Sukhdev and Rajguru.

The Naujawan Bharat Sabha was one of the most radical organisations in the country against the British Government and serves as a model for the students and youth today.

In *Colour of the Cage: A Prison Memoir*, its young author, Arun Ferreira, had written about the Naujawan Bharat Sabha in Mumbai that he joined in the late 1990s. The Naujawan Bharat Sabha was involved in the struggle of Mumbai slum dwellers protesting the demolition of their homes. He, who had spent some years in jails as a political prisoner, also tells us in his book that September 13 is commemorated every year as the martyrdom day of Shaheed (martyr) Jatin Nath Das who died on the 63rd day of his hunger strike, that he went on along with Bhagat Singh. The day is observed as an occasion to demand recognition of political prisoners.

The students of Panjab University, Chandigarh have formed Students for Society (SFS), an organisation on the lines of the Naujawan Bharat Sabha and the inheritor of the Sabha's ideology of Scientific Socialism. This organisation is led by the ideology of Bhagat

Singh. There was a headline in a newspaper; '*Shaheed Bhagat Singh Gets Fielded in Panjab University Polls*'. This was evident as his photo captioned *Inquilab Zindabad* (Long Live the Revolution) stood out on a wall in the University put up by the Students For Society during one of the annual Panjab University Students' Council elections. He was above all religions, was a staunch atheist and believed in class consciousness and class politics. His ideology was Scientific Socialism as is also the ideology of 'Students for Society'. It is a matter of pride and that like a whiff of fresh air, the students of the Panjab University, Chandigarh have elected Kanupriya, a candidate of the Student for Society, as the first woman President of their University Campus Students' Council.

4

Tracts Society

A well-planned programme for educating the masses, especially the youth, on the Sabha's ideology, was chalked out. It was decided to produce small pamphlets and leaflets and distribute these at a very low price. A Tract Society under the leadership of Principal Chhabildas, a reputed Marxist scholar in those times, was set up. He wrote a number of sixteen-page tracts priced at just two pices, so that the poorest could have the same. These were mostly written in '*Urdu*', the prevailing language and were very popular in the then Punjab [Haryana, East Punjab, Himachal Pradesh and the West Punjab of Pakistan] Delhi, UP, Rajasthan and in the princely states where these pamphlets were distributed in a clandestine manner.

Some of these tracts were declared objectionable and proscribed by the British Government as well as by the princely states. Our (author) family residing at Mansa, a town in the then princely state of Patiala, used to receive these tracts and my uncle used to distribute them to many Praja Mandal (a political organisation like the Congress in British India) activists as well as Kirti Party workers in the rural areas. A few people in Mansa town, who were illiterate, but were politically conscious, would gather in the evening at our residence, situated in the centre of the town, when my uncle would read out to them those publications as well as the daily newspaper received by him from the newspaper hawker, who was also a teacher running a small school. The teacher-cum-hawker used to receive just 20 copies of an Urdu Daily dispatched from Lahore by a train reaching Mansa at 4 pm. The hawker carrying the copies of the newspaper would pass through the main market shouting "*Akhbar lailo, Tazian Khabaran*" [Buy the newspaper, with the latest news]. I [the author], then a student of sixth class, fairly well-versed in Urdu, also sometimes used to read them. Principal Chhabildas remained active long after Bhagat Singh and his two comrades had been hanged and the publication and distribution of his tracts continued till the late 1930s.

Mansa, that is now a district headquarter in Punjab, used to be a small town surrounded by the villages which were strongholds of *muzzaras* (landless peasants and serfs) movement against the *Biswedars* [feudal landlords] led by the Communist and *Kirti* [workers'] Party stalwarts such as Jagir Singh Joga [later on, MLA in PEPSU and Punjab Legislative Assemblies] Dharam Singh Fakkad, Ajmer Singh Tamkotia and others. In the rural areas, there used to be often skirmishes and clashes between the *Muzzaras* and the *Biswedars*. These rural areas had become known as the 'Red Zone'. The revenue officials of the government were afraid of visiting these areas. The *Muzzaras*' leaders also used to hold meetings in Mansa attended by a huge gathering of not only the town's people but also by the many farmers who had brought their produce for sale in the grain market of Mansa. The meetings were held at night in front of our Commission Shop in the Grain Market at which Jagir Singh Joga would sometimes make me preside over the same. Addressing these gatherings, Jagir Singh Joga and other 'muzzara' leaders such as Ajmer Singh Tamkotia, would tell the audience [mostly farmers] that they (Communist Leaders) would show them their cruel ruler (Maharaja Bhupender Singh) "*Nu Thuada Kamma Banake, Thuhade Beddey Dian Khurlian Vich Pasuan Nu Sani karde Dikha Dian Gai*". (We shall show him (the Maharaja) working as your serf, tending and feeding the cattle in your cowsheds). The Maharaja was at that time, Chancellor of the Chamber of Princes as well. He, like all kings from Ashoka "The Great" to Akbar to Jehangir and Bahadur Shah Zaffar and "Sher-e-Punjab" Maharaja Ranjit Singh, had more than one queen. In Maharaja Bhupender Singh's case, however, it was said he had more than 100 Ranis [Queens] residing in his numerous palaces in Patiala City, the state's capital and there were many spicy tales circulating among his subjects about how he used to acquire his

'Ranis'. It was due to the brutal treatment, under his rule in Patiala Central Jail, meted out to Sardar Sewa Singh Thikriwala, a senior and popular Praja Mandal leader, that Sardar Thikriwala attained martyrdom after a nine-month long hunger-strike at the young age of 45 in 1935. He (Maharaja Bhupinder Singh) was the grandfather of Captain Amrinder Singh, who is serving as a Congress Chief Minister of Punjab.

The tracts of the Naujawan Bharat Sabha written by Principal Chhabildas, its manifesto authored by Bhagat Singh and the articles written by Bhagat Singh in *Kirti* (Labourer), published in Urdu and Punjabi languages, made a powerful impact on the masses, especially, the youth and the students, in raising their revolutionary political consciousness. They felt greatly attracted towards the Naujawan Bharat Sabha taking part in its activities. Bhagat Singh wrote illuminating articles on the various philosophical and political currents going on in the European countries such as France, Germany, Italy, Czarist Russia. He wrote in a series of three articles on 'Anarchism' as well as one on 'Russian Nihilists'. Bhagat Singh had expressed his intention to write articles on 'Communism' and 'Socialism' also but these, have not been found as yet.

In his articles on 'Anarchism', Bhagat Singh wrote: [extracts] "the word 'Anarchist' has become so unpopular that those who want to change the political establishment are called 'anarchists' simply to defame them. Dr. Bhupendra Nath Dutta had written in his unpublished book *The Political History*, Volume I that the "government may call us 'Anarchists' in order to defame us but actually we are a group of those who want to change the political establishment."

Bhagat Singh wrote further: "Anarchism is actually a very great ideal. Our ordinary public cannot even conceive such a great thing, for they have not seen even those who are less than the Anarchists. The word 'Anarchism' has been badly defamed. As the selfish capitalists have defamed the words 'Bolsheviks', 'Socialists', etc., so has this word been defamed, although 'Anarchists' are carefree persons who are well-wishers of the world. Even when we may differ from their ideas, we cannot doubt their seriousness, love for their people, spirit of sacrifice and truthfulness".

On 'Russian Nihilists', Bhagat Singh wrote: "Nihilism was then a philosophy which was opposed to religious blind beliefs, social injustice, narrow-mindedness, and the government's oppression. It also propagated such ideas which opposed these things... The Nihilists were also greatly oppressed. They were not allowed to preach good things... Many young Russian men and women had fled to Western Europe in 1871. Most of them were in Switzerland. They were allowed to come home by the government. These people arrived with new ideas of Communism. They started propagating these ideas. The moment they landed in Russia, the Czar got these young men arrested and sent them to Siberia. The young men changed their tactics. They did their work secretly.They were good public servants [*jansevaks*] endowed with a great spirit of sacrifice, they loved people.

Anarchism and Nihilism, like Socialism and Communism were popular philosophical currents attracting a large following in 19th century Europe. Proudhon, a French philosopher is called the 'father' of Anarchism. Subsequently, Prince Kropotkin, John Mast and many others came. Michael Bukanin is amongst the greatest of Anarchists. In the Paris Commune in 1871, many communards were followers of Proudhon and Michael Bukanin. Garibaldi, the well-known Italian revolutionary had also joined the Anarchists. Mrs. Emma Goldman and Alexander Brakeman were the propagandists of Anarchism in America according to Bhagat Singh. And where and what was India in the 19th century?

In India of the 19th century, all the socio-political ideologies prevailing in the Western world, especially in France, Germany and Russia remained subdued by the predominant religious thoughts such as preached by the Brahmo Samaj, the Ramakrishna Ashram movement, Arya Samaj and Sanatan Dharma movements, as well as the various gurukuls (Schools of Hindu religious thought), 'Singh Sabhas' (preaching Sikh religion) and 'Madrasas' (schools) of Islamic thought. Due to the lack of modern education and knowledge, people remained prone to superstitious beliefs. The dominance of religion-based movements impeded the development of political consciousness and the growth and quality of the revolutionary movement.

A small section of wealthy upper classes such as big landlords, industrialists, merchants, lawyers and other professionals, who had prospered by collaborating with the British rulers, were able to get themselves educated in England and other Western countries. They, however, had very few links with the vast majority of Indians. They lived in a world far apart from the masses and did not understand their plight.

5

Birth of the Hindustan Socialist Republican Association

At the initiative and insistence of Bhagat Singh, (He was just about 20 years old) an all-India meet of the revolutionaries was held on September 8-9, 1928 on the Ferozeshah Kotla ground in New Delhi. At the meeting, two major decisions taken, besides others, were the addition of the word 'Socialist' to the name of the Party [The Hindustan Republican Association] and the establishment of 'Socialism' besides the attainment of independence as its aims. Another important decision taken was the formation of the Party's Army Wing.

The meeting, according to Manmath Nath Gupta, was attended by Bhagat Singh, Bejoy Kumar Sinha, Shiv Varma, Kundan Lal, Manmohan Banerji, Sukhdev, Jaidev Gupta, Brahm Dutt Mishra, Surendra and Phanindra Ghosh. For obvious reasons, Chandra Shekhar Azad (He was absconding in the Kakori Case), did not attend the meeting. He had been consulted about the agenda and had agreed completely. He was appointed the Commander-in-Chief of the Party's Army Wing that was named 'The Hindustan Socialist Republican Army' and the Party's name was 'The Hindustan Socialist Republican Association'.

A Remarkable Marxist Postulation: The Party had formulated a remarkable Marxist postulation that if today the present British Government was handed over to the Congress and the system of administration remained just the same, the Hindustan Socialist Republican Association would be as much against the Congress Rule as against the British Government at present. If during the regime of the Congress Government as described above, the British [Great Britain] Government would establish a parallel Government in India, based on socialist principles, the Party would help the British Government and not the Government of the Congress in the country. [*The Tribune,* April 11, 1931]

Other rules of the Party were:

A member must be between the age of 16 and 35.

The member must have sufficient education to enable him to understand political literature. Mostly revolutionary literature was in English and Urdu. The members had to read books like *Ten Days That Shook the World* and *Swadhinta Ke Pujari.*

The member whose parents were living, had to abscond from his place to work for the Party as he could not serve the Party freely living with his parents.

The people who were addicted to alcohol could not become members of the Party.

A member had to undergo all sorts of examinations—physical, psychological, literacy, political knowledge, etc. before he could be enlisted as a member.

He must not have any physiological defect in his body.

He was not to entertain any conservative religious views. He could not be a member of any communal or religious body.

He could not be a member of the Congress Party unless it was in the interests of the Party, otherwise the Party was against the Congress Creed and its programme as it was not based on socialist principles. [*The Tribune,* April 11, 1931]

It was after this meeting that Bhagat Singh shed his hair and beard [religious symbols] in order to be more mobile and safe. This was done ceremoniously in Ferozepore. Bhagat Singh and the Party, thus, got new looks. In this meeting, Sukhdev, Kundan Lal, Phanindra Ghosh and Shiv Varma were made responsible for the organisation in Punjab, Rajasthan, Bihar and UP respectively. It was resolved that as there was a paucity of arms and money, they should be judiciously used.

In a short piece of about four pages of their Manifesto, the

Party of the revolutionaries elucidated on revolution, violence and non-violence, terrorism and the role of the youth. They boldly and unambiguously stated that their Party (Association) stood for revolution to liberate their country from foreign domination by means of organised armed rebellion, adding open rebellion by a subject people must always be preceded by secret propaganda and secret preparations.

6

Manifesto of the Hindustan Socialist Republican Association

The Party's Manifesto. is one of the most important statements reflecting its ideology and is reproduced as a part of the text. Written by Bhagat Singh, as the Party's General Secretary, it was typed, printed and published by Bhagwati Charan Vohra, as the Party's Propaganda Secretary. It was issued under the name of Kartar Singh, a fictitious name. [It was widely distributed during the Lahore Session of the Congress in December 1929.]

"The food on which the tender plant of liberty thrives is the blood of the martyr."

[For decades the life blood to the plant of India's liberty is being supplied by revolutionaries. There are few to question the magnanimity of the noble ideals they cherish and the grand sacrifices they have offered, but their normal activities, being mostly secret, the country is in the dark as to their present policy and intentions. This has necessitated the Hindustan Socialist Republican Association to issue this Manifesto.]

This Association stands for revolution in India in order to liberate the country from foreign domination by means of organised armed rebellion. Open rebellion by a subject people must always, in the nature of things, be preceded by secret propaganda and secret preparations. Once a country enters that phase the task of an alien government becomes impossible. It might linger on for a number of years but its fate is sealed. Human nature, with all its prejudices and conservatism, has a sort of instinctive dread of revolution. Upheavals have always been a terror to holders of power and privilege.

Revolution is a phenomenon which nature loves and without which there can be no progress either in nature or in human affairs. Revolution is certainly not unthinking, brutal campaign of murder and incendiarism. It is not a few bombs thrown here and a few shots fired there; neither is it a movement to destroy all remnants of civilisation and blow to pieces time-honoured principles of justice and equity. Revolution is not a philosophy of despair or a creed of desperadoes. Revolution may be anti-God but is certainly not anti-Man. It is a vital, living force which is indicative of eternal conflict between the old and the new, between life and living death, between light and darkness. There is no concord, no symphony, no rhythm without revolution. 'The music of the spheres of which poets have sung, would remain an unreality if a ceaseless revolution were to be eliminated from the space. Revolution is Law. Revolution is order and Revolution is the Truth.

The youths of our nation have realised this Truth. They have learnt painfully the lesson that without revolution there is no possibility of enthroning order, law and love, in place of chaos and legal vandalism and hatreds which are reigning supreme today. Let no one, in this blessed land of ours, run with the idea that the youths are irresponsible. They know where they stand. No one knows better than these youth, that their path is not strewn with roses. From time to time, they have paid a fairly decent price for their ideals. It does not, therefore, lie with anybody to say that youthful impetuosity has feasted upon platitudes. It is no good to hurl denunciatory epithets at our ideology. It is enough to know that our ideas are sufficiently active and powerful to drive us on, even to the gallows.

It has become fashionable these days to indulge in wild and meaningless talk of non-violence. Mahatma Gandhi is great and we mean no disrespect to him if we express our emphatic disapproval of the methods advocated by him for our country's emancipation. We would be ungrateful to him if we do not salute him for the immense awakening that has been brought about by his non-cooperation movement in the country. But to us the Mahatma is an impossible visionary. Non-violence may be a noble ideal, but is a thing of the morrow. We can, situated as we are, never hope to win our freedom by mere non-violence. The world is armed to the very teeth. And the world is too much with us. All talk of peace may be sincere but is false ideology. What logic, we ask, is there in asking the country to traverse a non-violent path when the world atmosphere is surcharged with violence and exploitation of the weak? We declare with all the emphasis we can command that the youths of the nation cannot be lured by such midsummer nights' dreams.

We believe in violence, not as an end itself but as a means to a noble end. And the votaries of non-violence, as also the advocates of caution and circumspection, will readily grant this much at least that we know how to suffer for and to act upto our convictions. Shall we here recount all those sacrifices which our comrades have offered at the altar of our common mother? Many heart-rending and soul-stirring scenes have been enacted inside the four walls of His Majesty's prison.

We have been taken to task for our terroristic policy. Our answer is that terrorism is never the object of revolutionaries, nor do they believe that terrorism alone can bring independence. Undoubtedly, the revolutionaries think, and rightly, that it is only by resorting to terrorism alone that they can find a most effective means of retaliation. The British Government exists, because the British have been successful in terrorising the whole of India. How are we to meet this official terrorism? Only counter-terrorism on the part of revolutionaries can checkmate effectively this bureaucratic bullying. A feeling of utter helplessness pervades society. How can we overcome this fatal despondency? It is only by infusing a real spirit of sacrifice that lost self-confidence can be restored. Terrorism also has its international aspect. England's enemies, which are many, are drawn towards us by effective demonstration of our strength. That in itself is a great advantage. India is writhing under the yoke of imperialism. Her teeming millions are today a helpless prey to poverty and ignorance. Foreign domination and economic exploitation have unmanned the vast majority of the people who constitute the workers and peasants of India.

The position of the Indian proletariat is, today, extremely critical. It has a double danger to face. It has to bear the onslaught of foreign capital on the one hand and the treacherous attack of Indian capital on the other. The latter is showing a progressive tendency to join forces with the former. The leaning of certain politicians in favour of Dominion Status shows clearly which way the wind blows.

Indian capital is preparing to betray the masses into the hands of foreign capital and receive as a price of this betrayal, a small share in the government of the country. The hope of the proletariat is, therefore, now centred on Socialism which alone can lead to the establishment of complete independence and the removal of all social distinctions and privileges. The future of India rests with the youth. They are the salt of the earth. Their promptness to suffer, their daring courage and their radiant sacrifice prove that India's future is perfectly safe in their hands. In a moment of realisation, the late Deshbandhu Dass said:

> The youths are at once the hope and glory of the Motherland. Theirs is the inspiration behind the movement. Theirs is the sacrifice. Theirs is the victory. They are the torch-bearers on the road to freedom. They are the pilgrims on the road to liberty.

Youths, ye soldiers of the Indian Republic, fall in: Do not stand easy, do not let your knees tremble. Shake off the paralysing effects of long lethargy. Yours is a noble mission. Go out into every nook and corner of the country and prepare the ground for future revolution which is sure to come. Respond to the clarion call of duty. Do not vegetate. Grow every minute of your life. You must think of devising means so that your ancient land may arise with flaming eyes and fierce strength. Sow the seeds of disgust and hatred against British imperialism in the fertile minds of your fellow youths. And the seeds shall sprout and there shall grow a jungle of sturdy trees, because you shall water the seeds with your warm blood. Then a grim and terrible earthquake having a universally destructive potentiality shall inevitably come along with portentous rumblings, and this edifice of imperialism will crash and crumble to dust, and great shall be the fall thereof. And then, and not till then, a new Indian nation shall arise and surprise humanity with the splendour and glory, all its own. The wise and the mighty shall be bewildered by the simple and the weak.

Individual liberty shall be safe. The sovereignty of the proletariat shall be recognised. We court the advent of such a revolution. Long Live the Revolution!

–Kartar Singh, President

7

Demonstration Against the Simon Commission

The Party decided to stage a demonstration protesting against the Simon Commission as well as the British Government's move to decide the fate of the Indian people. They affirmed their refusal to accept Britain's sovereignty over India as well as its 1919 Act. The Party opposed the Commission on the ground that the British colonial power had no right to decide the fate of the Indian people and the British Government and its Parliament could claim no sovereignty over India.

The stand of the Congress, on the other hand, was different from that of the Hindustan Socialist Republican Association. It (The Congress) opposed the Commission on the ground that it was composed of only the Englishmen and that no Indian, especially, Congressmen had been taken in it. It didn't oppose the India Act 1919 itself. The Congress had no objection to the sovereignty of the British Parliament to decide the fate of the Indian people.

Sir John Simon, on arrival in India, had written to the Viceroy Lord Irwin that the Commission would take the form of a Joint Free Conference between the English seven members and the seven Indian members who would be chosen by the Central Legislative Assembly. All the documents relating to the Commission including its Report would be made available to the whole Conference of these fourteen members for consideration on free and equal terms. The objection of the Congress against the Commission was, thus, flimsy and had no sense. In this context, the objective of the demonstrations against the Commission at Lahore or at other places including one at Lucknow headed by Pt. Jawaharlal Nehru and G.B. Pant had, therefore, no relevance.

The Seven Member Statutory Commission headed by Sir John Simon had been set up under Section 84A of the India Act 1919. Mr. Clement Attlee, a future Prime Minister of England, was its member. It was under his Prime Ministership in 1947, that the British Government had granted independence to India.

According to Manmath Nath Gupta, the Naujawan Bharat Sabha members along with the members of the Congress Party were in the vanguard of the huge demonstration headed by Lala Lajpat Rai against the Simon Commission.

On the October 30, 1928, the youths of the Sabha held an umbrella over the head of Lala Lajpat Rai. Dhanwantari and Ehsan Ellahi of the Sabha openly led the people, whereas Bhagwati Charan and Sukhdev avoided the limelight. When the mild lathi-charge failed to disperse the crowd, J.A. Scott, the Police Chief ordered an all-out attack. Under his orders, his deputy (Saunders) fell upon the crowd followed by the Indian policemen. His blow smashed the umbrella held over the head of Lala Lajpat Rai and the second blow fell on the Lalaji's shoulder.

Later, at a public meeting in the evening convened to protest against the Simon Commission, Lala Lajpat Rai declared that the blows hurled at him would be the last nails in the coffin of the British rule in India.

Lala Lajpat Rai died on November 17, 1928. More than 1,50,000 people accompanied the funeral procession covering a four-mile distance to the cremation grounds.

8

Vindiction of Lala Lajpat Rai's and the Nation's Honour

"Beware Ye Bureaucracy": "Beware Ye Tyrants": "Beware"

A few days after Lala Lajpat Rai's death, a secret meeting of the Party (HSRA) was held in Lahore and it was decided to liquidate the officer responsible for the death of Lalaji. They intended to kill J.A. Sott, the District Police Chief, but by mistake, J.P. Saunders, the Assistant District Police Superintendent was killed, although both the officers were responsible for inflicting lathi blows on Lalaji. Both deserved to be shot. Jai Gopal was to give the signal and Bhagat Singh and Rajguru were to open fire. On the appointed day, Saunders, who was mistaken as Scott, slowly reached the spot and Rajguru shot him on the head and he collapsed along with his motorcycle. Bhagat Singh also fired to be sure. In the meantime, head constable Chanan Singh chased them on his bicycle. Chandra Shekhar Azad saw that Chanan Singh was hot in pursuit and then Azad raised his pistol and killed Chanan Singh. The road was clear and they (revolutionaries) reached their hide-outs.

When the news of this "action" spread, it was greeted with joy among the public and there was fright in Government circles. The next morning the revolutionary Party's proclamation, The Hindustan Socialist Republican Army's Notice, Beware Ye Bureaucracy in the form of posters appeared pasted on the walls of the city of Lahore as well as published with banner headlines on the front pages of the newspapers, spread all over the country.

9

"Beware, Ye Bureaucracy, Beware"

THE HINDUSTAN SOCIALIST REPUBLICAN ARMY'S NOTICE

"Really, it is horrible to imagine that so lowly and violent a hand of an ordinary police official, J.P. Saunders could ever dare to touch in such an insulting way the body of one so old, so revered and so loved by 300 million people of Hindustan and thus cause his death. The youths and manhood of India was challenged by blows hurled on India's nationhood. And let the world know that India still lives; that the blood of its youths has not been totally cooled and that they can still risk their lives, if the honour of their nation is at stake. And it is proved through this act of the obscure who are ever persecuted, condemned and denounced even by their own people."

"Beware, Ye Tyrants: Beware"

Do not injure the feelings of a downtrodden and oppressed country. Think twice before perpetrating such diabolical deeds, and remember that despite the 'Arms Act' and strict guards against the smuggling of arms, the revolvers will continue to flow in–if not sufficient at present for an armed revolt, then at least sufficient to avenge the national insults. In spite of all the denunciations and condemnation of their own kith and kin, and ruthless repression and persecution by the alien government, the Party of young men will ever live to teach a lesson to the haughty rulers. They will be so bold as to cry even amidst the raging storm of opposition and repression, even on the scaffold: "Long Live the Revolution"!

Sorry for the death of a man. But in this man has died the representative of an institution which is so cruel, lowly and so base that it must be abolished. In this man has died an agent of the British authority in India—the most tyrannical government of governments in the world.

Sorry for the bloodshed of a human being; but the sacrifice of individuals at the altar of the Revolution that will bring freedom to all and make the exploitation of man by man impossible, is inevitable.

"Long Live the Revolution"

sd/-

Dated: December 18, 1928 Balraj

Commander-in-Chief

Immediately after eliminating Saunders, Bhagat Singh and Jaigopal headed for their hideout and entered the nearby DAV College hostel. Seeing them entering the hostel gate, some policemen including an inspector, named W.J.C. Fern,who had started giving them a hot chase, stopped. The DAV institution was known to be a stronghold of the students, sympathetic to the cause of the revolutionaries and, therefore, a hostile territory for the police.

Bhagat Singh remained in the DAV College hostel for a few hours and by midnight, he along with Sukhdev reached the residence of Comrade Sohan Singh Josh. Josh's house was not found to be under suspicion and surveillance.

"This is how Sohan Singh Josh has recorded in his book titled, *My Meetings with Bhagat Singh*.

I opened my door and to my utter surprise, I found Bhagat Singh and Sukhdev standing outside. I welcomed them, but told them that it was rather risky to have come to my house because the police might raid it any time. But Bhagat Singh said, "Don't worry, we have made all arrangements". They came in and said, "*We are hungry, give us something to eat.*" I could offer only two '*chapatis*', some vegetables and a glass of milk. I told them we could cook fresh food but they said, "nothing doing. We shall talk and sleep"."

"Bhagat Singh was wearing a felt hat and an English style suit. He was quite unrecognisable in those clothes. Sukhdev too was wearing an English hat and suit. Bhagat Singh took off his hat and placed it on a table nearby. He hung his pistol on a peg above the cot. Then after finishing the meagre meal, the first question he shot at me was *"what is the reaction in general to Saunders's murder?"*"

"The youths are happy", I replied. "But they would have been much happier if Scott had been killed."

"We had gone there only for him [Scott] but the other devil came out", he said "and we could not go empty-handed after all the pains taken for the preparations." And then he added, "anyway, some beginning has been made".

"There is another opinion also about this murder", I added, "that of Gandhi's followers". "We knew it beforehand", he said. "We discussed this before deciding upon the action". Then he contemptuously added, *"Gandhi stabbed"* the nation in the back by withdrawing the non-cooperation movement [1921-22] after the Chauri-Chaura incident. The people are still under the cloud of frustration and demoralisation which he brought to this country".

"But leave that aside", he continued, "do you know what has been the effect of Saunders's murder on the British rulers ?"

"I do not know, it is too early to know that". "There is a great panic among them", he said. "Some of them have already booked their wives' and children's passages for England. They are really frightened."

"But this panic is temporary", I gave my opinion. "It will wear off soon."

"What do you think of this action?"

"My views you know. We have talked about this matter several times. Our Naujawan Bharat Sabha workers will be arrested. There will be greater repression, and the movement will suffer, will be retarded." "I don't agree", he said. "This action will rouse the masses and strengthen the movement."

During this entire talk, Sukhdev did not say a word. He had met me for the first time. Then he asked me when I was going to Calcutta for the conference.

I replied tomorrow, "tomorrow".

"You go your way, we go ours". That ended our talk.

There were only two cots in the house. Sukhdev slept on one and Bhagat Singh and I shared the bigger one. They woke up slightly before four in the morning to be ready to go. A book *Liberty and the Great Libertarians* by T. Sprading, was lying on the table. This was a quotation book of bourgeois revolutionaries which helped me a lot to come to the communist movement. I got it while being tried in the *Akali Leaders Conspiracy Case* in the Lahore Fort. There was the censor's stamp on it. I was reluctant to part with it. But he promised to return the book after reading it and took it away.

We embraced each other and parted company. He did not give any indication as to where he was going.

As was to be expected, on 19th December large-scale arrests of youth belonging to the Naujawan Bharat Sabha and students' unions took place in Lahore. Since I [Sohan Singh Josh] had crossed the Punjab boundary, the Punjab Government sent a wire to the Government of India to arrest me. The Government of India referred the arrest telegraphically to the Bengal Government which replied, as Sohan Singh Josh is to preside over the Workers' and Peasants' Conference, his arrest has been postponed at the request of the Bengal Government till after the Conference (As if it was a conference of the Bengal Government officials).

Surprisingly, one may ask, why this generosity and friendliness towards Sohan Singh Josh, an eminent workers' and peasants' leader by both the British Government of India and the British Government of Bengal? Why was he allowed to preside over a patently and obviously anti-British Conference of Workers' and Peasants' Party and also not arrest him ? And why was such a Conference being allowed to be held? A large number of Naujawan Bharat Sabha members were being arrested and Sohan Singh Josh was one of the senior most leader of the Sabha, one would ponder over. Sohan Singh Josh has not explained it in his *My Meetings with Bhagat Singh* and in his other writings. It may be mentioned here that the Communists were working through the Workers' and Peasants' Party throughout the country at that time.

[Josh was arrested three months later, on the March 20, 1929 in the Meerut Conspiracy Case along with 32 other Communist Trade Union and Peasants' and Workers' Party leaders]

On December 24, 1928, Bhagat Singh again met Sohan Singh Josh at Calcutta.

"I was flabbergasted," writes Josh. "Just think, Josh entering a shaving saloon with a flowing beard and all the Sikh paraphernalia about him, and the CID shadowing and hunting everywhere for Bhagat Singh. That was not only creating suspicious circumstances but inviting the enemy to come and arrest us. I chided him for doing this foolish thing. He laughed and replied nonchalantly as usual. "Don't worry; nothing is going to happen. We have made all arrangements." What arrangements he had made, I don't know till today.

Then, showing an interest in the Conference, [which was being presided over by Josh] he asked me about its proceedings, the prominent leaders attending it, the provinces represented, etc. After having all this information, he said, "You do the organising of the workers and peasants and we shall do the disorganising of the British rulers. Let us have this division of work".

This conversation showed Bhagat Singh and his Party had serious political differences with Comrade Josh and his Party, albeit, the Communist Party.

He and his revolutionary comrades did not think of joining the Communist Party that had been functioning in one form or the other since 1925. The revolutionaries, under Bhagat Singh's leadership, had formed their own, The Hindustan Socialist Republican Association as well as its armed wing, called The Hindustan Socialist Republican Army with Chandra Shekhar Azad as its Commander-in-Chief.

Their Party, in its Manifesto, had laid down the establishment of a Socialist [Scientific Socialism] Republican State as its main aim. Their Manifesto called upon the youth to work, with all the devotion, spending their evenings and nights in the hovels of the working class, with the peasants in their hearths in their villages and with tribals in their *jhugies* [huts] in the jungles, teaching them, their women and grown-up children, what Socialism was and how to bring about revolution to free their motherland from the clutches of the British imperialism that would usher in a truly workers' state.

The Communists, on the other hand, kept themselves busy in organising trade unions of mill workers, railway workers and peasants on economic issues. They [Communists] claimed to be disciples of Karl Marx and V.I. Lenin often quoting them dogmatically but seemed to be following Bernstein and Karl Kautsky more than Karl Marx and V.I. Lenin.

At present, unfortunately, most of the industrial centres, mills in the then industrial cities and consequently the industrial workers have vanished and in their place sky-high domes, and towers comprising thousands of flats, each costing crores of rupees, have come up. The question now is: 'What is to be done?'

10

Fascinating Historic Escape

How did Bhagat Singh reach Calcutta? The ingeniousness of the revolutionariers and the glorious role played by Durga Bhabhi [wife of Bhagwati Charan Vohra] in the annals of the revolutionaries' struggle, for the establishment of an independent Socialist Republic of India, was manifested in the spectacular escape of Bhagat Singh from Lahore to Calculta on December 20, 1928.

This has been described by Professor Hazara Singh, a freedom fighter in a first-hand account based on his interview with Durga Bhabhi in May 1984 in his article published by M.M. Juneja in his *Selected Collections on Bhagat Singh.* Some extracts are provided below:

"Sukhdev called on Durga Bhabhi at about 8 pm on December 19, 1928, to ascertain if she could travel with a member of the HSRA not known to her. When she agreed readily, Sukhdev elaborated his query in a hesitating tone 'posing to be his wife'. He was doubtful whether a Hindu woman, who looked upon her husband as her god on earth, would accept the suggestion. She said that she was prepared to disregard all traditional beliefs for the sake of the Party and the motherland. Sukhdev was relieved with her categorical assurance. After 10 pm when the CID picket retired for the night, Sukhdev arrived with two other visitors, a tall young man dressed in European style and a servant humbly dressed. Both looked strangers to Durga Bhabhi. She kept talking to Sukhdev as she prepared meals for the guests.

After a few minutes, Sukhdev, unable to control himself any longer, burst out that the wheat-complexioned 'Sahib' was the rustic Jat Bhagat Singh. The identity of the other visitor was neither disclosed nor enquired about. Everyone was assured that if Durga Bhabhi could not recognise Bhagat Singh, he could even travel out of Lahore without being detected by the police. Durga Bhabhi, later on, regretted that the servant, about whom she later learnt was Rajguru, was casually served meals in brass utensils and treated unequally throughout".

Tongas (horse-driven carriages) were available round the clock as local transport. Keeping the light of the bedroom on, Bhagat Singh in a European dress carrying Durga Bhabhi's sleeping infant son, and she in her most impressive attire and Rajguru following shuffling under luggage, left the house at about 5 am, long before the arrival of the CID picket.

Reaching the station, Bhagat Singh kept his facial profile reasonably covered on one side with a slightly raised collar of the overcoat and on the other side by the sleeping infant, purchased two first class tickets and one for the servant. Bhagwati Charan Vohra, before leaving for Calcutta, had left a sum of Rs. 500 with his wife with specific instructions to hand over the amount to Sukhdev. The 'Escape', it seemed, had been well-planned much earlier. Durga Bhabhi too, it seemed, knew about the plan and well-prepared for it. The revolutionaries, after all, were people of extraordinary brilliance. They would leave nothing to chance and only those involved with the 'plan of action' would know of it.

That is how Bhagat Singh saying to Sohan Singh Josh at Lahore and subsequently at their meeting at Calcutta "Don't worry, nothing is going to happen, we have made all arrangements", could be explained and which Josh had said "did not know till the last."

The Lahore railway station junction looked like the Lahore police-station junction, bristling with the *"omnipotent"* and "*omniscient*" government CID men in plain clothes as well as in uniform looking with vigilant eyes at every coming and going passenger. The couple, Bhagat Singh [in his European style-dress with the felt-hat on his head] and Dugra Bhabhi with the infant child and a servant following them, dodged all the hawk-like CID of the British Empire, walked towards the first class compartment. The policeman standing outside whispered: "They are 'Sahibs', a British government official travelling with his family," saluted them and then escorted them to their seats. The European style dress and the first class tickets commanded their own awe and respect and they boarded the train under the very noses of the stupendous CID force without the least suspicion.

They broke their journey at Kanpur on 21st December and went to Lucknow. That was considered advisable because the CID at Howrah kept a close watch on passengers coming directly from Lahore. Both the cities were the nerve centres of the revolutionaries and the freedom struggle.

From Lucknow, a telegram was sent to Sushila Devi, another active worker of the HSRA. She was working as a tutor of the children of Seth Sir Chhajju Ram at his residence at Calcutta. The telegram text conveyed "Reaching Calcutta with brother". It was a coded message for Bhagwati Charan. At Lucknow, Rajguru parted company with them and left for Banaras. Bhagat Singh and Durga Bhabhi changed their guise to typical Bihari milk-vendors. They were received at Howrah by Bhagwati Charan dressed also in the guise of a milk-vendor.

At Calcutta, Bhagat Singh stayed with Seth Sir Chhajju Ram, a big merchant. Both he and his wife were great admirers of the revolutionaries and were now of Bhagat Singh as well. He stayed with them for two days during which time, Jatinder Nath Das made another arrangement in a hostel.

During his short stay in Calcutta, Bhagat Singh met a number of revolutionaries such as Prafulla Ganguli, Jyotish Ghosh, Phanindra Nath Ghosh and Trilokya Nath Chakraborti. The main issue discussed was, 'how to accelerate the disorganisation of the British Rule'. Trilokya Nath Chakraborti who had spent thirty years of his life in prisons, suggested that Bhagat Singh should build a volunteer corps of 5,000 young men. Bhagat Singh did think on the same lines and the Naujawan Bharat Sabha had been formed keeping in view this very idea. However, it takes time to build such an organisation.

> He told them that the rank and file of the Congress Party as well as the people in general did not believe in Gandhi's creed of non-violence and they are mostly sympathetic to the programme and policies of the revolutionaries. But they are afraid of the British Government's might. The task of a revolutionary was set with thorns. It was easier said than done. They had to pass through extremely adverse conditions–imprisoning, torturing, detaining for long periods without trial, deprivation of all the civic rights of expression and association and then the hanging. The non-violent satayagrahis of Gandhi's civil disobedience movement were, on the other hand, treated softly and with light punishment. So most of the Congressmen felt reluctant to be openly with the revolutionaries. It was an open secret that Mahatma Gandhi, Pt. Jawaharlal Nehru and other Congress leaders were provided with all comforts and facilities including the food of their choice in the jails.

The Bengal revolutionaries were highly impressed and were in complete agreement with him and offered their whole-hearted support to him. Bhagat Singh sought their help in manufacturing the bombs. Jatinder Nath Das immediately offered himself to accompany Bhagat Singh to help the Punjab revolutionaries in this task. Bhagat Singh wanted to meet more Bengal revolutionaries but he could not expose himself further. Trilokya Nath Chakraborti again suggested that Bhagat Singh should organise a volunteer corps of youths to which he replied they would keep it in view. Bhagat Singh returned from Calcutta in the first week of January 1929 while Jatinder Nath Das joined him in Agra in February when a bomb manufacturing factory was set up. It was at Agra that the decision to throw bombs in the Central Legislative Assembly was taken. Two controversial

Bills—the Public Safety Bill and the Trade Disputes Bill, being discussed, in the Assembly, had aroused country-wide interest and which were being largely opposed both within the Assembly as well as outside by the public. It seemed the French revolutionary Auguste Vaillant's historic action was in Bhagat Singh's mind when he sought the Bengal revolutionaries' help in manufacturing bombs.

11

A Loud Explosion to Make the Deaf Hear

April 8, 1929 is one of the most significant dates not only in the constitutional history of the country but more so in the annals of the freedom struggle of India. Two controversial bills—the Trade Disputes Bill and the Public Safety Bill were under discussion in the Central Legislative Assembly—the so-called Parliament of India. The first Bill was intended to curtail the trade union rights of the workers while the second Bill was directed against persons not being British Indian subjects or subjects of Indian princely states. Through this measure, the government was to get powers to remove British and foreign communists from India.

The real purpose was to crush the rising militant trade union movement in the industrial cities of Bombay, Calcutta, Sholapur, Ahmedabad, Kanpur, etc. as well as the rising unorganised and organised revolutionary movement led by *The Hindustan Socialist Republican Association* all over the country. Massive militant strikes were increasingly influenced by the ideology of Communism. In those years, a number of British trade union and communist leaders such as Charles Asleigh in 1922, Percy Glading in 1925, George Alison in 1926 and Ben Bradley, Phillip Sprat, Hutchinson in 1927-28 along with the Indian trade union leaders used to take an active part in the working class movement in India. In the Meerut Conspiracy Case, the last three among them, namely, Ben Bradley, Phillip Sprat and Hutchinson were sentenced for four and a half years. The Communist Party of Great Britain had organised the Meerut Defence Committee, in order to create public opinion in favour of the Meerut accused as well as to render help otherwise. The Trial inspired the 1932 play 'Meerut' by the Manchester street theatre group, 'Red Megaphones', highlighting the detrimental effects of colonialism and industrialisation. Ultimately, the sentences of the Meerut prisoners were reduced and they were released in 1933. Surprisingly and deplorably, the British Communist Party did not set up a Bhagat Singh-Sukhdev-Rajguru Defence Committee nor pleaded to the Labour Party Government for their release or commutation of death sentences.

Mr. Shapurji Saklatvala, an Indian from the province of Gujarat, was a Member of the British Parliament elected as a communist candidate of Great Britain's Communist Party. He was amongst the most active members espousing India's cause for independence in the British Parliament and denouncing British imperialism.

> Speaking on the evils of the foreign rule during one of the debates on India in the House of Commons, in 1928, Mr. Saklatvala made it clear that "the people of India will never be content to remain under foreign rule. They are just the same as the people of Great Britain or of any other country. The first problem every morning when Indians rise and the last problem when they go to bed, is the curse of the foreign rule in their country in their minds which they must fight to overthrow with all their might and with all the resources at their power. As long as British Rule continues in India or in anybody else's country, even though it may be under the Labour Party's Government, it can only be a rule of oppression, of degradation, of tyranny, of exploitation and of inhumanity".
>
> "I know some honourable friends on the treasury benches condemn me for the communist preaching of revolution but I would tell them that I would preach a revolution to put an end to the British murder of 6,00,000 lives year after year due to hunger and starvation and due to diseases like TB and malaria. It does not disturb the conscience of some people who say they are against physical violence and acts of terrorism. This is a condition which must continue under imperialism and capitalism. The real issue, they need to know, is, for how long the British imperialism is to be permitted to suppress a human race of 30,00,00,000 people."

During this period a report on the pathetic and ghastly living conditions of the Indians was published by the Trade Union

Congress of Great Britain. It stated that the Indian workers were half-starved, badly clothed and horribly housed smitten with diseases in the 20th century after having lived 150 years of British rule. The report had been prefaced by Mr. A.A. Purcall, Member of Parliament of Great Britain and Mr. J. Hallsworth—two British trade union leaders. They had spent over three months in India travelling 2,700 miles, investigating the living and working conditions of the Indian workers in the railways, coal mines, textile mills, woollen mills, tea gardens and plantations. It held the British Government responsible for keeping so many millions of human beings in mental darkness, intellectual and material poverty. The remedy, the report recommended, was in strengthening the trade unionism for they were in frightful distress. "Is it too much to expect that out of Great Britain—the one land which has made millions of profits from its association with India, a really practical and lasting form of help may be afforded to these millions of human beings who, if they had the wherewithal, are sufficient in number to set going the whole of world industry at high speed," the report concluded.

Alarmed by these developments, the British Indian Government decided to acquire extraordinary powers to curb all such activities through the two bills, namely, the Public Safety Bill and the Trade Disputes Bill.

How the spectre of Communism was haunting the British Indian Government and its bureaucracy was evinced when Sir James Crerar, the Home Member, presented the Public Safety Bill in the Central Legislative Assembly on February 6, 1929.

> He said, "Communism works to destroy the existing social and economic order as well as the existing form of government. Its policy is to influence every source of discontent, manufacture and create it, if necessary, in order to collect sufficient inflammable material whereupon it may be possible to light a conflagration destroying an orderly society."

After having gone through the usual procedural discussion for and against the two Bills during the past few months in the Legislative Assembly, the final voting on the same was to be held on April

8, 1929. Both the Trade Disputes Bill and the Public Safety Bill had aroused the keenest controversy in the country, especially, the expected ruling of the President of the Assembly on the Public Safety Bill. An unprecedented large number of visitors were present in the Chamber.The visitors' gallery had accommodation for about 200 persons but as many as about 400 persons were present. Not an inch of space was unoccupied. The gallery was like a big box of sardines. The benches, corridors, gangways and approaches were all packed.

The Trade Disputes Bill after the division, had been declared carried by 56 voters for and 38 votes against by the President. The announcement, of the result of the division, was followed by tumultuous clappings and then there was pin-drop silence.The President had again stood up to give his ruling on the Public Safety Bill. The attention of everyone was riveted to the President who started to give his ruling on the Public Safety Bill.

There was a hustle in the visitors' gallery. Suddenly like a bolt from the blue, two bombs, one after the other, struck the Chamber of the Central Legislative Assembly, situated in the heart of the capital city of New Delhi. The high and the mighty of the then British Imperialist Empire, where it was claimed, "the sun never set", were stunned and terrified. Was it some artillery from the Heavens? They could neither divine nor could find any clue. And then two pistol-shots were heard with shouts of "Long Live the Revolution", "Down with Imperialism", "Workers of the World Unite". Also tumbled down many Red Leaflets bearing the heading "To Make the Deaf Hear"-Notice of the Hindustan Socialist Republican Association issued by the Hindustan Socialist Republican Army and signed by its Commander-in-Chief, Balraj. (the Party name of Chandra Shekhar Azad)

[A typed leaflet was thrown into the Central Assembly by Bhagat Singh and B.K. Dutt, after exploding the bombs. It was written by Bhagat Singh in his Sitaram Bazar den. The typing was also done by Bhagat Singh himself. He typed about 30 to 40 copies of it on the Party letterhead. The typing arrangement was made by Jaidev Kapoor with the help of the drill master of a Marwari School. A full-size block of the leaflet was published by *The Hindustan Times* in its special evening edition the same day. (April 8, 1929)]

> **"It Takes a Loud Voice to Make the Deaf Hear",** With these immortal words uttered on a similar occasion by Auguste Vaillant, a French anarchist martyr, do we strongly justify this action of ours.
>
> Without repeating the humiliating history of the past ten years of the working of the reforms (Montague-Chelmsford Reforms) and without mentioning the insults hurled at the Indian nation through this House—the so-called Indian Parliament, we want to point out that, while the people expecting some more crumbs of reforms from the Simon Commission, and are always quarrelling over the distribution of the expected bones, the government is thrusting upon us new repressive measures like the Public Safety and the Trade Disputes Bills, with the Press Sedition Bill reserved for the next session. The indiscriminate arrests of labour leaders working in the open field clearly indicate where the wind blows.
>
> In these extremely provocative circumstances, The Hindustan Socialist Republican Association, in all seriousness, realising their full responsibility, had decided and ordered its army to do this particular action, so that a stop be put to this humiliating farce and to let the alien bureaucratic exploiters do what they wish, but they must be made to come before the public eyes in their naked form.
>
> Let the representatives of the people return to their constituencies and prepare the masses for the coming revolution and let the government know that while protesting against the Public Safety and Trade Disputes Bills and the callous murder of Lala Lajpat Rai, on behalf of the helpless Indian masses, we want to emphasise the lesson often repeated by history, that it is easy to kill individuals but you cannot kill the ideas. Great Empires crumbled but the ideas survived. The Bourbons and Czars fell, while the revolution marched ahead triumphantly.

We are sorry to admit that we, who attach so great a sanctity to human life, who dream of a glorious future, when man will be enjoying perfect peace and full liberty, have been forced to shed human blood. But the sacrifice of individuals at the altar of the 'Great Revolution' that will bring freedom to all, rendering the exploitation of man by man impossible, is inevitable.

"Long Live The Revolution.", "Down with Imperialism",

–Balraj
Commander-in-Chief

12

Imperialists are Paper-Tigers

After the two bombs were dropped and the Red Leaflet thrown into the Central Assembly Chamber, there were cries and shrieks and there was immediately a rush for the exit. People were running in all directions.

Members ran helter-skelter for safety. Everyone was terrified. Chaos and confusion prevailed. Red fire had stormed the lair of the twin ferocious tigers of imperialism and capitalism.

Sir John Simon [of the Simon Commission] took to his heels running in panic from the President's gallery taking shelter in the Assembly Superintendent's room closing himself therein. Sir Hari Singh Gaur, an official member ran out into the bathroom. Some official Members took shelter under the desks. Sir George Schuster, the Finance Member, was so terrified that he took cover under a desk nearby. Some other Members had hidden themselves behind the 'almirahas' [cupboards] while many more crawled out into the lobbies. There were other stories as well. Fear of a sort of *coup d'etat* or a revolution, it seemed, had begun to haunt the minds of many of the crony members of the Empire in the Assembly.

Sitting on the Micro-Film-Reader on the first floor of the Nehru Memorial Library Hall in the Teen Murti House, New Delhi, browsing through the valorous actions of Bhagat Singh and his revolutionary comrades, banner-headlined on the front pages of national Dailies such as *The Tribune, The Hindustan Times, Amrit Bazar Patrika, Civil & Military Gazette, The Statesman* and *The Hindu*, I was reminded of Vo Nguyven Giap, the great Ho Chi Minh's General, acknowledged to be one of the world's greatest military strategist and how he had exposed the myth of Uncle Sam's invincibility of the US armed might. Facing a stinging defeat at the hands of Giap, the Viet Cong General and eating humble pie, Uncle Sam was forced to beg an invitation from Mao Tse Tung in 1971 to make a personal request for help to get himself [Uncle Sam] rescued from the iron-like grip of Ho Chi Minh's General.

Throwing dust into the eyes of the sleuthhounds, some amongst them Scotland Yard-trained, of the Empire's supposedly omniscient Criminal Investigation Department, Bhagat Singh, one of the world's greatest revolutionary strategists along with B.K. Dutt, another gallant revolutionary, made John Bull collapse and fall flat, while sneaking into the Central Legislative Assembly in the highly-fortified, flaunting imperial pomp and arrogance, newly-built Capital Complex.

Wading through the April 1929 *Hindustan Times*, eyes again ran over the headline "Sir John Simon Took To His Heels" and immediately the brain machine excavated Mao's "Imperialists Are Paper-Tigers" dictum. They [imperialists and capitalists] would fire hundreds of rounds of ammunition at the innocent and non-violent people, butchering hundreds and thousands without qualms and demur as they had done in Jallianwala Bagh, Amritsar in 1919. But when they are confronted with an enemy more powerful than themselves, they would, in no time, eating crow, humble themselves.

After sometime the smoke disappeared. The members had all collected in the hall. The President adjourned the House. In the Visitors' gallery, there remained a few persons. Among them were two young men who offered themselves for arrest. Observing the policemen including the senior ones, feeling hesitant to move forward to arrest them, they placed their pistol on a nearby bench and threw up their hands. Sergeant Terry and a constable arrested them. The names of the arrested young men were Bhagat Singh, a graduate of the National College and son of Sardar Kishan Singh and B.K. Dutt of Kanpur. The bombs were considered to be of Jam Pop Fuse quality and not the dangerous type. The police took charge of the Assembly premises and started the investigations.

13

High and Mighty of the Empire Horrified

Crossing oceans and continents, the thunderous reverberations of this action by Bhagat Singh and B.K. Dutt, and their loud shouts of "Long Live the Revolution", "Down with Imperialism" and "Workers of the World Unite" struck the stone-walls of Buckingham Palace in London shaking the foundations of the British Empire and terrifying her rulers. How shaken the British imperialists had become, could be judged from the "expression of horror" of His Majesty the King George of England conveyed through the exchange of telegrams between the Secretary of State of India and the Viceroy as well as the comments in the Press.

King George of England Horrified

From the Secretary of State to the Viceroy dated April 9, 1929:

"His Majesty desires me to convey to you an expression of his horror at the murderous outrage that was committed in the Assembly yesterday and of his sympathy with the injured to whom he wishes speedy recovery. He trusts that their injuries will not prove serious and is relieved to learn that less harm was done than might have been feared."

Reply from the Viceroy to the Secretary of State, dated April 10, 1929:

Your telegram of April 9: On behalf of India, I desire respectfully to acknowledge His Majesty's gracious message expressing his horror at the outrage that was committed in the Assembly on April 8. By less than a miracle, the injuries and damage caused were not serious and I am glad to assure His Majesty that the injured are all progressing favourably. I have communicated to them His Majesty's gracious message of sympathy. His Majesty's Government have also expressed their horror at the outrage and their sympathy with those who were wounded.

British Press Comments

The horror and the threat the British colonists felt, and the fear of losing their grip on India was evident in the British Press. The comments of Sir Michael O'Dwyer, the "notorious" Lt. Governor of Punjab, and the official responsible for the Jallianwala Bagh massacre of 1919 in Amritsar were published by British newspapers-and further reproduced in the Indian national media:

The Manchester Guardian, reported:

Sane Counsel Sir Michael O'Dwyer, the incessant apostle of the policy of the strong man's rule for India says in *The Evening News* that: "Indians are beginning to think that we are no longer capable of governing." For Sir Michael, the whole issue is one of "Govern or Go." He says that the growth of the menace, that culminated in the recent outrage, can be traced to since the discovery of the Communist Conspiracy in 1919." Adding further, Sir Michael says that "the Delhi outrage is the direct result of the misguided policy of bestowing representative institutions." Sir Michael concluded that "It is a case of Govern or Go". I assert, he says that "not one in a thousand wants us to go but Indians are beginning to think that we are no longer capable of governing."

The Daily Telegraph editorialised that considerable moral responsibility for terrorist outrages must be borne by the political leaders, who during a succession of years, have been inflaming the tempers of the ignorant masses by furious and incessant vilification of British rule in India.

'Unbalanced Fanatics'–ran the headline in *The Daily News*. It thought that the Simon Commission is the least of all likely to fall into the error of judging the capacity of India by unbalanced fanatics. The paper welcomes Sir John Simon's suggestion that there should be no more decennial revisions of the Constitution, and considers that this creation of a date put a premium on agitation and even occasioned yesterday's outrage.

The Times of London commented that "outrage is a warning to political India accepting partisans of class war as allies of nationalism".

Indian Press Comments

The Indian newspapers pretending to speak on behalf of Indian citizens, while mostly owned and funded by rich businessmen, were not far behind in expressing slavish and contrived outrage, as seen below:

> *The Civil and Military Gazette,* Lahore April 10, 1929: "*Government and Revolutionary Movement*": "One thing is quite certain, however, there must be no more shilly-shallying by the government. Ample evidence exists of dire revolutionary movement, and the normal man has shaken his head sadly as he sees it developing unchecked. The duty has been laid upon government but that does not exempt it during the training period from ruling India firmly and well. Blowing hot and blowing cold dismays friends and encourages enemies."

The Hindustan Times, Delhi, April 11, 1929 in its editorial captioned '*The Assembly Outrage*' was somewhat balanced. "We expressed yesterday in no uncertain or unequivocal terms our condemnation of the action of two young men who were responsible for the bomb outrage in the Assembly. In expressing our views, we did, we are sure, we were voicing the feelings and sentiments of a large majority of our countrymen. We condemn their action because we ourselves are pledged to strict non-violence, and because we feel that such exhibitions of violence cannot lead to any result of lasting benefit to the country. The perpetrators of yesterday's outrage had no person in view but wanted to kill as many officers and sympathisers of government as they possibly could by their misdeed". "...The question we ask is, will this event serve as an eye -opener to the Government of India? Will it make it realise that it is not resolute government that is wanted but popular government."

The Tribune, Lahore, April 11,1929 in its editorial titled 'Bomb Outrage' wrote: "If ideas cannot be killed by killing individuals, no more can political systems and institutions, no matter how unsound, can be killed by killing individuals, and after all, bombs, revolvers and pistols can only kill individuals. The man who thinks that he is going to uproot either bureaucratic rule in India or government by throwing bombs into the Legislative Chamber is not only devoid of political sanity and common sense but entirely ignorant of history, however glibly he may talk of the Bourbons and the Czars.

"...Happily in our own case, these men of weak intellect and perverted moral sense, even if their advocacy of a revolution is not a pose, are only a handful and the country has no sympathy with them. If the bureaucracy is wise, it will not for one moment of madness permit these sporadic exhibitions of mad men to influence its policy. To do so would be to decisively play the revolutionaries' game".

Amrit Bazar Patrika wrote: "Public opinion will strongly condemn the outrage for it is nothing less than that though it might easily have been more dangerous. Two persons are said to have been arrested in this connection with pistols and revolvers. We trust there will be impartial investigation and the whole truth will come out in connection with this unfortunate incident"

The Statesman had this to state: "This is a crime of the type which by no stretch of language can be called political. It should excite the indignation of every man of every Party, for the intention is simply indiscriminate murder. It is of importance that the people should keep their tempers calm ... Law is strong enough to punish and it must be allowed to take its course."

Exercising his authority conferred upon the Governor-General under Section 72 of the Government of India Act, Lord Irwin, the Viceroy issued an Ordinance giving the Governor-General-in-Council, the requisite powers envisaged and asked for through the Trade Disputes Bill and the Public Safety Bill.

14

High and Mighty Should Have Been Grateful to Bhagat Singh

Right from King George of England and Lord Irwin, the Viceroy of India to Pt. Motilal Nehru, the President of the Indian National Congress and its General Secretary, Pandit Jawaharlal Nehru and Mahatma Gandhi and to the scores of official and non-official members of the Central Legislative Assembly and, of course, the press, both the British and the Indian, all of them, in unison, damned the two young revolutionaries to their heart's content. They started abusing them with the choicest curses such as "lunatics", "madmen", "wicked men", "fanatics", "men of perverted moral sense", "devoid of political sanity", "enemies of India's progress", "ignorant of history", "misguided hair-brained", impatient, immature, impulsive, politically insane, morally weak-minded, etc. and their actions "sinful" and "criminal".

Neither a thought, had been given to the fact that the two bombs were thrown as a protest against the unjust and oppressive foreign rule and that they were country-made of inferior quality and not dangerous and not meant to kill, nor that they threw away their pistol after firing two shots in the air and then raising their hands, offered themselves voluntarily for arrest, thereby, assuring Sergeant Terry and the police constables that they could arrest them without fear.

None of the high and the mighty of the Empire considered another fact that, had the revolutionaries intended, they, with the pistol, could have easily killed Sir John Simon, Sir George Schuster, the Finance Member, Sir James Crerar, the Home Member and some others on the Treasury Benches.

Freed from any danger after the revolutionaries had voluntarily surrendered, they did not bother to think of how the two young men, had, after throwing dust in the eyes of their notoriously cunning and crafty CID, covering every hole and corner of the Empire, sneaked into the Assembly Building, one of the most protected fortresses. The High and Mighty also did not realise that, had the revolutionaries intended, they would have smuggled inside the Assembly, the really dangerous bombs, causing immense harm and loss of lives. After all, many other revolutionaries had, elsewhere, been shooting the high dignitaries of the government such as the Governors, District Magistrates, Senior Police officers, etc.

And shouldn't, for this consideration of the safety of human lives of even their British enemies present in the Chamber, the high and the mighty of the British Empire, have, in their statements, remembered and expressed their gratitude to Balraj, the Commander-in-Chief of the Hindustan Socialist Republican Army and his revolutionary colleagues—Bhagat Singh and B.K. Dutt?

15

Revolutionaries Damned by Nationalist Leadership

Immediately after the Assembly Bomb Episode, the Nationalists and Swarajists started condemning the episode and damning the two revolutionaries. Pt. Jawaharlal Nehru damned it as an act of "lunatics". Mahatma Gandhi dubbed it as "Mad Act of Two Youngsters".

His Majesty King George of the British Empire had been horrified at the Delhi Assembly bomb outrage but no less horrified were the 'Swarajists' and Nationalists of India. They started, one after the other, issuing statements vilifying and abusing the two valorous revolutionaries without having a look at the Red Leaflet dropped in dozens in the Central Hall along with the two harmless bombs in which they [the two revolutionaries] had explained why they did so with the 'Loud Explosion'. The first to do so were Pt. Motilal Nehru, the then President of the Indian National Congress, Pt. Jawaharlal Nehru, the then General Secretary of the Congress and Mahatma Gandhi and followed by others.

Pt. Motilal Nehru condemned the action in a statement published by *The Hindustan Times* dated April 11, 1929 under the title, 'The Disease and its Remedy':

> All sensible men must condemn the outrage perpetrated in the Assembly Chamber, but it must not be allowed to deflect either the government or the representatives of the people from their plain duty. Crime must, of course, be put down and the criminals brought to justice in every case but the peaceful citizen must at the same time be protected in the exercise of his legitimate rights. When a grave crime, such as that of yesterday, is committed, the zeal to punish the guilty is apt to outrun

> the obligation to protect the innocent. The inevitable result is that the remedy proves worse than the disease. While, therefore, I fully admit the right of the government to use all the legitimate powers to preserve peace and order in the country, I can not too strongly emphasise the need of keeping a cool head in dealing with this deplorable affair.

It is wise statesmanship alone which can, by strengthening the force of non-violence, effectively meet the counter-force of violence. India does not mean a few misguided hair-brained youths. Real India does not believe in the cult of bombs nor does she believe in the cult of statutory commissions. India believes in suffering, and if the government does not weaken the hands of Mahatma Gandhi, she will one day stagger the world by the magnitude of her suffering for freedom. Let the people and the government both see things in their true perspective. The choice lies between Mahatma Gandhi and "Balraj".

Diwan Chaman Lal, a Labour leader (*The Tribune*, April 10,1929)said:

> It was a dastardly crime against the nationalist movement itself. Everything should be done to take the strongest measures against the rule of violence which makes us hide our head in shame.

Pt. Madan Mohan Malaviya (*The Tribune*, dated April 10, 1929) also characterised the event as "abhoring and most deplorable".

Mahatma Gandhi's reaction to the Assembly outrage was reported in *The Tribune* dated April 13,1929 with the caption—'Mad Act of Two Youngsters':

> Crimes of any kind are the manifestation of a mind full of vice and each act of violence renders the vision of 'Swaraj' more and more distant. The mad act of the two youngsters in the Assembly has made the accomplishment of 'Swaraj' more difficult and we have distinctly gone a step backward in our striving for it.

Immediately after the Assembly Bomb Episode, in an article, "View it in Its True Perspective" Pt. Jawaharlal Nehru, as reported in *The Hindustan Times* dated April 11,1929, stated:

> Feeling very much grieved on learning of the Assembly outrage, I can

> only conceive of a lunatic indulging in such an act. It is sure to be exploited by the government in favour of repressive measures that they are taking. Obviously the individual acts like this have or should have nothing to do with the general policy of either the Nationalists or the government. Unfortunately, however, they do often affect such a policy. I hope the momentary excitement in the Assembly yesterday has cooled down and that people can view the incident in the proper perspective.

Did Pt. Jawaharlal Nehru forget his own observation of the nature and behaviour of the tigers of imperialism and capitalism which could not be tamed?

Didn't the non-violent movement such as non-cooperation and civil disobedience amount to and proved just gentle and affectionate pats to the tigers of imperialism and capitalism? Such movements did not touch their hearts and heads. It was the loud sound of two bomb explosions that made them not only stir from their slumber but also stunned and terrified them and ultimately led them to quit India in 1947.

Neither the nationalist leaders and nor the nationalist press, for days after the Bomb Episode, uttered or wrote a word in appreciation of the historic 'Red Leaflet,' through which the revolutionaries had raised their "Loud Voice to Make the Deaf Hear" the heart-rending cries and agonies of the semi-starved, helpless and enslaved thirty crore Indians. Instead, they were condemned by the national leadership. Pt. Motilal Nehru, called the incident a "grave crime", deserving to be condemned by all sensible men.

Justifying their action and exposing, through their 'Red Leaflet', the humiliating farce of the Central Legislative Assembly, the so-called Indian Parliament, they, the revolutionaries, on behalf of the Indian masses, protested against the new repressive measures such as the Public Safety and the Trade Disputes Bills, the ensuing Press Sedition Bill and the callous murder of Lala Lajpat Rai, which Pt. Jawaharlal Nehru took to mean the vindication of the honour of Lala Lajpat Rai and of the Indian nation. Yet he [Pt. Jawaharlal Nehru] conceived the revolutionary action as an act of lunatics.

They, Bhagat Singh and B.K. Dutt exhorted the representatives of the people sitting comfortably in the Assembly Chambers, among whom was Pt. Motilal Nehru, the President of the Indian National Congress, to go to the people in their respective constituencies and spending some evenings with them in their slums and villages enlightening the masses about how their miseries could be ended.

They reminded the collaborating nationalist leadership with the tyrannical British rulers and the alien and Indian bureaucratic exploiters, the lesson often repeated by history that it is easy to kill individuals but that they cannot kill ideas while Bourbons and Czars fell and the great Empires crumbled but the revolution marched ahead triumphantly.

Further on, they restated their dream of a glorious future when man will be enjoying perfect peace and full liberty. Feeling sorry for having been forced to shed human blood, though they attached great sanctity to human life, but made it clear that the sacrifice of individuals at the altar of the 'Great Revolution', that will bring freedom to all, rendering the exploitation of man by man impossible, is inevitable, ending the 'Red Leaflet' with "Inquilab Zindabad" and "Long Live the Revolution". It was signed by Balraj, Commander-in-Chief, The Hindustan Socialist Republican Army.

Their "action", through the Assembly Bomb Episode was not at all meant to murder anyone. It was an attack on the institution. Lord Irwin, the Viceroy too recognised it as such and made it clear in his Address to the Joint Session of the Assembly.

Sitting comfortably in the drawing room of his Buckingham Palace in London, thousands of miles away from India, His Majesty King George was justified in experiencing a feeling of discomfort, a trembling and fright and a sense of horror, on having a look at the Red Leaflets and the phrases in it such as "the coming revolution", "great Empires crumbled "Bourbons and Czars fell", "revolution marched ahead", "Long live the revolution". He saw at the hands of the revolutionaries, the prospect of losing India, his Empire's jewel. A spectre of revolution started haunting him. It was indeed a spectacle of horror for him.

But what justification was there for Pt. Motilal Nehru, Pt. Jawaharlal Nehru, Pt. Madan Mohan Malaviya, Diwan Chaman Lal, and other nationalist leaders to feel grieved at the Delhi bomb incident. Being amongst the senior most leaders of the Congress Party and of the country, they were expected to conceive not of lunatics but of gallant patriots and valorous revolutionaries performing an extraordinarily daring act, shaking the foundations of the Empire. The nationalist leadership should have felt proud of Bhagat Singh and B.K. Dutt, the two valiant revolutionary heroes. They did not intend to harm anybody; the bombs were of a harmless type; had thrown away their pistols and had surrendered voluntarily. These facts should have been highlighted by the nationalist leadership, especially Pt. Motilal Nehru and Pt. Jawaharlal Nehru. They, regrettably, forgot that Bhagat Singh and his revolutionary colleagues had, as appreciated by them earlier, vindicated the honour of Lala Lajpat Rai as well as of the Indian Nation by their revolutionary act of killing a devil—Saunders.

Calling the Assembly bomb incident a 'grave crime' deserving to be condemned by all sensible men implying those, who did not do so, were not sensible people, Pt. Motilal Nehru, the then President of the All India Congress Committee as well as the leader of the Congress Party in the Legislative Assembly, did injustice to the revolutionaries in general, and Bhagat Singh and B.K. Dutt in particular, by calling them misguided, hair-brained youth, and believers in the cult of bombs.

This unique act of 'Ahimsa' (non-violence) performed by the two great revolutionaries should have been appreciated by Mahatma Gandhi. Terming the Assembly bomb incident a crime and a "mad act of two young men" manifesting a "mind full of vice" and ignoring what was written in their Red Leaflet and how non-violently, the two revolutionaries had offered themselves for arrest, and voluntarily surrendered, Mahatma Gandhi's harsh reaction did not behove a Mahatma. Theirs was an unique act of 'Ahimsa' (non-violence) but called "outrage". Mahatmaji should have appreciated the way the revolutionaries had acted. There was no vice in their minds and there was no madness in their act. Such abusive wordings are used by the imperialists and not by nationalists against their patriots.

There were many other mainstream politicians of various shades expressing their horror and calling the Assembly incident dastardly and condemning the revolutionaries. Among them was Diwan Chaman Lal, a prosperous politician and a Congressman also guising himself as a socialist and a labour leader, thereby, making himself eligible to be sponsored, as an official labour representative, at the International Labour Conferences by the government. He called the Assembly incident a dastardly crime against the nationalist movement itself making him hide his head in shame and urging the government to take the harshest measures against the rule of violence.

Many expletives, such as 'lunatics, insane, madmen, had been used while denouncing the revolutionaries by all sorts of politicians but that was not enough. There were numerous editorials, notes and comments on the revolutionaries and their daring actions and so there were invectives for them to the heart's pleasure of the British rulers and their Indian collaborators.

Here is one more piece under the column—'Notes and Comments' on the editorial page of *The Tribune*, the leading nationalist newspaper of Punjab to which Bhagat Singh had pointed out in one of his writings:

'Those who imagine that because a deplorable outrage has been perpetrated by two mad men in the name of liberty, therefore, all efforts for the attainment of liberty by legitimate constitutional means must for the moment be suspended, could not have been the victims of a graver delusion. Such a thing has nowhere happened and can never happen. In every country in which liberty has, far too long a time, been withheld, unconstitutional efforts, by a few impatient, immature, impulsive, politically insane and morally weak minds, for the winning of liberty, have synchronised with the constitutional efforts by the overwhelming majority of politically-minded people. But we are not aware of a single case in which responsible men, on the other side, have suggested the suspension of the constitutional movement, pending the elimination of crime.'

16

Auguste Vaillant's Court Room Speech

A miserable and woefully oppressive situation existed in every other part of the capitalist world, in the 19th century as it exists at present as well. And so it was in France, another imperialist power, occupying vast territories of the continents of Africa, Asia and South America where also the governing capitalist classes remained insensitive to the cries of the starving masses. Auguste Vaillant, a French anarchist, is most famous for his bomb attack on the French Chamber of Deputies on December 9, 1893. The Government's reaction was the passing of the infamous repressive *Lois Aceierates* (an oppressive law). His speech before the French Chamber of Deputies is as fresh, interesting and relevant today as it was more than a century ago and mirrors the prevailing miserable situation in our society in the capitalist world and it is reproduced:

Courtroom Speech: Before the French Chamber of Deputies, December 9, 1893 prior to receiving sentence of death for a political crime:

> "Gentlemen, in a few minutes you are to deal your blow, but in receiving your verdict, I shall have at least the satisfaction of having wounded the existing society, that cursed society in which one may see a single man spending, uselessly, enough to feed thousands of families; an infamous society which permits a few individuals to monopolise all the social wealth, while there are hundreds and thousands of unfortunates who have not even the bread that is not refused to dogs, and while entire families are committing suicide for want of the necessities of life.
>
> Ah, gentlemen, if the governing classes could go down among the unfortunates. But no, they prefer to remain deaf to their appeals. It seems that a fatality impels them, like the royalty of the 18th century,

towards the precipice which will engulf them, for woe be to those who remain deaf to the cries of the starving, woe to those who, believing themselves of superior essence, assume the right to exploit those beneath them. There comes a time when the people no longer reason; they rise like a hurricane, and pass away like a torrent. Then we see bleeding heads impaled on pikes.

Among the exploited, gentlemen, there are two classes of individuals. Those of one class, not realising what they are and what they might be, take life as it comes, believe that they are born to be slaves, and content themselves with the little that is given them in exchange for their labour. But there are others, on the contrary, who think, who study, and who, looking about them, discover social iniquities. Is it their fault if they see clearly and suffer at seeing others suffer? Then they throw themselves into the struggle, and make themselves the bearers of the popular claims.

Gentlemen, I am one of these last. Wherever I have gone, I have seen unfortunates bent beneath the yoke of capital. Everywhere I have seen the same wounds causing tears of blood to flow, even in the remoter parts of the inhabited districts of South America, where I had the right to believe that he who was weary of the pains of civilisation, might rest in the shade of the palm trees and there study nature. Well, there even, more than elsewhere, I have seen capital come, like a vampire, to suck the last drop of blood of the unfortunate pariahs.

Then I came back to France, where it was reserved for me to see my family suffer atrociously. This was the last drop in the cup of my sorrow. Tired of leading this life of suffering and cowardice, I carried this bomb to those who are primarily responsible for social misery. I am reproached with the wounds of those who were hit by my projectiles. Permit me to point out in passing that, if the bourgeois had not massacred or caused massacres during the Revolution, it is probable that they would still be under the yoke of the nobility. On the other hand, figure up the dead and wounded on Tonquin, Madagascar, Dahomey, adding thereto the thousands, yes, millions of unfortunates who die in the factories, the mines, and wherever the grinding power of capital is felt. Add also those who die of hunger, and all this with the assent of our Deputies. Beside all this, of how little weight are the reproaches now brought against me!

It is true that one does not efface the other; but, after all, are we not acting on the defensive when we respond to the blows which we receive from above? I know very well that I shall be told that I ought to have confined myself to a speech for the vindication of the people's claims. But what can you expect? 'It takes a loud voice to make the deaf hear'. Too long have they answered our voices by imprisonment, the rope, rifle volleys. Make no mistake; the explosion of my bomb is not only the cry of the rebel Vaillant, but the cry of an entire class which vindicates its rights, and which will soon add acts to words. For, be sure of it, in vain will they pass laws. The ideas of the thinkers will not halt; just as, in the last century, all the governmental forces could not prevent the Diderots and the Voltaires from spreading emancipating ideas among the people, so all the existing governmental forces will not prevent the Reclus, the Darwins, the Spencers, the Ibsens, the Mirabeaus, from spreading the ideas of justice and liberty which will annihilate the prejudices that hold the mass ignorance. And these ideas, welcomed by the unfortunate, will flower in acts of revolt as they have done in me, until the day when the disappearance of authority shall permit all men to organise freely according to their choice, when everyone shall be able to enjoy the product of his labour, and when those moral maladies called prejudices shall vanish, permitting human beings to live in harmony, having no other desire than to study the sciences and love their fellows.

I conclude, gentlemen, by saying that a society in which one sees such social inequalities as we see all about us, in which we see every day suicides caused by poverty, prostitution flaring at every street corner, a society whose principal monuments are barracks and prisons, such a society must be transformed as soon as possible, on pain of being eliminated, and that speedily, from the human race. Hail to him who labors, by no matter what means, for this transformation. It is this idea that has guided me in my duel with authority, but as in this duel, I have only wounded my adversary, it is now its turn to strike me.

Now, gentlemen, to me it does not matter what penalty you may inflict, for, looking at this assembly with the eyes of reason, I can not help smiling to see you, atoms lost in matter, and reasoning only because you possess a prolongation of the spinal marrow, assume the right to judge one of your fellows.

Ah! gentlemen, how insignificant a thing is your assembly and your verdict in the history of humanity; and human history, in its

> turn, is likewise inconsequential in the whirlwind which bears it through immensity, and which is destined to disappear, or at least to be transformed, in order to begin again the same history and the same facts, a veritably perpetual play of cosmic forces renewing and transferring themselves forever".

Auguste Vaillant (From Wikipedia, the free encyclopedia): (1861, Mezieres, Ardennes—February 3, 1894) was a French anarchist, most famous for his bomb attack on the French Chamber of Deputies on December 9, 1893. The government's reaction to this attack was the passing of the infamous repressive *Lois Scelerates* (a repressive law).

He threw the home-made device from the public gallery and was immediately arrested. The weakness of the device meant that the explosion only caused slight injuries to twenty deputies. At his trial in Paris he was defended by Fernand Labori. Vaillant claimed that his aim was not to kill but to wound as many deputies as possible in revenge for the execution of Ravachol. Despite this, Vaillant was sentenced to death and execution followed on February 3, 1894. His bombing and execution in turn inspired the attacks of Emile Henry and Sante Geronimo Caserio (who, with a dagger on which Vaillant's name was written, stabbed to death Marie Francois Sadi Carnot, President of the French Third Republic). Bhagat Singh (who threw a low intensity bomb into the Central Legislative Assembly in British India, and was hanged later was slightly more than 23 years old while Auguste Vaillant was about 33 years old when he was hanged. Auguste Vaillant is now also called the "French Bhagat Singh". Both of them were sentenced to death in similar circumstances and faced the gallows with smiles. Vaillant's last words were "Death to the Bourgeoisie" "Long Live Anarchy!" Bhagat Singh's last words were "Long Live the Revolution", "Long Live the Proletariat", "Down with Imperialism".

17

Trial and Statement of Bhagat Singh in the Sessions Court

Soon after the Central Legislative Assembly was bombed "making the deaf hear" the agonies of the 30 crore oppressed Indians by Bhagat Singh and B.K. Dutt, their trial as accused, began on May 7, 1929 in the Court of Mr. F.B. Pool, Additional District Magistrate in the Delhi Central Jail, near Ferozeshah Kotla Ground. As soon as they were ushered in, they hailed the Court with their war cries, "Long Live the Revolution" and "Down with Imperialism". These greetings became their norm and routine in the Sessions Court as well as in the Special Tribunal, every time they were brought in before the Court and the Judges. The judges initially were irritated and upset, but gradually adjusted themselves taking the same as a routine and a part of the daily proceedings. Mr. Asaf Ali was B.K. Dutt's Counsel as Bhagat Singh had decided to represent his case himself.

They were committed to the Sessions after they had refused to make any statement. Mr. Asaf Ali, as the defence counsel, argued that "so long as the Indian Penal Code was in existence, no other law should be employed". "You cannot deal with the accused under the ordinary law and a special enactment for one and the same offence". He said:

> The fact is that not even a cat was killed. It was only a demonstration and rather a rash act. Red Leaflets should be taken as a mere school boy's joke.

Their trial, in the Sessions Court of Mr. Middleton, started on June 4, 1929. On their (Bhagat Singh and B.K. Dutt) entering the Court, after the usual greetings with "Long Live the Revolution" and

"Down with Imperialism", the Judge read out the charges to both the accused. When asked by the Court whether they pleaded guilty, they replied "We claim to be tried".

Bhagat Singh and B.K. Dutt explained in their statement on June 6, 1929 why they had thrown the bomb. They said, headlined by *The Tribune* dated June 8, on its front page: "We Wanted to Make the Deaf Hear"; "No Faith in Utopian Non-Violence"; "Assembly is Only a Hollow Show"; "We Could Have Ambushed Simon"; "But That Was Not Our Intention"; Accused Quote Law Member!

Bhagat Singh and Dutt accused in the Assembly Bomb Case, admit that they threw bombs in the Assembly. "It was only a danger signal to the government to change their system of administration". They said:

> "Out of our sincerest good will and love for humanity have we adopted this method of warning to prevent untold sufferings which we, like millions of others, clearly foresee". Quoting the words of the late Mr. S.R. Das, the late Law Member, they declared that:
>
> "The bombs were regarded as necessary to awaken England from her dream". The accused stated that "they had no intention to take human life which they hold to be very dear, but believed in revolution which they defined as reconstruction of society on Socialist lines".

Statement in the Sessions Court

(A policy document explaining the aims and objectives of the revolutionary movement.) Full Text of the Statement of Bhagat Singh and B.K. Dutt in the Assembly Bomb-Case, read in the Court on June 6, 1929, by Mr. Asaf Ali on behalf of Bhagat Singh and B.K. Dutt.

"We stand charged with certain serious offences, and at this stage it is but right that we must explain our conduct. In this connection, the following questions arise.

Were the bombs thrown into the Chamber, and, if so, why?

Is the charge, as framed by the Lower Court, correct or otherwise?

To the first half of the first question, our reply is in the affirmative, but since some of the so-called 'eye-witnesses' have perjured themselves and since we are not denying our liability to that extent, let our statement about them be judged for what it is worth. By way of an illustration, we may point out that the evidence of Sergeant Terry regarding the seizure of the pistol from one of us is a deliberate falsehood, for neither of us had the pistol at the time we gave ourselves up. Other witnesses, too, who have deposed to having seen bombs being thrown by us, have not scrupled to tell lies. This fact had its own moral for those who aim at judicial purity and fairplay. At the same time, we acknowledge the fairness of the Public Prosecutor and the judicial attitude of the Court so far.

Viceroy's Views Endorsed

In our reply to the next half of the first question, we are constrained to go into some detail to offer a full and frank explanation of our motive and the circumstances leading up to what has now become a historic event.

When we were told by some of the police officers, who visited us in jail that Lord Irwin in his address to the joint session of the two Houses described the event as an attack directed against no individual but against an institution itself, we readily recognised that the true significance of the incident had been correctly appreciated. We are next to none in our love for humanity. Far from having any malice against any individual we hold human life sacred beyond words.

We are neither perpetrators of dastardly outrages and therefore a disgrace to the country as the pseudo-socialist Dewan Chaman Lal is reported to have described us nor are we lunatics as *The Tribune* of Lahore and some others would have it believe.

Practical Protest

We humbly claim to be no more than serious students of the history and conditions of our country and her aspirations. We despise hypocrisy. Our practical protest was against the institution, which since its birth, has eminently helped to display not only its worthlessness but its far-reaching power for mischief. The more we have been convinced that it exists only to demonstrate to the world,

India's humiliation and helplessness, and it symbolises the overriding domination of an irresponsible and autocratic rule. Time and again the national demand has been pressed by the people's representatives only to find the waste-paper basket as its final destination.

Attack on Institution

Solemn resolutions passed by the House have been contemptuously trampled under foot on the floor of the so-called Indian Parliament. Resolutions regarding the repeal of the repressive and arbitrary measures have been treated with sublime contempt, and the government measures and proposals, rejected as unacceptable by the elected members of the legislatures, have been restored by a mere stroke of the pen. In short, we have utterly failed to find any justification for the existence of an institution which, despite all its pomp and splendour, organised with the hard-earned money of the sweating millions of India, is only a hollow show and a mischievous make-believe. Alike, have we failed to comprehend the mentality of the public leaders who help the government to squander public time and money on such a manifestly stage-managed exhibition of India's helpless subjugation.

No Hope for Labour

We have been ruminating upon all these matters, as also upon the wholesale arrests of the leaders of the labour movement. When the introduction of the Trade Disputes Bill brought us into the Assembly to watch its progress, the course of the debate only served to confirm our conviction that the labouring millions of India had nothing to expect from an institution that stood as a menacing monument to the strangling exploiters and the serfdom of the helpless labourers.

Finally the insult of what we consider, an inhuman and barbarous measure, was hurled at the representatives of the entire country, and the starving and struggling millions were deprived of their primary right and the sole means of improving their economic welfare. None, who has felt like us for the dumb driven drudges of labourers, could possibly witness this spectacle with equanimity. None, whose heart bleeds for them, who have given their life-blood in silence to the building of the economic structure, could repress the cry, which this ruthless blow, had wrung out of our hearts.

Bomb Needed

Consequently, bearing in mind the words of the late Mr. S.R. Das, once Law Member of the Governor-General's Executive Council, which appeared in the famous letter he had addressed to his son, to the effect that the 'Bomb was necessary to awaken England from her dreams', we dropped the bomb on the floor of the Assembly Chamber to register our protest on behalf of those who had no other means left to give expression to their heart-rending agony. Our sole purpose was "to make the deaf hear" and to give the heedless a timely warning. Others have, as keenly felt, as we have done, and from under the seeming stillness of the sea of Indian humanity, a veritable storm is about to break out. We have only hoisted the "danger-signal" to warn those who are speeding along without heeding the grave dangers ahead. We have only marked the end of an era of Utopian non-violence, of whose futility, the rising generation has been convinced beyond the shadow of doubt.

Ideal Explained

We have used the expression Utopian non-violence, in the foregoing paragraph which requires some explanation. Force, when aggressively applied, is "violence" and is, therefore, morally unjustifiable, but when it is used in the furtherance of a legitimate cause, it has its moral justification. The elimination of force at all costs is Utopian, and the new movement, which has arisen in the country, and of that dawn we have given a warning, is inspired by the ideal which guided Guru Gobind Singh and Shivaji, Kamal Pasha and Riza Khan, Washington and Garibaldi, Lafayette and Lenin. As both the alien government and the Indian public leaders appeared to have shut their eyes to the existence of this movement, we felt it as our duty to sound a warning where it could not go unheard. We have so far dealt with the motive behind the incident in question, and now we must define the extent of our intention.

No Personal Grudge

We bore no personal grudge or malice against anyone of those who received slight injuries or against any other person in the Assembly. On the contrary, we repeat that we hold human life sacred beyond words, and would sooner lay down our own lives in the service of humanity than injure anyone else. Unlike the mercenary soldiers of the imperialist armies who are disciplined to kill without compunction, we respect, and, in so far as it lies in our power, we attempt to save human life. And still we admit having deliberately thrown the bombs into the Assembly Chamber. Facts, however, speak for themselves and our intention would be judged from the result of the action without bringing in Utopian hypothetical circumstances and presumptions.

No Miracle

Despite the evidence of the government expert, the bombs that were thrown in the Assembly Chamber resulted in slight damage to an empty bench and some slight abrasions in less than half a dozen cases, while government scientists and experts have ascribed this result to a miracle, we see nothing but a precisely scientific process in all this incident. Firstly, the two bombs exploded in vacant spaces within the wooden barriers of the desks and benches, secondly, even those who were within two feet of the explosion, for instance, Mr. P. Rau, Mr. Shankar Rao and Sir George Schuster were either not hurt or only slightly scratched. Bombs of the capacity deposed to by the government expert (though his estimate, being imaginary, is exaggerated), loaded with an effective charge of potassium chlorate and sensitive (explosive) picrate would have smashed the barriers and laid many low within some yards of the explosion.

Again, had they been loaded with some other high explosive, with a charge of destructive pellets or darts, they would have sufficed to wipe out a majority of the members of the Legislative Assembly. Still again we could have flung them into the official box which was occupied by some notable persons. And finally we could have ambushed Sir John Simon whose luckless Commission was loathed by all responsible people and who was sitting in the President's gallery at the time. All these things, however, were beyond our intention and bombs did no more than they were designed to do, and the miracle consisted in no more than the deliberate aim which landed them in safe places.

We then deliberately offered ourselves to bear the penalty for what we had done and to let the imperialist exploiters know that by crushing individuals, they cannot kill ideas. By crushing two insignificant units, a nation cannot be crushed. We wanted to emphasise the historical lesson that *lettres de cachets* and Bastilles could not crush the revolutionary movement in France. Gallows and the Siberian mines could not extinguish the Russian Revolution. Bloody Sunday, and Black and Tans failed to strangle the movement of Irish freedom.

Can Ordinances and Safety Bills snuff out the flames of freedom in India? Conspiracy cases, trumped or discovered and the incarceration of all young men, who cherish the vision of a great ideal, cannot check the march of revolution. But a timely warning, if not unheeded, can help to prevent loss of life and general sufferings. We took it upon ourselves to provide this warning and our duty is done.

(Bhagat Singh was asked in the lower court what he meant by the word 'Revolution'). In answer to that question, he said, "Revolution does not necessarily involve sanguinary strife, nor is there any place in it for individual vendetta. It is not the cult of the bomb and the pistol. By 'Revolution' we mean that the present order of things, which is based on manifest injustice, must change. Producers or labourers in spite of being the most necessary element of society, are robbed, by their exploiters, of the fruits of their labour and deprived of their elementary rights. The peasant who grows corn for all, starves with his family, the weaver who supplies the world market with textile fabrics, has not enough to cover his own and his children's bodies. Masons, smiths and carpenters who raise magnificent palaces, live like pariahs in the slums. The capitalists and exploiters, the parasites of society, squander millions on their whims. These terrible inequalities and forced disparity of chances are bound to lead to chaos. This state of affairs cannot last long, and it is obvious, that the present order of society in merry-making is on the brink of a volcano.

The whole edifice of this civilisation, if not saved in time, shall crumble. A radical change, therefore, is necessary and it is the duty of those, who realise it, to reorganise society, on the socialist basis. Unless this thing is done and the exploitation of man by man and of nations by nations is brought to an end, sufferings and carnage with which humanity is threatened today cannot be prevented. All talk of ending war and ushering in an era of universal peace is undisguised hypocrisy.

By 'Revolution', we mean the ultimate establishment of an order of society which may not be threatened by such a breakdown, and in which the sovereignty of the proletariat should be recognised and a world federation should redeem humanity from the bondage of capitalism and misery of imperial wars. This is our ideal, and with this ideology as our inspiration, we have given a fair and loud enough warning.

If, however, it goes unheeded and the present system of government continues to be an impediment in the way of the natural forces that are swelling up, a grim struggle will ensue involving the overthrow of all obstacles, and the establishment of the dictatorship of the proletariat to pave the way for the consummation of the ideal of revolution. Revolution is an inalienable right of mankind. Freedom is an imperishable birthright of all. Labour is the real sustainer of society. The sovereignty of the people is the ultimate destiny of the workers.

For these ideals, and for this faith, we shall welcome any suffering to which we may be condemned. At the altar of this revolution we have brought our youth as an incense, for no sacrifice is too great for so magnificent a cause. We are content, we await the advent of Revolution. 'Long Live the Revolution.'

Himself appreciating and rightly so like every patriotic Indian, Bhagat Singh and B.K. Dutt's statement in the Sessions Court and realising the fact of very general appreciation of it among Congress circles, Pt. Jawaharlal Nehru had published it in the *Congress Bulletin* but was taken to task by Mahatma Gandhi for doing so. Beating a pathetic retreat like an obedient follower from his stand, Pt. Nehru offered apologies to Bapuji for doing the unpardonable.

Leaving aside the *Congress Bulletin*, Pt. Jawaharlal Nehru got so chastened that he, afterwards, never uttered a word on the revolutionaries' trial and harsh and unjust punishment inflicted on them under the British judicial system in the country till the execution of Bhagat Singh and his two comrades. He could have at least safely said a word or two on what even the Viceroy had already acknowledged stating that it was not an attack directed against an individual but was against an institution.

There seemed to be an effort by all the nationalist forces to belittle Bhagat Singh's genius. At the outset of the trial in the Sessions Court, asking and persuading Bhagat Singh to expunge certain portions of his statement showed Mr. Asaf Ali's indecorousness and that too to oblige the Prosecution Counsel, "a very great friend of mine" as stated by him in his article titled "An Outstanding Maker of History" first published in the *Commonweal* (Pune) and later in *Selected Collections on Bhagat Singh* by M.M. Juneja. Mr. Asaf Ali should have detailed the portion he got expunged. [The significant deletion made by Mr. Asaf Ali was of the concept of 'The Dictatorship of the Proletariat' and replacing it with 'Sovereignty' to please the Prosecutor, his friend. The statement with the original wording had already been procured by *The Hindustan Times*, and published it in its Evening Edition.]

Mr. Asaf Ali, who remained in close touch with the two revolutionaries for a fairly long time during their trial in the Sessions Court and later on in the High Court, was not able to realise that their statements and "actions" were to highlight and serve their political aims while escaping the punishment, however harsh, was of least consideration. Similarly Mr. Asaf Ali claiming "the actual language and sequel of sentence had to be mine", showed his arrogance, lies, falseness and political opportunism. This claim is glaringly false. It was a part of the efforts to undermine Bhagat Singh's intellect by the social democrats of various hues like Mr. Asaf Ali. Bhagat Singh did not need Mr. Asaf Ali's language. His own English in his writings and knowledge was far more superior and superb than that of Mr. Asaf Ali.

Likewise, in 'just one other incident' in March 1931 before the execution of the martyrs, Mr. Asaf Ali, had shown his incapability of understanding how shocked Bhagat Singh would have been, had a draft prepared by him (Mr. Asaf Ali), signifying a repudiation of the 'cult of violence,' been put up before Bhagat Singh for his signature. Mr. Asaf Ali, it might be added, was the Governor of Orissa [Odisha] at the time when he wrote his article on Bhagat Singh and it seemed he wanted to please his superiors. Earlier he was also a Minister for a while in Pt. Jawaharlal Nehru's Interim Cabinet in 1946.

18

Statement Before the Lahore High Court Bench

[Through this brilliant statement Bhagat Singh demolished the basis of the Sessions Court judgment and emphasised the importance of motive. The motive of action, he argued, should be the main consideration while judging the offence of an accused.]

My Lords,

We are neither lawyers nor masters of the English language, nor holders of degrees. Therefore, please do not expect any oratory from us. We, therefore, pray that instead of going into the language mistakes of our statement, Your Lordships will try to understand the real sense of it.

Leaving other points to our lawyers, I will confine myself to one point only. The point is very important in this case. The point is as to what were our intentions and to what extent we are guilty. This is a very complicated question and no one will be able to express before you that high mental elevation, which inspired us to think and act in a particular manner. We want that this should be kept in mind while assessing our intentions behind our offence. According to the famous jurist Solomon, one should not be punished for his criminal offence if his aim is not against law.

We had submitted a written statement in the Sessions Court. That statement explains our aim and, as such, also explains our intentions. But the learned judge dismissed it with one stroke of the pen, saying that:

> Generally the operation of law is not affected by how or why one

committed the offence. In this country the aim of the offence is very rarely mentioned in legal commentaries.

My Lords, our contention is that under the circumstances the learned judge ought to have judged us either by the result of our action or on the basis of the psychological part of our statement. But he did not take any of these factors into consideration.

The point to be considered is that the two bombs, we threw in the Assembly, did not harm anybody physically or economically. As such the punishment awarded to us is not only very harsh but also revengeful. Moreover, the motive of the offence of an accused cannot be found out without knowing his psychology. And no one can do justice to anybody without taking his motive into consideration. If we ignore the motive, the biggest generals of the world will appear like ordinary murderers; revenue officers will look like thieves and cheats. Even judges will be accused of murder. This way the entire social system and the civilisation will be reduced to murders, thefts and cheating. If we ignore the motive, the government will have no right to expect sacrifices from its people and its officials. Ignore the motive and every religious preacher will be dubbed as a preacher of falsehoods, and every prophet will be charged of misguiding crores of simple and ignorant people.

If we set aside the motive, then Jesus Christ will appear to be a man responsible for creating disturbances, breaking peace and preaching revolt, and will be considered to be a "dangerous personality" in the language of the law. But we worship him. He commands great respect in our hearts and his image creates vibrations of spiritualism amongst us. Why? Because, the inspiration behind his actions was that of a high ideal. The rulers of that age could not recognise that high idealism. They only saw his outward actions. Nineteen centuries have passed since then. Have we not progressed during this period? Shall we repeat that mistake again? If that be so, then we shall have to admit that all the sacrifices of mankind and all the efforts of the great martyrs, were useless and it would appear, as if we are still at the same place where we stood twenty centuries ago.

From the legal point of view also, the question of motive is of special importance. Take the example of General Dyer. He resorted to firing and killed hundreds of innocent and unarmed people. But the military court did not order him to be shot. It gave him lakhs of rupees as an award. Take another example. Shri Kharag Bahadur Singh, a young Gurkha, killed a Marwari in Calcutta. If the motive be set aside, then Kharag Bahadur Singh ought to have been hanged. But he was awarded a mild sentence of a few years only. He was even released much before the expiry of his sentence. Was there any loophole in the law that he escaped capital punishment? Or, was the charge of murder not proved against him? Like us, he also accepted the full responsibility of his action, but he escaped death. He is free today. I ask your Lordship, why was he not awarded capital punishment? His action was well calculated and well planned. From the motive end, his action was more serious and fatal than ours. He was awarded a mild punishment because his intentions were good. He saved the society from a dirty leach who had sucked the life-blood of so many pretty young girls. Kharag Singh was given a mild punishment just to uphold the formalities of the law.

The principle (that the law does not take motive into consideration) is quite absurd. This is against the basic principles of the law, which declares, that:

> "The law is for man and not man for the law." As such, why are the same norms not being applied to us also? It is quite clear that while convicting Kharag Singh, his motive was kept in mind, otherwise a murderer can never escape the hangman's noose. Are we being deprived of the ordinary advantage of the law, because, our offence is against the government, or because our action has a political importance?

My Lords, under these circumstances, please permit us to assert that a government which seeks shelter behind such mean methods has no right to exist. If it exists, it is for the time being only, and that too with the blood of thousands of people on its head. If the law does not see the motive, there can be no justice, nor can there be stable peace.

Mixing of arsenic (poison) in the flour will not be considered to be a crime, provided its purpose is to kill rats. But if the purpose is to kill a man, it becomes a crime of murder. Therefore, such laws which do not stand the test of reason and which are against the principle of justice, should be abolished. Because of such unjust laws, many great intellectuals had to adopt the path of revolt.

The facts regarding our case are very simple. We threw two bombs in the Legislative Assembly on April 8, 1929. As a result of the explosion, a few people received minor scratches. There was pandemonium in the chamber, hundreds of visitors and members of the Assembly ran out. Only my friend B.K. Dutt and myself remained seated in the visitors' gallery and offered ourselves for arrest. We were tried for attempt to murder, and convicted for life. As mentioned above, as a result of the bomb explosion, only four or five persons were slightly injured and one bench got damaged. We offered ourselves for arrest without any resistance.

The Sessions judge admitted that we could have very easily escaped, if we had any such intention. We accepted our offence and gave a statement explaining our position. We are not afraid of punishment. But we do not want to be wrongly understood. The judge removed a few paragraphs from our statement. This we consider to be harmful for our real position.

A proper study of the full text of our statement will make it clear that, according to us, our country is passing through a delicate phase. We saw the coming catastrophe and thought it proper to issue a timely warning with a loud voice, and we gave the warning in the manner we thought proper. We may be wrong. Our line of thinking and that of the learned judge may be different, but that does not mean that we should be deprived of the permission to express our ideas, and wrong things be propagated in our name. In our statement we explained in detail what we mean by "Long Live the Revolution" and "Down with Imperialism". That formed the crux of our ideas. That portion was removed from our statement. Generally a wrong meaning is attributed to the word 'revolution'. That is not our understanding. Bombs and pistols do not make revolution. This is not our understanding. The sword of revolution is sharpened on the whetting-stone of ideas. This is what we wanted to emphasise. By revolution we mean the end of the miseries of capitalist wars. It was not proper to pronounce judgment without understanding our aims and objects and the process of achieving them. To associate wrong ideas with our names, is out and out injustice. It was very necessary to give the timely warning that the unrest of the people is increasing and that the malady may take a serious turn, if not treated in time and properly. If our warning is not heeded, no human power will be able to stop it. We took this step to give proper direction to the storm. We are serious students of history. We believe that, had the ruling powers acted correctly at the proper time, there would have been no bloody revolutions in France and Russia. Several big powers of the world tried to check the storm of ideas and were sunk in the atmosphere of bloodshed. The ruling people cannot change the flow of the current. We wanted to give the first warning. Had we aimed at killing some important personalities, we would have failed in the attainment of our aim. My Lords, this was the aim and the spirit behind our action, and the result of the action corroborates our statement.

There is one more point, which needs elucidation, and that is, regarding the strength of the bombs. Had we had no idea of the strength of the bombs, there would have been no question of our throwing them in the presence of our respected national leaders like Pandit Motilal Nehru, Shri Kelkar, Shri Jayaker and Shri Jinnah. How could we have risked the lives of our leaders? After all, we are not mad and had we been so, we would have certainly been sent to the lunatic asylum, instead of being put in jail.

We had full knowledge about the strength of the bombs and that is why we acted with so much confidence. It was very easy to throw the bombs on the occupied benches, but it was difficult to have thrown them on unoccupied seats. Had we not been of saner mind or been mentally unbalanced, the bombs would have fallen on occupied benches and not in empty places. Therefore I would say that we should be rewarded for the courage we showed in carefully selecting the empty places. Under these conditions, My Lords, we think we have not been understood properly.

We have not come before you to get our sentences reduced. We have come here to clarify our position. We feel we should not be given any unjust treatment, nor should any unjust opinion be pronounced about us. The question of punishment is of secondary importance before us.

—Bhagat Singh

19

Epoch-Making Hunger-Strike

Shackled behind the iron bars of the high-security prisons of the British Indian administration, after having been sentenced to life imprisonment on June 6,1929 and the damocle's sword of gallows and stringent sentences in a possible verdict in the ensuing Lahore Conspiracy Case, hanging on the heads of Bhagat Singh and his revolutionary comrades, the Indian white rulers as well as their brown collaborators were perceiving a sense of respite from the terrifying "actions" of the Hindustan Socialist Republican Army. After the Delhi Judgment, B.K. Dutt had been put in the Lahore Central Jail while Bhagat Singh was sent to a far-flung Mianwali Jail in Punjab. Since the hearing of the Lahore Conspiracy Case was to commence on June 26, 1929, Bhagat Singh, through a letter to the jail authorities, pointed out the difficulties in pursuing his case from Mianwali, a distance of 200 miles and requested the authorities to transfer him to Lahore Central Jail. Realising their folly, the jail authorities set right the wrong done to him and transferred him to Lahore.

Bhagat Singh and B.K. Dutt while they were in Delhi Jail, were treated well, given good food and provided with other facilities. But in Mianwali and Lahore Jails, they were treated as ordinary criminals and given very poor food which they refused to eat. Thus, they began their epoch-making hunger-strike. Not only they, all the other political prisoners were also not treated properly. Bhagat Singh and B.K. Dutt were not the ones to lie low and keep quiet. They wrote the following letter to the Home Member, Government of India, putting before the government their demands and listing the other facilities which all the political prisoners should be given.

The Home Member,
Government of India, New Delhi

Central Jail Lahore
June 24, 1929

Sir,

We, Bhagat Singh and B.K. Dutt, were sentenced to life transportation in the Assembly Bomb Case, Delhi, on June 12, 1929. As long as we were under-trial prisoners in Delhi Jail, we were accorded very good treatment and were given a very good diet. But since our transfer from that jail to the Mianwali and Lahore Central Jails respectively, we are being treated as ordinary criminals. On the very first day, we wrote an application to the higher authorities asking for a better diet and a few other facilities, and refused to take the jail diet.

Our demands are as follows:

1. We, as political prisoners, should be given a better diet and the standard of our diet should be at least the same as that of European prisoners. (It is not the sameness of dietary that we demand, but the sameness of standard of diet)
2. We shall not be forced to do any hard and undignified labour at all.
3. All books, other than those proscribed, along with writing materials, should be allowed to us without any restriction.
4. At least one standard daily newspaper should be supplied to every political prisoner.
5. Political prisoners should have a special ward of their own in every jail, provided with all necessities as those of the Europeans. And all the political prisoners in one jail must be kept together in their ward.
6. Toilet necessities should be supplied.
7. Better clothing.

We have explained above the demands that we made.They are the most reasonable demands. The jail authorities told us one day that the higher authorities have refused to comply with our demands.

Apart from that, they handle us very roughly while feeding us artificially, and Bhagat Singh was lying quite senseless on June 10,1929, for about 15 minutes, after the forcible feeding which we request to be stopped without any further delay. In addition, we may be permitted to refer to the recommendations made in the UP Jail Committee by Pt. Jagat Narain and K.B. Hafiz Hidayat Husain. They have recommended the political prisoners to be treated as "Better C class prisoners."

We request you to kindly consider our demands at your earliest convenience.

By "Political Prisoners", we mean all those people who are convicted for offences against the state, for instance, the people who were convicted in the Lahore Conspiracy Cases, 1915-17, the Kakori Conspiracy Cases, and Seditition Cases in general.

Yours

Bhagat Singh -B.K. Dut

The citizens of Lahore, Amritsar and other cities led by Naujawan Bharat Sabha and the local Congressmen started holding meetings in support of the demands of the hunger-strikers and condemning the conduct of the government. A call was given by Naujawan Bharat Sabha to observe June 30 as the Bhagat Singh B.K. Dutt Day throughout the country. In response to their call, huge public meetings were held everywhere.

> In order to observe 'The All India Bhagat Singh-Dutt Day,' the General Secretary, Naujawan Bharat Sabha had issued a statement as follows:
>
> Bhagat Singh and Dutt had been on a hunger-strike for about five weeks now. They are fighting for the just and legitimate rights of all political prisoners. They are determined to win or die in this struggle. Other prisoners in the Lahore Conspiracy Case have also stopped having food in sympathy with their comrades. Fighting as all of them are, for the rights of political prisoners, they deserve every encouragement and sympathy. The Naujawan Bharat Sabha has decided to celebrate Sunday, the 21st July as All India Bhagat Singh-Dutt Day. They,

> therefore, appeal to all Congress, youth and labour organisations in the country to observe the 21st July by 1)Fasting, 2) Taking out processions and collecting funds for the defence of the accused in the Lahore Conspiracy Case, 3) Organising meetings in the evening to explain the significance and importance of the struggle in the cause of the country's freedom and to record the country's protest against the treatment meted out to these prisoners.Wherever possible their photos and copies of their statements in the Assembly bomb episode and in the Sessions Court should be distributed. [*The Tribune,* July 19,1929]

Soon after the General Secretary Naujawan Bharat Sabha's appeal to the political organisations, and especially the Congress, to support Bhagat Singh and B.K. Dutt's cause to improve the lot of the political prisoners and their hunger-strike for the same, Mr. Harihar Nath Shastri, a member of the AICC, proposed to move a resolution congratulating Bhagat Singh and B.K. Dutt on their bold step to improve the conditions of the political prisoners. The resolution to be moved at the forthcoming meeting of the All India Congress Committee stated as follows:

> While adhering to the principle of non-violence in our fight for freedom, the AICC appreciates the courage and patriotism of Messrs. Bhagat Singh and Butkeshwar Dutt, and while congratulating them upon the bold step they have taken to better the lot of political prisoners in the country, the Committee feels about the present state of their health and looks with contempt upon the callousness of the government and its not moving rightly in the matter. The Committee proposes that the 4th day of August be observed throughout India as "Political Sufferers' Day" when every lover of the country's youth should observe a 23-hour fast and pray for their health and recovery. The meetings should be held that evening for the same purpose. [*The Tribune,* July 20, 1929]

Pt. Motilal Nehru, the President of the AICC, however, disallowed Mr. Harihar Nath Shastri's resolution regarding the Bhagat Singh-B.K. Dutt hunger-strike at the AICC meeting held at Allahabad,

The Tribune, date-lined July 27, 1929 stated:

> The President disallowed as being contrary to the creed of non-violence of the Congress the motion regarding Messrs, Bhagat Singh and Dutt.

> In another report published by *The Tribune* dated August 16, 1929, it was stated that Pt. Motilal Nehru, the Congress President had not allowed the Bhagat Singh Dutt resolution to avoid discussion as Gandhiji had said, "he would oppose it".
>
> *The Tribune* datelined Banaras, August 11, 1929 stated:
>
> "Explaining his position about Pt. Motilal's statement regarding the disallowance of the resolution of the Lahore hunger-strikers in the All India Congress Committee, the mover, Mr. Harihar Nath Shastri in the course of a letter to the 'AJ' says that he agreed to any alterations to make the resolution in conformity with the Congress creed. He could not say what was the real reason of its being disallowed. He learnt from Pt. Jawaharlal Nehru [Pt. Nehru was the General Secretary at the time] that Mahatma Gandhi desired that the resolution should be withdrawn, otherwise he would oppose it".

How the resolution of Harihar Nath Shastri or the hunger-strike was against the Congress creed, was not explained by either Pt. Motilal Nehru, the Congress President or Pt. Jawaharlal Nehru, the Congress General Secretary. The hunger-strike was to improve the lot of all the political prisoners and not just of the revolutionary prisoners. The political prisoners also meant the civil disobedience movement prisoners. It was an exemplary act of non-violence, satyagraha and truth. The hunger-strikers were neither using any physical force nor had they ever intended it. Their hunger-strike was the purest soul force against the British Government to arouse a sense of justice and humanly feelings in the hearts of the British rulers as fellow-human beings.

There was a serious "Janus" like behaviour of the official Congress Party platform regarding their position on Bhagat Singh. On the one hand, Congress at Mahatma Gandhi's behest did its best to officially dissociate itself from the actions of the revolutionaries, while on the other hand, sensing the growing popularity of Bhagat Singh, they thought of mouthing platitudes.

Thus, on August 8, 1929, Pt. Jawaharlal Nehru visited the Central Jail and Borstal Jail, Lahore to meet the hunger-strikers.

Later, Pt. Jawaharlal Nehru, addressing a mammoth public

meeting at Lahore, referred, to the suffering which the hunger-strikers were undergoing in the Lahore Jails.

> "They", are not undergoing the manifest suffering, which it is in the power of a few to endure, for themselves, but for all poltical prisoners. How can we help these brave souls, these national heroes? Not by raising shouts at public meetings or in the streets of Lahore, but by joining in the national army of freedom. Let us extend and perfect the organisation of the Congress and let us free our country from bondage. Then there will be no political prisoners.

Raising and shouting "Inquilab Zindabad" "Bhagat Singh and B.K. Dutt Zindabaad" were called "shouts" by Pt. Nehru. Holding meetings in sympathy with the hunger-strikers and in support of their demands was not the way the hunger-strikers could be helped, according to Pt. Nehru. He, on the other hand, asked the young men to support and strengthen the Congress Party–the Party that had disallowed Mr. Harihar Nath Shastri's resolution in support of Bhagat Singh-B.K. Dutt and their comrades' hunger-strike at its meeting held at Allahabad on July 27,1929 [*The Tribune*, July 30,1929].

Mr. Ganesh Shankar Vidyarthi MLC, Editor, '*Pratap*', Kanpur and a distinguished public figure had visited Lahore and interviewed Bhagat Singh as well as other hunger-strikers. He, on his return, had issued a statement giving Bhagat Singh's view-point on the issue of the hunger-strike [*The Tribune,* August 2, 1929]. A few extracts of his statement are given here below:

> "I went to Lahore being pressed by some friends and relatives of the accused on the hunger-strike. I saw all the accused lodged in the Central and Borstal jails. I had a long talk with Sardar Bhagat Singh lying all alone in a condemned cell. He told me he stood for better treatment of political prisoners as a matter of right. By political prisoners he meant persons convicted of offences of a political nature. He holds that the government can confiscate their liberty of action and movement. But can they confine them with the worst type of criminals and cause their intellectual death by not letting them read even scientific and literary books and kill them slowly by giving a very poor diet, to which they are not used to and on which they can make no improvement without

resorting to objectionable methods as is done by many. Then, the one and only duty of political prisoners who know how to dare and die, is to fight out the issue to the bitterest end."

"Bhagat Singh added, he did not care about himself. He was ready to die in that very cell but he could not, under any circumstances, brook the intolerable conditions in which the political prisoners were, as a rule, putting. He did not believe in the bona fides of the officials who offered diet on medical advice, as such a course was nothing new, being already provided under the Jail Manual. The hollowness of the government advocate's assertion of diet on a liberal scale and better arrangements became apparent, when the three accused who were not on hunger-strike and who attaching credence to the government declaration demanded better food, were taunted with the remark that they were not in Nedoes Hotel, but in jail."

"Sardar Bhagat Singh emphatically refused to yield as long as the government did not declare that the under-trial persons and persons convicted of political offences would have, as a matter of right, proper food, books and light labour in jail. After a good deal of discussion he, like a Mahatma, agreed to ask other young men, who had gone on hunger-strike in sympathy, to abandon the same, as he thought that he and Dutt were enough to fight the issue to a finish. At this stage, the latter was brought into the cell on a stretcher. He looked very weak and emaciated."

यतीन्द्र नाथ दास 1904-1929
JATINDRA NATH DAS

"Mr. Jatindra Nath Das was the worst case. I understand that two tubes were used in this case. One was introduced through his nostrils

> and another through his mouth which caused intense pain and profuse bleeding. When I saw him he was lying in a half-conscious condition and had temperature as well. He could hardly speak and when I spoke to him about my mission he could speak under great strain and in a very low voice."
>
> "I asked all the hunger-strikers to let Sardar Bhagat Singh and Mr. Dutt fight alone for the cause and commence such a strike again, if after conviction, they were reduced to the common level. They, however, rejected my position as they thought their combined effort would finish the struggle sooner. Were Sardar Bhagat Singh and Mr. Dutt alone to do it, the affair would last longer and be rather more painful."
>
> "Mr. Jatindra Nath Das was against the hunger-strike but when he began it once, he would not yield as long as the government would not give way. Despite his physical agony which made him toss on the bed, his mind was very clear. Quite unequivocally, he expressed his deliberate determination to die if the reasonable demands were not conceded."

In the meanwhile, the condition of Jatindra Nath Das continued to deteriorate. The British rulers refused to budge from their position and refused either to release him or concede the demands of the hunger-strikers. Mr. Das ultimately attained martyrdom on September 13, 1929 on the 63rd day of his hunger-strike. As had been desired by him, his body was taken to Calcutta for cremation. Mr. Subhas Chandra Bose had by telegraphic money order sent a sum of Rs. 600, the requisite amount of railway fare for the same. At every railway station at which the train had a stoppage, huge crowds of people were present to pay their homage to the martyr putting wreaths and flowers on his body and cries of 'Long Live Jatin', 'Inquilab Zindabad' rent the air. In Calcutta, more than six lakh people had joined the funeral procession.

Mr. Bankim Behari Das, father of Jatindra Nath Das, helped Kiran Chandra Das, his elder son, in performing the last funeral rites at the burning ghat. The old man burst into tears while meeting Subhas Chandra Bose. They took some time to control each other. The following message of Mr. Bankim Behari Das was read at the cremation ground when the earthly remains of Mr. Jatin Das were being placed on the pyre:

> "As a penance for the treachery of which our forefathers, both Hindus and Muslims, were guilty of when they cheated Nawab-Siraj-ud-Daula whose salt they had eaten and handed over Bengal, nay the whole of India, to the foreigners, I surrender my dearly loved son, Khendu, at your feet, Oh Lord, with tributes of tears. May India wake up as a result of his sacred self-immolation." [*The Tribune*, September 19, 1929]

After Jatindra Nath Das's martyrdom, the stupendous upsurge of sympathy with the hunger-strikers and in support of their demands amongst the people all over the country, forced the Congress Party leadership to come out in favour of the hunger-strikers and contact the British administration to agree to accept their demands.

During this long life and death struggle of the hunger-strikers, Mahatma Gandhi had maintained a stone-hearted silence. However, the popular upsurge made Mahatma Gandhi relent somewhat, as he did not oppose the resolution issued by the AICC in support of the demands of the hunger-strikers, when it met at Lucknow on September 28, 1929. It passed a resolution on hunger-strikers in jails which, while deeply appreciating the motive of the prisoners, expressed the opinion that a hunger-strike should not be undertaken except upon the gravest emergencies. The Committee advised those who had imposed the sacrifice upon themselves to end their strike, especially, in view of the self-immolation of Jatindra Nath Das in a Lahore jail after 63 days' starvation and the fact that the government had at the eleventh hour yielded to most of the demands of the hunger-strikers and an effort is being made to secure full redress. They ended their starvation on October 4, 1929 after 112 days. Since the British Government did not fulfil the acceded demands, Bhagat Singh wrote another letter to the Government of India on January 28, 1930.

A Press Communique had been published by the Government of India on February 19, 1930 framing rules for the classification of political prisoners. The word 'political' was sedulously omitted, despite the fact that for ten years previously, the government had been freely using the expression though within inverted commas in their annual publication of India. According to the above government order on the classification of prisoners, the 'A' class was there only nominally. The 'B' class was given in a niggardly spirit. Men with large property and refined standards of life and fulfilling the conditions set by the Government would get 'B' class. 'C' class prisoners were set to stone-breaking, oil grinding and pump work in jails. The treatment to 'Satyagrahis' soon revealed that the government order of February 1930 was an eye-wash. The treatment given was brutal. [*The History of the Indian National Congress,* p. 403 by Pattabhi Sitaramayya] The political prisoners have not been recognised as a category even in a free India.

During this long Bhagat Singh, Dutt, Jatin and other hunger-strikers' life and death struggle, Mahatma Gandhi maintained a stony-hearted silence. His conscience didn't prick even when, on Jatindra Nath Das's death, the whole country was weeping and he did not feel like expressing a word of condolence to the martyr's family.

The AICC had to change its stance and all the leaders of the Party, except Mahatma Gandhi, started supporting the demands of the hunger-strikers publicly, when Jatindra Nath Das died on September 13, 1929. It was only after Das's death, the All India Congress Committee had passed the resolution as stated above on September 28, 1929 at Lucknow appreciating the motive of the hunger-strikers and appealing to them to end their fast.

Bhagat Singh and his revolutionary comrades were on hunger-strike for the right to be recognised as political prisoners and that right they neither got during Pt. Jawaharlal Nehru's reign as Prime Minister nor that of his successors. Sadly, Pt. Nehru during his 17 long years of Prime Ministership had forgotten, it seemed, what he had written at a time when power did not seem to be within reach.

So, continued the situation during Shri Lal Bahadur Shastri's Prime Ministership. He too had been declaring at public meetings before independence that in a free India, political prisoners would be accorded humane treatment.

20

Bhagat Singh's Jail Diary

Bhagat Singh wrote his famous 'Jail Diary' while he was a prisoner in the Central Jail Lahore serving a life sentence and the expected death sentence. He, a voracious reader and a prolific writer, would take down notes from the books he went through. His 'Jail Diary' includes the notes from the books of more than 110 world-renowned philosophers, poets and other authors.

These included Karl Marx, Friedrich Engels, V.I. Lenin, Trotsky, Bukharin, Kautsky, Bernstein, Maxim Gorky, Upton Sinclair, Rousseau, Plato, Socrates, Aristotle, Thomas Carlyle, Danton, Thomas Paine, Bertrand Russell, Dostovesky, Charles Dickens, Tennyson, Wordsworth, to name a few. Besides these 110 authors noted in the *'Jail Note Book'*, there were some others such as Bukanin, the greatest amongst the anarchists, Proudhon, Peter Kropotkin, Karlo Kafiars, Mala Tamta, Stepniak, Bhagat Singh had read. He had written four articles on 'Anarchism' and 'Russian Nihilists'. These are cited by some of his critics as proof of Bhagat Singh's leaning towards Anarchism, instead of appreciating the sweep of his study and reach of his knowledge. It might be a surprise to his detractors that he had read Marx's *Capital* before the formation of his Party [HSRA] in 1928. And the number of books estimated to have been read by him would go upto 300 or more if the books, he had gone through during his National College and Dwarka Das Library days, were counted.

Jitendra Nath Sanyal, one of his revolutionary colleagues in his book, *Bhagat Singh, A Biography*, wrote:

> "It was marvellous how he procured contraband and rare literature inside the jail. He studied and finished a detailed history of the

> revolutionary movement in India. For this purpose, he had learnt Bengali to the fullest extent... He was also able to send out drafts for some of the revolutionary pamphlets, notably 'The Philosophy of the Bomb'. Only a short time before his execution, he drafted and sent out a statement 'An Address to the Young Political Workers' which is regarded as his will and testament to the nation".

Another example of Bhagat Singh's resourcefulness could be seen in procuring the then Premier of Great Britain, Mr. J. Ramsay MacDonald's book captioned *The Government of India* and on the basis of which he sent a notice for the then Legislative Assembly. It was reported in *The Tribune* of January 7, 1931 on its first page. It is being reproduced here:

"Last Chapter in History of Bureaucrats is Repression".

Mr. Bhagat Singh has given notice of the following question for the forthcoming session of the Legislative Assembly.

'Will the government be pleased to state whether they have taken note of the following passage occurring in the chapter on "Press" in the present Premier, Mr. J. Ramsay MacDonald's book on *The Government of India?*

> "The Indian Press, though its foundation may be to act as a part of the constitutional opposition to the government, cannot do its work in the full way that 'papers' in this country [England] do, until there is really a free Press in India, but the Press Act will never finally disappear there, though both their contents and their administration may vary in stringency, while the government is a bureaucracy. To demand the complete abolition of the Press Act is equivalent to demanding that the government itself should be put on a more liberal foundation. The problem of the Indian Press is at the root that of inherent conflict between a bureaucracy and public opinion. The last chapter in the history of bureaucracies is repression. They pass away like an old monarch, driven from his throne, hurling accusations of sedition against his approaching successor."

21

Judgment by the Tribunal

The judgment in the Lahore Conspiracy Case was delivered by the Lahore Conspiracy Case Special Tribunal, on October 7, 1930. Bhagat Singh, Sukhdev and Rajguru were given death sentences. Bejoy Kumar Sinha, Kamalnath Tiwari, Jaidev Kapur, Shiv Varma, Gaya Prasad, Kishorilal and Mahabir Singh were sentenced to transportation for life. Kundanlal was given 7 years rigorous imprisonment, Premdutt, 3 years rigorous imprisonment. The others were released. It was a fifty-page document.

It could not be kept secret and people came to know of it immediately. It resulted in a spontaneous 'hartal' [closing of business establishments] and a wave of anger gripped the country. On 8th October not only Lahore, but all cities in the country were convulsed with strikes. Naturally, Lahore was the most agitated. Many students including women were arrested. The police entered DAV College and beat up a large number of students. The sky was rent with the cries of "Bhagat Singh, Rajguru, Sukhdev Zindabad" "Inquilab Zindabad". The government was using its oppressive bulldozers. The Naujawan Bharat Sabha convened a meeting of students and youths at Bradlaugh Hall, once the hub of activities of Bhagat Singh and Bhagwati Charan Vohra. In this meeting, the revolutionary leaders were extolled and the government was condemned. In the city outside Mori gate, twelve thousand men and women collected at a meeting presided over by the veteran freedom fighter Parvati Devi.

Bhagat Singh, Rajguru and Sukhdev were kept in condemned cells. Now that the Court room was no longer available to carry on revolutionary propaganda, they sent an appeal to the Privy Council, to highlight the high-handedness of the Tribunal and proclaimed the fact that the revolutionary Party in India stood for Scientific Socialism. The agitation to get Bhagat Singh's death sentence commuted spread. Had Mahatma Gandhi taken over the agitation in the form of the civil disobedience movement, it would have turned into a hurricane from the Khyber Pass to Kanyakumari forcing the British Government to commute the death sentences on the revolutionaries.

But Mahatmaji was afraid of the revolution. He hated the revolutionaries and struggled all his life, supported by Pt. Jawaharlal Nehru and other Congress leaders as well as their Congress Party, against them in various covert and overt ways.

22

No Hanging, Please Shoot Us

(The main charge against the LCC accused was that of waging war against His Majesty the King of England. The three condemned comrades, therefore, claimed that they should be treated as war prisoners. In army, the death sentence is carried out not by hangmen but by a firing squad. It was with this request that the three comrades addressed this letter to the Governor of Punjab.)

Letter to Governor, Punjab

To
The Punjab Governor
Sir,

With due respect we beg to bring to your kind notice the following:

That we were sentenced to death on October 7, 1930 by a British Court, LCC Tribunal, constituted under the Special Lahore Conspiracy Case Ordinance, promulgated by the H.E. the Viceroy, the Head of the British Government of India, and that the main charge against us was that of having waged war against H.M. King George, the King of England.

The above-mentioned finding of the Court pre-supposed two things:

Firstly, that there is a state of war between the British nation and the Indian nation and, secondly, that we had actually participated in that war and were, therefore, war prisoners.

The second pre-supposition seems to be somewhat flattering, but nevertheless, it is too tempting to resist the desire of acquiescing in it.

"As regards the first, we are constrained to go into some detail. Apparently there seems to be no such war as the phrase indicates. Nevertheless, please allow us to accept the validity of the presupposition taking it at its face value. But in order to be correctly understood we must explain it further."

"Let us declare that the state of war does exist and shall exist so long as the Indian toiling masses and the natural resources are being exploited by a handful of parasites. They may be purely British capitalist or mixed British and Indian or even purely Indian. They may be carrying on their insidious exploitation through mixed or even on purely Indian bureaucratic apparatus. All these things make no difference. No matter, if your government tries and succeeds in winning over the leaders of the upper strata of Indian society through petty concessions and compromises and, thereby, cause a temporary demoralisation in the main body of the forces. No matter, if once again the vanguard of the Indian movement, the Revolutionary Party, finds itself deserted in the thick of the war. No matter if the leaders to whom personally we are much indebted for the sympathy and feelings they expressed for us, but nevertheless, we cannot overlook the fact that they did become so callous as to ignore and not to make a mention in the peace negotiation of even the homeless, friendless and penniless of female workers who are alleged to belong to the vanguard and whom the leaders consider to be enemies of their utopian non-violent cult which has already become a thing of the past; the heroines who had ungrudgingly sacrificed or offered for sacrifice, their husbands, brothers, and all that were nearest and dearest to them, including themselves, whom your government has declared to be outlaws. No matter, if your agents stoop so low as to fabricate baseless calumnies against their spotless characters to damage their and their Party's reputation. The war shall continue."

"It may assume different shapes at different times. It may become now open, now hidden, now purely agitational, now a fierce life and death struggle. The choice, of the course, whether bloody or comparatively peaceful, which it should adopt, rests with you. Choose whichever you like. But that war shall be incessantly waged without taking into consideration the petty (illegible) and the meaningless ethical ideologies. It shall be waged ever with new vigour, greater audacity and unflinching determination till the Socialist Republic is established and the present social order is completely replaced by a new social order, based on social prosperity and thus every sort of exploitation is put an end to and humanity is ushered into the era of genuine and permanent peace. In the very near future the final battle shall be fought and final settlement arrived at."

"The days of capitalist and imperialist exploitation are numbered. The war neither began with us nor is it going to end with our lives. It is the inevitable consequence of the historic events and the existing environments. Our humble sacrifices shall be only a link in the chain that has very accurately been beautified by the unparalleled sacrifice of Mr. Das and most tragic but noblest sacrifice of Comrade Bhagawati Charan and the glorious death of our dear warrior Azad."

"As to the question of our fates, please allow us to say that when you have decided to put us to death, you will certainly do it. You have got the power in your hands and the power is the greatest justification in this world. We know that the maxim "Might is right" serves as your guiding motto. Our entire trial was just a proof of that. We wanted to point out that according to the verdict of your court we had waged war and were, therefore, war prisoners. And we claim to be treated as such, i.e. we claim to be shot dead instead of to be hanged. It rests with you to prove that you really meant what your court has said."

"We request and hope that you will very kindly order the military department to send its detachment to perform our execution."

Yours

–Bhagat Singh

23

To the Gallows

One of the men who saw Bhagat Singh when he was confined in the Condemned Cell was Prannath. He wrote:

> "On that day I was privileged to stay near Bhagat Singh's cell for nearly an hour. I had met him many times at the same place. I had witnessed him as a hunger-striker, and had seen him in action in the Courts, but had never felt that he was that courageous and so great. He and I both knew that he was walking through the valley of the shadow of death. The hands of the clock were moving fast towards the zero hour of hanging but I found him cheerful. His face glistened as always. When I approached his cell, he was pacing it like a tiger in a cage". As soon as I stepped inside the cell he asked: "Did you bring the book? I handed over the book quietly. He was very pleased at the sight of the book. It was probably a book on Lenin or by Lenin, I don't remember. I asked him: "Would you give a message to the country? He said, "Down with Imperialism, Long Live the Revolution." I asked him; 'How do you feel today"? He said briefly, 'I am feeling fine'. I persisted and asked, 'have you any last wish? He answered, 'May I be reborn and serve the motherland again.' He conveyed his thanks to the leaders, who had taken an interest in the case and expressed his good wishes to his friends, specially the absconding ones. In that atmosphere of death, I felt shaken, but he seemed to be entrenched firmly in the faith that looks through death. He seemed to be so much at peace with himself, he was so free from fear and unattached that he appeared to be divine.

During these last days Bhagat Singh wrote to a friend:

> "It is but natural that I should desire to live. I do not want to conceal this, but it is conditional in the sense that I do not want to have my freedom curbed. My name has become a symbol of revolution and the ideals and sacrifices of revolutionary parties have placed me on a high

pedestal. It is such a high pedestal that I may not be able to do justice to it as a living being. My weaknesses are not known to the public. If I am saved from the gallows, they would become known to everybody. Thus, the symbol of revolution would fade and even dissolve, but if I die wreathed with smiles, Indian mothers would wish their children to emulate Bhagat Singh, and thus the number of formidable freedom fighters would increase so much that it would be impossible for the satanic forces of imperialism to stop and stem the march of revolution. Of course, there lingers a hidden hankering in my heart that I have not accomplished even a thousandth part of what I proposed to do. Could I live, may be I could get the opportunity to fulfil the tasks and thus be happy.

Apart from this, there was never any temptation to be saved from hanging. Otherwise I am the luckiest man. Nowadays, I think too much of myself. I have no lurking desire. Now I am impatiently waiting for the last test. I wish it could be nearer."

Yours comradely,
Bhagat Singh.

Just one day before the hanging, the Sikh chief warder, Chatter Singh approached Bhagat Singh. Chatter Singh was re-employed in the jail department after retiring as Havildar from the British army. Knowing that Bhagat Singh had only a few hours left, as a devout Sikh he thought it is his duty to help him prepare properly for the next world. According to his religion, Chatter Singh was doing very pious work.

He went to Bhagat Singh and said, 'My son, death, the journey's end is round the corner. I am just like your father. Listen to me.'

Bhagat Singh was mildly surprised, he asked, 'What is the matter? Chatter Singh said, 'I have only one request to make. The end is very near. Now you take the name 'Wahe Guru' and read 'Gurbani' (Sikh Gita). Here I have brought the Gutka (the little book) for you.' Bhagat Singh laughed and said,

> Old man, I would gladly comply with your request, but now that the journey's end is very near, if now I pray to God, people would say that Bhagat Singh was chicken-hearted. I never prayed, and now that I am

> feeling the icy breath of death on my neck, if I started praying, people would misunderstand me. It would be better to let me go my own way. I might be abused because I am an atheist and do not believe in God, but nobody would say that Bhagat Singh was dishonest and flinched at the sight of death.

Bhagat Singh remained true to dialectical materialism, which is as much a part of Marxist philosophy as the head is a part of the body.

Prannath had given him a book on Lenin or by Lenin. Years later, Manmath Nath Gupta asked Prannath to confirm, but he could not remember whether it was a book on Lenin or by Lenin. When called upon to mount the scaffold, Bhagat Singh was reading this book. He continued his reading and said: 'Wait a while. A revolutionary is talking to another revolutionary.' There was something in his voice which made the executioners pause, otherwise befuddled as they are with drink. (officially, the excecutioner was given his thirty pieces of silver and a bottle of wine during the British rule) Backed by brute-force, they do not care for anybody. Bhagat Singh continued to read. After a few moments, he flung the book upward towards the ceiling and said, *'let's go.'* The trio Bhagat Singh, Sukhdev and Rajguru were hanged together. Bhagat Singh was in the middle, Sukhdev was on his right and Rajguru on his left. It is said that Bhagat Singh sang this couplet before going to his death:

Dil se na niklegi marker bhi watan ki ulfat
Meri mitti se bhi khushboo-e-watan aegi.

'Even after death, the love of motherland shall linger in my mind. My dead body shall emit the fragrance of my motherland.'

After he had sung the couplet, he told the Magistrate with a smile, 'You are really fortunate that you are witnessing how Indian revolutionaries march to their death.'

After this they were hanged and they passed into history. All the martyrs before and since Bhagat Singh, had been hanged in the morning, but in the case of these three, an exception was made and they were hanged at 7.33 in the evening on the 23rd of March. This was done to maintain secrecy, but the ordinary prisoners of the jail came to know of it and they raised slogans. Fearing that if the bodies were taken out of the jail gate, some lurking scout of the revolutionaries might notice, the high wall was breached at the back of the jail and the bodies were taken out for summary disposal to Ferozepur. The half-burnt bodies were thrown into the waters of the Sutlej. After the police party had left, the villagers came to know of dead bodies burnt with the collusion of the local police, they learnt of the truth. The news of these hangings was greeted with strikes and protest meetings all over the country.

24

Judas and Quislings Generously Awarded

[R.K. Kaushik, an IAS officer of the Punjab Cadre, a distinguished writer, seems to have done extensive research on Bhagat Singh. Recently he had written an article in 'The Tribune' of March 25, 2017 on the lavish rewards bestowed on India's renegades, the Judas and Quizlings of India, in the Lahore Conspiracy Case of 1928-1931. Shri R.K. Kaushik has given an account of the roles of many of them, they played in the trial and execution of Bhagat Singh and his two martyred colleagues, namely, Sukhdev and Rajguru as well as the others given various terms of imprisonment in Andamans and other jails. The details of such rewards are given below here:]

Hans Raj Vohra, Jai Gopal, Phanindra Nath Ghosh, and Manmohan Banerji, prominent revolutionaries of the Hindustan Socialist Republican Association and trusted comrades of Bhagat Singh had turned government approvers and gave statements against the revolutionaries in their trial.They were amongst the 457 witnesses brought by the Punjab Police Prosecution in the Case. After the execution, all four were rewarded. Vohra refused to accept monetary benefits. But he was sponsored by the Punjab government to study in the prestigious London School of Economics. After a Masters in political science, Vohra got a degree in journalism from London University and was the correspondent of the *Civil and Military Gazette* of Lahore till 1948. He later shifted to Washington and in the 1950s and 60s was the Washington correspondent of a leading Indian daily. He died in July 1995, in Washington.

Jai Gopal got an award of Rs. 20,000. Phanindra Nath Ghosh and Manmohan Banerjee got 50 acres of land each in Champaran district of Bihar (their home district) in lieu of their services and loyalty to the British government. The then jail superintendent, Major P.D. Chopra, was promoted as DIG, Prisons, Punjab, two days after the hangings.

The Deputy Jail Superintendent, Khan Sahib Mohammad Akbar Khan, wept after the execution of Bhagat Singh and his two companions. He was suspended, though later taken back as Assistant Jail Superintendent. His title of Khan Sahib was, however, withdrawn.

The IG, Prison, Punjab, Lt. Col. F.A. Barker, was honoured with the Knighthood of Sir and sanctioned ex-India leave before retirement. The DIG Prisons Punjab, Lt. Col. N.R. Puri, was promoted as IG Prisons Punjab after a few days of the execution.

The notorious Investigating Officer of the Lahore Conspiracy Case, Khan Bahadur Sheikh Abdul Aziz, SP, was given special favours as he was promoted out-of-turn as a selection grade SP, leading to his promotion as DIG three years later. His was the only example in 200 years of British rule in India, where a person who had joined as Head Constable retired as DIG (in July 1937). He had played the most decisive role in the Conspiracy Case leading to the execution of the martyrs. The revolutionaries had made many attempts on his life to bounce him off and each time he escaped miraculously.

Bhagat Singh's execution was supervised by the then District Magistrate, Lahore, A.A. Lane Robert, a 1909 batch ICS officer, along with G.T. Hamilton Hardinge, a 1915 batch IP officer, the then SSP of Lahore. Apart from them, the then IG Punjab Police Cherris Stead (1898 batch) and the then IG prisons (Punjab), Lt. Col. F.A. Barker were present. All the British and Indian officials who had played a role in conducting the Lahore Conspiracy Case were generously and lavishly awarded by the British Government. Abdul Aziz, the CID Inspector who had played the most significant and important role in the prosecution and execution of Bhagat Singh and his two colleagues, namely, Sukhdev and Rajguru, as well as in the sentences of other prisoners of the Lahore Conspiracy Case, was promoted to the post of the Superintendent of Police and his son was also appointed in a senior position in the Police.

There was, however, one more official, who, it is said, had tears in his eyes while the three martyrs were being hanged, was not given any reward.

Letter to the Lahore Conspiracy Case Associates

March 22, 1931

Comrades,

The desire to live is natural. It is in me also. I do not want to conceal it. But it is conditional. I do not want to live as a prisoner or under restrictions. My name has become a symbol of Indian Revolution. The ideal and the sacrifices of the revolutionary party have elevated me to a height beyond which I will never be able to rise if I live.

Today people do not know my weaknesses. If I escape the gallows, those weaknesses will come before them and the symbol of revolution will be tarnished or perhaps it may vanish altogether. On the other hand, if I mount the gallows boldly and with a smile, that will inspire Indian mothers and they will aspire that their children should also become Bhagat Singh. Thus the number of persons prepared to sacrifice their lives for the freedom of our country will increase enormously. It will then become impossible for imperialism to face the tide of the revolution, and all their might and their satanic efforts will not be able to stop its onward march.

Yes, one thing pricks me even today. My heart nurtured some ambitions even for doing something for humanity and for my country. I have not been able to fulfil even one thousandth part of those ambitions. If I live I might perhaps get a chance to fulfil them. If ever it occurred to me that I should not die, it came from this end only.

I am proud of myself these days and I am anxiously waiting for the final test. I wish the day may come nearer soon.

Your comrade,
–Bhagat Singh

Letter to B.K. Dutt

[This letter gives an idea as to what Bhagat Singh expected from those comrades who would escape capital punishment.]

Central Jail, Lahore
November, 1930

Dear Brother

The judgment has been delivered. I am condemned to death. In these cells, besides myself, there are many other prisoners who are waiting to be hanged. The only prayer of these people is that somehow or other they may escape the noose. Perhaps I am the only man amongst them who is anxiously waiting for the day when I will be fortunate enough to embrace the gallows for my ideal.

I will climb the gallows gladly and show to the world as to how bravely the revolutionaries can sacrifice themselves for the cause.

I am condemned to death, but you are sentenced to transportation for life. You will live and, while living, you will have to show the world that the revolutionaries not only die for their ideals but can face every calamity. Death should not be a means to escape the worldly difficulties. Those revolutionaries who have by chance escaped the gallows for the ideal also bear the worst type of tortures in the dark dingy prison cells.

Yours
–Bhagat Singh

25

The Indian National Congress, Gandhiji and Revolutionaries

"British Indians and Englishmen have come together by Divine Providence"... "I believe that two races, the British and Indian, have been brought not only for their own mutual advantage, but to leave an impress on the history of the world." "I trust, it is the mission of the English race, even where there are subject races, to raise them to equality with themselves, to give them free institutions and make them absolutely free men".

–M.K. Gandhi [*CWMG*, Vol. VIII, p. 246]

The administration in India, having been taken over by the Crown after the Mutiny in 1857, continued to be despotic and oppressive. There were complaints not loud but deep with regard to the costly and unsuitable civil courts, the corrupt and oppressive police and the rigid revenue system. There were famines which were not so much due to the scarcity of food grains as the lack of wherewithal to purchase them, resulting in the death of hundreds and thousands of people all over the country. The physical suffering of the many, acted on by the apathy and selfishness of the few, was rapidly bringing popular unrest to the danger point. The socio-economic situation was grave and India within measurable distance of a revolutionary outbreak.

It was only in time that Mr. Allan Octavian Hume, a retired civil servant of the British administration was inspired to intervene. Mr. Hume had impeccable evidence that the political discontent was going underground. He came into possession reports of the seething revolt incubating in various districts, based upon the communications of the disciples of various gurus to their religious heads. This was towards the end of Lord Lytton's rule, the seventies of the 19th century. Not that an organisd mutiny was ahead, but that the people pervaded with a sense of hopelessness, wanted to do something, by which was merely meant, "a sudden violent outbreak of sporadic crime, murders of obnoxious persons, robbery of bankers and looting of bazaars, acts really of lawlessness which by a due coalescence of forces might any day develop into a National Revolt." Such were the agrarian riots of the Deccan in the Bombay Presidency.

It was to frustrate and forestall such anti-imperialist, anti-feudal national liberation struggles that the organisation, named, 'The Indian National Congress' was founded in 1885.

The British rulers, shrewd and cunning, as they were, thought of opening a 'Safety-Valve' for this unrest. It will probably be news to many that The Indian National Congress, as it was originally started, and as it has since been carried on, was in reality the work of Lord Dufferin who was the Governor-General of India in 1885.

At 12 noon, on December 28, 1885, in the hall of the Gokuldas Tejpal Sanskrit College, Bombay, the first National Congress met. Mr. A.O. Hume, the Hon. Mr. S. Subrahmania Aiyer and Mr. K.T. Telang proposed, seconded and approved respectively the election of Mr. W.C. Bannerjee as the first President to preside over the first National Assembly of the Congress Party.

These sessions of the National Congress were held regularly in the month of December of each year at some metropolis or the other of the country. These were generally attended by the highly educated anglicised wealthy tiny class of big landlords, prosperous lawyers, doctors, retired Indian bureaucrats and other loyal Indian subjects of the Empire. They had few links with the millions of poor and miserable Indians living in the rural areas and the urban hovels, yet called themselves representatives and leaders of India, supposedly articulating their grievances and demands. The civil administration including the judiciary continued to be as oppressive, despotic and corrupt as was observed by Mr. A.O. Hume in the 19th century and so also the masses remained restless and discontented. [*The History of the Indian National Congress* by Pattabhi Sitaramayya, pp. 6-14]

It was on such Congress sessions that Aurobindo Ghosh wrote in the *Indu Prakash* in September 1893 that the self-appointed leaders would not forget the lessons of history of a country that is France where the "ignorant proletariat through purification of blood and fire blotted out in five terrible years the accumulated oppression of thirteen centuries."

In 1914, the Indian National Congress at its session at Madras resolved to convey to His Majesty, the King Emperor of England and the people of England its profound devotion to the Throne, its unswerving allegiance to their British association and their firm resolve to stand by the Empire at all hazards and at all costs. Lokmanya Bal Gangadhar Tilak, the then topmost Congress leader, on his release after six years of imprisonment, declared that at such a crisis, it is the duty of every Indian, be he great or small, rich or poor, to support and assist His Majesty's Government to the best of his ability. India's war effort, especially,the whole-hearted support from the mainstream political leadership surprised the British Government and the then British Prime Minister gratefully acknowledged the unstinted and bountiful support extended by "one and all" to Britain's war effort. 'An Indian Loyalist' in his own words:

Having been feeling deeply his own as well as of the Indians' "indebtedness" to the English rulers during his stay in South Africa and asserting repeatedly his loyalty to the Empire, Mahatma Gandhi, on his return to India in 1915, plunged himself whole heartedly into the drive for the enlistment of the recruits to the British Indian army. The following speech of Mahatma Gandhi [a Barrister-at-Law] gives an idea how untiringly he served the British imperialists.

My loyalty to the British Empire

April 24, 1915

Mr. Chairman, Mr. Lord Chief Justice, My Lords and Gentlemen.

"During my three months' touring in India as also in South Africa, I have often been questioned how I, a determined opponent of modern civilisation and an avowed patriot, could reconcile myself to loyalty to the British Empire of which India was such a large part. How it was possible for me to find it consistent that India and England could work together for mutual benefit?"

"It gives me the greatest pleasure this evening at this very great and important gathering to re-declare my loyalty to this British Empire and my loyalty is based upon very selfish grounds. As a passive resister, I discovered that I could not have that free scope which I had under the British Empire, I know that a passive resister has to make good his claim to passive resistance, no matter under what circumstances he finds himself, and I discovered that the British Empire had certain ideals with which I have fallen in love, and one of those ideals is that every subject of the British Empire has the freest scope possible for his energies and efforts and whatever he thinks is due to his conscience. I think that this is true of the British Empire as it is not true of any other government that we see. I feel as you have perhaps known that I am no lover of any government and I have more than once said that, that government is best which governs the least, and I have found that it is possible for me to be governed the least under the British Empire. Hence my loyalty to the British Empire."

[Speech at Madras (Chennai) Law Dinner-M.K. Gandhi-*CWMG,* Vol. 13, pp. 59-60]

The above speech delivered at a law dinner at Madras in honour of the Lord Chief Justice in 1915 by Mahatma Gandhi shows his loyalty to the British Rule. Many Indians might not know that he (Gandhiji) was awarded the Kaiser-e-Hind Medal by His Majesty, the King of England for his "untiring services" to the British Empire.

Here is Mahatma Gandhi as an Indian recruiting sergeant and a proponent of the use of arms.

His Appeal for Enlistment:

> "If we want to learn the use of arms with the greatest dispatch, it is our duty to enlist ourselves in the army."
>
> "There can be no friendship between the brave and the effeminate. We are regarded as a cowardly people. If we want to become free from that reproach, we should learn the use of arms."

> "Partnership of Empire is our definite goal. We should suffer to the utmost of our ability and even lay down our lives to defend the Empire. If the Empire perishes, with it perish our cherished aspirations."
>
> "Hence the easiest and the straightest way to win 'Swaraj' is to participate in the defence of the Empire. It is not within our power to give much money. Moreover, it is not money that will win the war. Only an army inexhaustible in number, can do it. That army India can supply. If the Empire wins mainly with the help of our army, it is obvious that we would secure the right we want". [Extracts from his appeal dated June 22, 1918 to the people of Kheda for enlistment to army.]
>
> –M.K. Gandhi [*CWMG,* Vol. 14, pp. 439-440]

In his appeals to the poor Indians, Mahatma Gandhi had been inducing them to join [to become cannon fodder] in the British perpetuation of the country's slavery. In his eagerness to get enlisted as many recruits as possible, he asked the Indians to bear arms so that they are not considered to be cowardly and effeminate, for "there could be no partnership and friendship between the brave and the effeminate," he would state.

The talk of the concepts of "Soul force", 'Satyagraha' and 'Truth', was not appropriate at this juncture to help the British rulers. He forgot his definitions of 'Satyagraha', and 'Passive Resistance.' [Satyagraha postulates the conquest of the adversary by suffering in one's own person and not the remotest idea of injuring the other" and that in Satyagraha physical force is forbidden, etc]. These would, however, become relevant again to save the British rulers from the "valorous actions" of the revolutionaries and Ghadrites.

"Indian Troops Under British Rule Used as 'Guinea Pigs' "

Hundereds of helpless Indian soldiers serving under the British rule were used as 'guinea pigs' in gas chambers to test the effects of poison gases on humans by scientists during the Second World War. Documents uncovered by *The Guardian* have revealed. The experiments were conducted more than 10 years before and during the world war in a military installation at Rawalpindi now in Pakistan. The newspaper report said the British military did not check the after-effects of the gas on the Indian skin. It is now being discovered that mustard gas can cause cancer and other diseases.

Newly discovered documents at the National Archives have shown for the first time the full scale of the experiments. [*The Tribune*, dated: February 3, 2007]

"Indian Soldiers Were Hired Assassins"

Former Press Council of India Chairman Justice (Rtd) Markandey Katju had, in a statement reported in the *Indian Express* on December 12, 2014, described the Indian soldiers who fought the First World War under the British flag as "hired assassins" questioning the need for honouring those soldiers on the 100th anniversary of the First World War. Justice Katju argued that "the Indian soldiers fought as hired assassins to kill Germans for Anglo-French interests and not for India's interests. "The war", he went on "was fought for distribution and redistribution of colonies. The Indian soldiers who fought in that war, were really mercenaries and hirelings of the British and the French."

Captain Amrinder Singh, then the Deputy Leader of the Congress Party in the Lok Sabha [Lower House of Parliament in 2015] and later on a Congress Chief Minister of Punjab (2017), was amongst the first to criticise justice Katju calling his statement an insult to the Indian army, advising him [Justice Katju] not to comment on issues of which he had no knowledge. He felt proud of his erstwhile royal princely State of Patiala, then ruled by his grandfather Maharaja Bhupender Singh, contributing one of the largest contingents of Indian soldiers to the Anglo-French war effort. Citing proudly Mahatma Gandhi's support to all those British Indian soldiers in the world war, he [Captain Amrinder Singh] contemptuously dismissed Justice Katju's comments.

With a view to highlight the deeds of bravery of the Indian soldiers and their sacrifices and imparting knowledge to the Indians about them, [Indian soldiers] Captain Amrinder Singh had written a book on the First World War. In his book, singing paeans to 1.3 million Indian soldiers, [equivalent to probably the present strength of the Indian Army] he had asserted that without their [Indian soldiers] sacrifices, the British Empire would have collapsed.

India Would Have Won Independence in 1918

Sadly, Captain Amrinder Singh did not state and could not think of it that in case, the British Empire had collapsed, Indians would have been freed from the clutches of the cruel British imperialist rulers there and then, instead of in 1947, as India would have won independence in 1918 itself. What a boon the collapse of the British Empire would have been to Indians, Captain Amrinder Singh seems to have failed to realise the same.

With the collapse of the British Empire and India regaining her independence in 1918, there would have been no 'Jallianwala Bagh Massacre' at Amritsar; thousands of Ghadrite prisoners, Babbar Akali Dal prisoners and other revolutionaries languishing in Andaman Island Jail and other jails in India would have been freed from the jails and gallows of the British. Shaeed-e-Azam Bhagat Singh, Sukhdev, Rajguru and others would not have been hanged. The Bengal Famine of 1943 would not have happened, thereby, saving the lives of lakhs of poor Indians and there might not have been any Second World War, etc.

Similarly, a book could be written eulogising the role of the troops, contributed to the British rulers by the then princes of the Indian princely states helping the British in the annexation of Punjab into the British Indian Empire by subjugating the descendants of Maharaja Ranjit Singh.

The Valorous Ghadrites

In contrast to this blind and depressing wave of loyalty to British imperialism, an inspiring revolutionary tide from the coasts of America and Canada crossing all oceans and continents landed on the shores of India. With the beginning of the First World War and finding Britain in mortal trouble, the Indian immigrants in America and Canada, the lands of Washington and Lincoln, took it as a golden opportunity to liberate their motherland from the imperialist clutches. They organised themselves into a revolutionary party called Ghadr Party and brought out a weekly paper naming it *Ghadr*, distributing which and other pamphlets, they began revolutionary propaganda exhorting people to overthrow the British Raj. They were led by Lala Hardayal, Baba Gurdit Singh, Baba Gurmukh Singh, Baba Rattan Singh, Baba Sohan Singh Bhakna, Bhai Santokh Singh, to name a few valorous Ghadrites. They made a strategic plan to organise a revolt in India during the war period. As many as 8,000 patriotic Ghadrites relinquished their prized careers in the USA and Canada. Separately another group of nearly 500 Ghadrites led by Baba Gurdit Singh reached Calcutta on a ship, named 'Komagatamaru' from Canada. The British Indian Police ordered the ship to land its passengers at Budge Budge near Calcutta where most of them were massacred. The incident has become known as the 'Budge Budge Massacre.'

Having become aware of the Ghadr Manifesto and their programme of action, the Government of India was quick to pass the Defence of India Act in March 1915 to prohibit their entry and residence in India and most of the Ghadrites were interned. The story of how they infiltrated into the British Indian army and how the Ghadr movement had spread all over the USA, Canada, Japan, Shanghai, Hong Kong, Singapore, Malaysia, Burma and Thailand and their plans for the revolt in the Indian Army, is an inspiring saga.

As a brief introduction of those brave Indians, it may be stated that they were living comfortably on well-paid vocations earning in hundreds and thousands of dollars during those days. Seeing Great Britain in trouble, they considered it a golden opportunity to liberate their country from the yoke of the British rulers and, therefore, spread themselves in cantonments in India, Burma, Malaysia, Singapore, Thailand, etc. and hatched a grand plan to rise in simultaneous revolt against the British. A large number of Indian soldiers in all those cantonments had secretly joined with them. Their plan, however, misfired. The reason was the treachery of some of those in the cantonments acting as informers. The result was hundreds and thousands of them were executed or sentenced to life imprisonment in the Andamans. They were patriots to the core of their hearts sacrificing not only their well-paid jobs but also their lives at the altar of freedom of their country. They were known as the 'Ghadrites'.

It is they (Ghadrites), as a symbol of our gratitude to them, whose centenary we should be feeling duty-bound to commemorate and not those who, for the sake of a few rupees, were forced to agree, due to their poverty, to assassinate Germans and in return get themselves assassinated by them (Germans), for a cause for the perpetuation of the enslavement not only of their own countrymen but also of millions of those living in other colonies of England, France and Belgium, in Africa, Asia and South America. Our colonial masters as a symbol of their gratitude to them had erected India Gate in New Delhi dedicating it to the dead of the Indian armies who fell in the First World War. We should, on the other hand, erect a Memorial at India Gate in New Delhi in memory of the Ghadrites and revolutionaries who died for the liberation of their motherland.

It was awful to observe that Mahatma Gandhi showed no hint of any awareness of the great revolutionary movement of the world's Indian immigrants under the leadership of the Ghadr Party raging in India for overthrowing the British rule. His deadly silence over the great independence struggle was loathsome. The reason one could think of was his unflinching loyalty to the British Empire.

Rabindranath Tagore Renounced His Knighthood

The letter written by Rabindranath Tagore to Lord Chelmsford, the then British Viceroy, protesting against the Jallianwala Bagh Massacre is a contrast to how Mahatma Gandhi acted and reacted.

Your Excellency,

The enormity of the measures taken by the government in the Punjab for quelling some local disturbances has, with a rude shock, revealed to our minds, the helplessness of our position as British subjects in India. The disproportionate severity of the punishments inflicted upon the unfortunate people and the methods of carrying them out, we are convinced, are without parallel in the history of civilised governments, barring some conspicuous exceptions, recent and remote.

Considering that such treatment has been meted out to a population, disarmed and resourceless, by a power, which has the most terribly efficient organisation for destruction of human lives, we must strongly assert that it can claim no political expediency, far less, moral justification. The accounts of the insults and suffering by our brothers in Punjab have trickled through the gagged silence, reaching every corner of India, and the universal agony of indignation roused in the hearts of our people has been ignored by our rulers-possibly congratulating themselves for imparting what they imagine as salutary lessons.

The time has come when badges of honour make our shame glaring in the incongruous context of humiliation, and I, for my part, wish to stand, shorn, of all special distinctions, by the side of those of my countrymen who, for their so-called insignificance, are liable to suffer degradation not fit for human beings.

And these are the reasons which have compelled me to ask Your Excellency, with due reverence and regret, to relieve me of my title of Knighthood, which I had the honour to accept from His Majesty the King at the hand, of your predecessor, for whose nobleness of heart I still entertain great admiration.

Yours faithfully,
–Rabindranath Tagore
Calcutta, May 30, 1919

The day May 30, 1919, Rabindranath Tagore wrote his letter to the Viceroy of India [Lord Chelmsford] renouncing his Knighthood in protest against the Jallianwala Bagh Masscare, Amritsar. Mahatma Gandhi also wrote a letter as follows to the Viceroy.

Mahatma Gandhi's Letter to Viceroy Lord Chelmsford

Clarifying his position on the tragic happening [Jallianwala Bagh Masscare], he stated that he had not only not condemned the Martial Law but in order to avoid causing any irritation to the local administration, had refrained from issuing any statement as well. Mahatma Gandhi, in his letter, on the other hand, showing his sympathies and support to the British rulers, advised the Viceroy to appoint a Committee to soothe the public mind and restore confidence in the administration.

Laburnum Road Bombay
May 30, 1919

Dear Mr. Hignell, [Private Secretary to the Viceroy]

"It is within His Excellency's knowledge that I have made no public declaration regarding the events in the Punjab. Even at the risk of being misunderstood by my countrymen, I have refrained from saying anything in public because I had no reliable data to enable me to form an opinion. I was not prepared to condemn Martial Law as such; I was unwilling to do anything calculated needlessly to irritate local authority; and lastly I was not prepared to infer from Sir Michael O' Dwyer's reported severe administration during the peace period that Martial Law measures would be unduly hard.

It is suggested that a committee comprising both officials and non-officials may be appointed. It would calm the public mind to restore confidence [much shaken by the events in Punjab] in the good intentions of the government ..."

–M.K. Gandhi [*CWMG*, Vol. 15, pp. 334-335]

In a letter to Mr. V.S. Srinivasa Sastri on June 6, 1919, Mahatma Gandhi commented on the poet's letter [Rabindranath Tagore] to the Viceroy renouncing his Knighthood and expresed his disapproval. "The Punjab horrors have produced a burning letter from the poet. I personally think it is premature."

–M.K. Gandhi [*CWMG*, Vol. 15, pp. 345-346]

Mahatma Gandhi himself had been awarded by the British, a Boer Medal, a Zullu Medal besides the Kaiser-e-Hind Medal for his services to them. These, he did not renounce as a protest against the Jallianwala Massacre by the British imperialists as the poet, Rabindranath Tagore had done.

When questioned by the President of the 'Disorders Inquiry Committee' on January 9, 1920 about the objects of the Rowlatt Bills, "if he [Mahatma Gandhi] had any doubts that the objects were to put down revolutionary and anarchical crimes."Mahatma Gandhi replied, "he had no doubt that the objects were laudable" [*CWMG,* Vol. 16, pp. 378].

Mahatma Gandhi's Views on Socio-Political Issues

"It will be of interest to know Mahatma Gandhi's views on various socio-political issues then facing the country, as written by Pt. Jawaharlal Nehru in his *An Autobiography*. Even after 70 years of independence, the people of the country are still facing the same issues. Pt. Nehru in a chapter titled 'paradoxes' on page 535 stated:

"I have discovered during the last year or so that Gandhiji approves of the 'Taluquadari' [landlordism] system as such and wants it to continue. He said in July 1934 at Kanpur that he was never in favour of abolition of the 'Taluquadari' or 'Zamindari' system, and those, who thought that it should be abolished, did not know their own minds. He [Gandhiji] further said: "I shall be no party to dispossessing propertied classes of their property without just cause" ... "But supposing that there is an attempt unjustly to deprive your property, you will find me fighting on your side ..."

Pt. Nehru further continued on page 510 of his Autobiography: "India's salvation consists", he [Gandhiji], wrote in 1909, "In unlearning what she has learnt during the last fifty years, the railways, telegraphs, hospitals, lawyers, doctors and such—like have all to go; and the so-called upper classes have to learn consciously, religiously and deliberately, the simple peasant life, knowing it to be a life giving true happiness." Pt. Nehru adds: "Personally I dislike the praise of poverty and suffering. I do not think they are at all desirable and they ought to be abolished" ... "Nor do I appreciate in the least the idealisation of the simple peasant life. I have almost a horror of it and instead of submitting to it myself, I want to drag out even the peasantry from it ...crushed and exploited for innumerable generations, the peasant only barely removed from the animals who keep him company."

"He, [Gandhiji]" observed Pt. Nehru on page 516 of his *Autobiography*, had also no desire to raise the standards of the masses beyond a certain very modest competence, for higher standards and leisure may lead to self-indulgence and sin ..." "he [Gandhiji] has had a fixed basis for all his ideas, and his mind is hardly an open mind. He listens with the greatest patience and attention to people who make new suggestions to him, but behind all his courteous interest one has the impression that one is addressing a closed door."

The following lines on pages 6 and 475 of *CWMG,* Vol. 42 explicate Mahatma Gandhi's views on the position of women and varnadharma (caste system) respectively.

Women: That mutual lust too has played an important part, in bringing about the disqualifications of the fair sex, hardly needs any demonstration. Woman has circumvented man in a variety of ways, in her unconsciously subtle ways, as man has vainly and equally unconsciously struggled to thwart woman in gaining ascendancy over him. The result is a stalemate. Thus viewed, it is a serious problem, the enlightened daughters of Bharat Mata are called upon to solve. They may not ape the manner of the West which may be suited to its environment. They must apply methods suited to the Indian genius and Indian environment. Their must be the strong, controlling, purifying, steadying hand, conserving what is the best in our culture and unhesitatingly rejecting what is base and degrading. This is the work of Sitas, Draupadis, Savitris and Damayantis, not of amazons and prudes.

Mahatma Gandhi seemed to be oblivious to the suffering of millions of Sitas and Draupadis, their oppression, exploitation and injustice meted out to them by the men in their day-to-day lives. He expressed no concern about the daily domestic violence inflicted on them by the men as well as the gender inequality faced by them. He had no word of advice to the men. He had rather blamed the women and urged them to act like Sitas and Draupadis as exemplary ones.

Varnadharma: Mahatma Gandhi believed in the caste system and justified varnadharma eulogising the same. He explained how the sages had divided society into four sections for its welfare and, thereby, attempted to root out rivalry which is fatal to society. Therefore, they made one varna responsible for the growth of knowledge in society, the second responsible for protection of life and property in society, the third for trade in society, and the fourth for service to society. All four functions were and are equally essential; therefore, there was no reason to consider one high and the other low. ...In varnadharma the work of each varna was for the welfare of society. Livelihood was not the motive. Gain or no gain, the Kshatriya had to defend the people. The Brahmin had to impart knowledge whether he received alms or not. The Vaishya had to trade and the Shudra had to farm and tend cattle whether he earned money or not. ...Disparities will always be there, but like the several leaves of a tree they will look beautiful and pleasant.

As in the case of women, Mahatma Gandhi had disregarded the criminal social and political discrimination, exploitation and oppression of the Shudras [Scheduled Castes] by the upper castes [Kshatriyas, Brahmins, Vaishyas]. He did not feel concerned about the inequalities suffered by the lower castes and offered no concrete solution to root out the same. [*CWMG,* Vol. 42, pp. 6 and 475]

No Political Strikes: Mahatma Gandhi was against the political strikes by the industial workers. He writes: "In India, we want no political strikes. We are not yet instructed enough for them. Not to have political strikes is to forward the cause of freedom. We do not need an atmosphere of unsettled unrest. It hampers our progress towards the final stages of our programme. A soldier who runs amok is unfit to be in an army. We must gain control over all the unruly and disturbing elements to isolate them as we are isolating the government. (*CWMG,* Vol. 20, p. 228)

Against Tenants and Labour: Mahatma Gandhi was against

tenants fighting for their rights against the oppression of the landlords. He focused on "on the agrarian disturbances and deplored the action of the 'Kisans' (tenants) who committed violence... Gandhiji condemned violence most strongly and unequivocally, and said that he considered it a sin against God and man. He deprecated all attempts to create discord between landlords and tenants and advised the tenants to suffer rather than fight, for they had to join all forces for fighting against the most powerful Zamindar, namely, the Government..." "...thirty crores of souls, he said, were a power and could bring Swaraj, without violence, by non-cooperation. The sword was described as a weapon of the weak. He pleaded for organisation, the adoption of the spinning-wheel and for funds.

"We seek not to destroy capital or capitalists, but to regulate the relations between capital and labour. We want to harness capital to our side. It would be folly to encourage sympathetic strikes. [*CWMG,* Vol. 20, p. 228].

Mahatma Gandhi Praised Hitler: Mahatma Gandhi had a few words of praise for Hitler. Speaking at a meeting of the Gram Sewak Sangh and Charkha Sangh at Wardha on June 22, 1940, he said: "We have to live and move and have our being in 'Ahimsa' [Non-violence], even as Hitler does in 'Himsa '[Violence]. It is the faith, perseverance and single-mindedness with which he has perfected his weapons of destruction that commands my admiration. That he uses them as a monster is immaterial for our purpose. We have to bring to bear the same single-mindedness and perseverance in evolving our 'Ahimsa'. Hitler is awake all 24 hours of the day in perfecting his 'Sadhana' [Aim]. He wins because he pays the price. His inventions surprise his enemies. But it is his single-minded devotion to his purpose, that should be the object of our admiration and emulation. Although he works all his waking hours, his intellect is unclouded and unerring. Are our intellects unclouded and unerring? [*CWMG*, Vol. 72, p. 193]

Speech at Bardoli on December 17, 1941: "Even a votary of violence is capable of self-sacrifice. Hitler too is said to be self-sacrificing. He is violence incarnate. It is said he is a vegetarian. I find it difficult to imagine how, if he is one, he is able to countenance so much slaughter. Anyway, his is said to be a life of self-sacrifice. He has no vice. He has not married. His character is said to be clean. He is always alert. What we require is both self-sacrifice and non-violence. Non-violence means love. [CWMG, Vol. 75, pp. 177]

Mahatma Gandhi Hailed Mussolini: Mahatma Gandhi hailed Mussolini as "one of the great statesmen of our time". According to a book entitled *Subhas Chandra Bose in Nazi Germany*, author Romain Hayes wrote that in late 1931, Gandhi accepted an invitation to visit Mussolini in Rome while the Mahatma was on his way back to India after attending the Round Table Conference in England. Reportedly, the two men—the vain Italian Fascist and the modest, unassuming Indian ascetic—got along extremely well and admired each other. Hayes wrote that, among other things, Gandhi reviewed a black-shirted fascist youth honour-guard during his visit.

Regarding his visit with Il Duce, Gandhi wrote in a letter to a friend: "Mussolini's care of the poor, his efforts to bring about coordination between capital and labour, seem to me to demand special attention. What strikes me is that behind Mussolini's implacability is a desire to serve his people. Even behind his emphatic speeches there is a nucleus of sincerity and of passionate love for his people. It seems to me that the majority of the Italian people love the iron government of Mussolini."

Mahatma Gandhi's views smacked of racialism. He called native black Africans 'Kafirs' (considered a racial slur in Africa) [*CWMG,* Vol. 1, p. 150]. This prompted Ghanian students in the University of Ghana in Africa to pull down Gandhiji's statue from the University premises according to a report in *The Times of India* of September 20, 2016.

Damned the Garhwali Soldiers

Mahatma Gandhi damned the Garhwali soldiers for refusing the orders to fire, murder and maim the peaceful and non-violent 'Khudai Khidmatgars' [servants of God] of Khan Abdul Ghaffar Khan in Peshawar in 1930. This historic event occurred soon after

Khan Abdul Ghaffar Khan, the leader of Khudai Khidmatgars [servants of God] and other Pathan leaders had been arrested during the civil disobedience movement of 1930 launched by Mahatma Gandhi. Following their arrest, protest demonstrations were held which were fired upon by the police and as a result of which several persons were killed by the police. At Peshawar there was a 'hartal' on April 23, 1930 and there were huge processions and demonstrations. The government called out the army. Two platoons of the Second Battalion of the 18th Royal Garhwal Rifles refused the order to fire, broke ranks, fraternised with the people and they handed over arms to the authorities. The determined resistance of the people and the Garhwali soldiers' refusal to murder and maim the peaceful and non-violent demonstrators, forced the British government on April 20, 1930 to withdraw from Peshawar and the city was in the hands of the people till May 4, 1930 when the powerful British forces, with air squadrons, were concentrated to 'recapture' Peshawar. There was no resistance. The government subsequently refused all demands for an enquiry into the happening. Sixty-seven Garhwali soldiers were court-martialled and were sentenced to long terms of imprisonment. Their leader Chandra Singh was sentenced to death that was commuted to transportation for life. [R.P Dutt in *India Today*, pp. 302-03 and S.K. Ghosh in *India and Raj*, pp. 352-53].

Mahatma Gandhi wrote: I did not like at all what happened in Peshawar. If the reins of the government fall into the hands of such persons, will they not rule in the same way? Will they not break the heads of the poor?" [*CWMG,* Vol. XLVIII, p. 101]

Later during his visit to the Round Table Conference in London, Mahatma Gandhi in an interview to a French journalist, Charles Petrsch, explained his reasons for disapproving of the Garhwali soldiers' action: "A soldier who disobeys an order to fire, breaks the oath which he has taken, renders himself guilty of criminal disobedience. I cannot ask officials and soldiers to disbey for when I am in power I shall in all likelihood make use of those same officials and those same soldiers. If I taught them to disobey, I should be afraid that they might do the same when I am in power." [Published in *Monde* on February 20, 1932—R.P. Dutt, *India Today*, p. 303]. What does Gandhiji's interview mean? No oath could give a human being much less a soldier who is armed, the right or compel a duty to fire on innocent and non-violent human beings. A soldier's first oath and duty is to protect mankind. The above interview is purported to have been given by Gandhiji.

Mahatma Gandhiji's Eleven Points: Mahatma Gandhi ignoring all the resolves of attaining complete independence, enunciated at the Lahore Congress Session in the first week of January, 1930, unexpectedly and astonishingly, announced his inconsequential Eleven Points as an offer to Lord Irwin, the Viceroy, for his acceptance and on the condition of his doing so, all the talk of the civil disobedience movement was to be dropped. In a more than five-page letter sent to the Viceroy on March 2, 1930, without intimating and consulting the Congress President [Pandit Jawaharlal Nehru] and the Congress Working Committee, Mahatmaji assured him (the Viceroy), on behalf of the AICC that the resolution of complete national independence should cause no alarm. The said resolution had to be passed to carry out the solemn resolution of the Congress passed earlier at its Calcutta Session. [*CWMG*, Vol. 43, pp. 2-8]

The Eleven Points highlighted as offer [to be in lieu of the recently passed complete independence resolution] were enumerated in his above-said letter. These were 1) Total prohibition. 2) Reduction of rupee exchange ratio to 1 s 4 d. 3) Reduction of land revenue at least by 50 per cent making it subject to legislative control. 4) Abolition of Salt Tax. 5) Reduction of military expenditure at least by 50 per cent to begin with. 6) Reduction of salaries of the highest grade services by half or less so as to suit the reduced revenue. 7) Protective tariff on foreign cloth. 8) Passage of the Coastal Traffic Reservation Bill. 9) Discharge of all political prisoners, except those condemned for murder, or attempt to murder, or their trial by ordinary judicial tribunals. Withdrawal of all political prosecution, abrogation of Section 124 A and Regulation 111 of 1818 and giving permission to all Indian exiles to return. 10) Abolition of the CID or its popular control. 11) To issue license to use fire-arms for self-defence subject to popular control. [*The History of the Indian National Congress*, p. 366]

Mahatmaji's Main Concern for the Party of Violence: While explaining his Eleven Points to the Viceroy and requesting him for their acceptance in his letter dated March 2, 1930, Mahatma Gandhi had stressed the urgency to set in motion the intensely active force of non-violence to be expressed through civil disobedience against the party of violence that is gaining ground and making itself felt. Expressing his deep concern about the growing activities of the revolutionaries [read Bhagat Singh and his Party], he added that "the conviction is growing deeper and deeper in me that nothing but unadulterated non-violence can check the organised violence of the British rule as [against] the unorganised violent force of the growing party of violence. To sit still would be to give rein to both the forces above-mentioned ... it would be sinful [against God] on my part to wait any longer ..."

In a prompt response, and rejecting Mahatma Gandhi's offer in Gandhiji's above-said letter, the Viceroy regretted that Gandhiji should be "contemplating a course of action which clearly is bound to involve violation of the law and danger to the public peace."

Movement of Non-Violence: A Safety-Valve Against Movement of Violence: In reply to a question as to "will not your movement lead to violence?" was a revelation of Mahatmaji's mind on the forces of violence. [Bhagat Singh and his party's revolutionary actions]. He [Gandhiji] said, "it may, though I am trying my best to prevent any outbreak of violence. Today there is greater risk of violence in the absence of any safety-valve in the shape of a movement of non-violence like the one I am contemplating. Upto now, it is growing upon me that it is only by setting the force of non-violence in motion that I can get those elements [the revolutionaries] under control." [*CWMG*, Vol. 43, pp. 43-45]

Mahatma Gandhi's repeated reference to the growing unorganised violent force in his communications to the Viceroy, his interviews to the Press and his questions and answers on or before March 11, 1930, which were recorded by Mahadev Desai, under the heading, "talks before the trek," gave enough evidence of his inner thought. Mahatma Gandhi seemed to be least interested in pursuing the demand for complete national independence. It was probably considered too "revolutionary." In the past at the Congress Sessions, he opposed its adoption as the agenda of the Congress. It was allowed by Mahatmaji at the Lahore Congress Session to counter the revolutionaries' growing influence because of their "programme", "statements" and "actions". It had already become a popular demand and that forced Gandhiji and other Congress leaders to own it as their demand. But there it stood. Mahatmaji immediately relegated it by bringing forward his insignificant and irrelevant Eleven Points and then finally only the repeal of the Salt Tax considered as the core issue facing the country by him. Non-compliance with these Eleven Points or the demand for the abolition of the Salt Tax would now mean civil disobedience movement, according to Mahatmaji.

Revolutionary Movement Gained Ground Heavily: An extract from Mahatmaji's interview to *Manchester Guardian*: "I admit that this may be my last chance and if I do not seize it, it may never come again. The revolutionary and, of course, violent movement has gained ground heavily. The need for the speediest action is absolutely necessary." [*CWMG*, Vol. 43, p. 38 also published in *The Hindu*, June 11, 1930]

Common Cause: "It is common cause that however disorganised and for the time being insignificant it may be, the party of violence is gaining ground and making itself felt ..." Mahatma Gandhi made his commitment to counter the Indian revolutionary force to the Viceroy emphasising its further delay would be sinful [sinful to God] on his part, thereby, making his counter-revolutionary movement [civil disobedience movement] as divinely sanctioned and ordered by God.

Lord Irwin, the Viceroy understood Mahatmaji's motive clearly and both of them [the Viceroy and Mahatmaji] had to play their unsaid due roles to make the civil disobedience movement a real and a great success.

None of the famous Eleven Points including the demand for the abolition of Mahatma Gandhi's Salt Tax had any relevance with the Lahore Congress Resolution for the attainment of the complete national independence. All these points were not the pressing economic issues for the dumb Indians. Even the point relating to the fifty per cent reduction in the land revenue was beneficial to the landlords only and not the landless poor farmers. Almost all the other points were the concern of the wealthy industrialists and other elite classes. In this respect, A.O. Hume seemed to be well-aware of the miserable lot of the poverty-stricken and famine-stricken Indian people when in the 1880s, he, in consultation with Lord Dufferin, constituted the Indian National Congress as a safety-valve to absorb the then growing political discontent of the masses.

After the Viceroy's curt "no", in his reply to Mahatmaji's letter dated March 2, 1930, Gandhiji left on foot from his Sabarmati Ashram on the, 12th March leading a procession of his 75 Ashram disciples reaching Dandi, a sea-side village, at a distance of 200 miles in 24 days to start his civil disobedience, by manufacturing salt, violating the Salt Law. Since the government authorities kept on watching and did not arrest him, Gandhiji also raided the salt works at Dharsana and Chharsada and, thereby, got himself arrested on the 15th May. After Gandhiji's arrest, there were widespread patriotic demonstrations and 'hartals' [closing of business shops] in big cities.

Jail going in any agitation against the government for a public or political cause was traditionally highly appreciated and respected by the people. This tradition had been going on since time immemorial against the rulers. The people showing their faith in Gandhiji courted arrest in thousands by raiding the shops selling salt. There was practically no political consciousness among the illiterate people. Jail going under Gandhiji's leadership was an easy affair. There was minimal police repression unlike under the revolutionary actions. Soon, the Congress officially joined the movement after the meeting of the Congress Working Committee in May at Allahabad. Raiding and picketing salt-selling shops in various cities became a common scene. Gandhiji and the Congress leadership were highly satisfied with the progress of the movement. It, however failed to move Lord Irwin—the Viceroy, towards any action to repeal the Salt Law or accept any one of Gandhiji's Eleven Points.

Gradually the civil disobedience movement started losing its momentum and there were signs of it heading towards failure. The Liberals such as M.R. Jayakar and T.B. Sapru, acting as mediators, had stepped in to bring about peace with some suggestions regarding the release of the prisoners and the restoration of the confiscated properties of the 'Satyagrahis' though these were vague. As a result of their efforts, the notification declaring the Congress Working Committee unlawful was withdrawn and members were released. Later on they met at Allahabad on February 6, 1931.

Mahatma Gandhi as well as the Party's leadership were keen to arrive at some settlement with the British Indian Government. It was decided to request the Viceroy for an interview for a frank talk and Gandhiji on February 14, 1931 wrote to the Viceroy for a meeting with him that was granted (It was not the Viceroy who invited Gandhiji as has been made out by some historians). Gandhiji immediately left for New Delhi followed by members of the Working Committee.

After numerous meetings with the Viceroy for more than two weeks, from February 17 to March 5, a settlement called the Gandhi Irwin Pact was signed on March 5, 1931. As a result of this Pact that could be called a "Surrender Pact", the civil disobedience movement was discontinued, although none of his Eleven Points had been conceded by the Viceroy.

How Pt. Jawaharlal Nehru reacted to the terms of the Pact, is recounted by him on page 257 of his *Autobiography*: "On the night of March 4, we waited till midnight for Gandhiji's return from the Viceroy's house. He came back at about 2 am., and we were woken up and told that an agreement had been reached. We saw the draft. I knew most of the clauses, for they had been discussed, but at the very top, clause 2, with its reference to safeguards, etc. gave me a tremendous shock. I was wholly unprepared for it ..."

Why was Pt. Jawaharlal Nehru shocked? Was it that Mahatma

Gandhi took a decision, unilaterally, on one of the most important issues relating to the fate of the thirty crore of the Indian people, without consulting not only members of the Working Committee but also the President of the Congress—Pt. Jawaharlal Nehru? It was not the first time that he took a decision on his own. Earlier he had conceived his Eleven Points and offered the same in his letter to the Viceroy showing total disregard to the Complete Independence Resolution passed just a few days back and without consulting Pt. Jawaharlal Nehru—the Congress President and the Working Committee.

The Pact was a Total Surrender

What a fall from the demand of a Dominion Status within a year at its Calcutta Congress presided over by the senior Nehru [Pt. Motilal Nehru] and the Resolution of Complete National Independence passed at the Lahore Congress Session presided over by his son [Pt. Jawaharlal Nehru] to a vague and delusional promise of discussions on the scheme of constitutional reforms in London?

The year 1931 was the saddest and the proudest year in India. A great upsurge of sympathy and admiration of people for their real heroes—Bhagat Singh, Sukhdev, Rajguru, was sweeping the whole country. The people were focused on somehow saving the lives of their heroes and not on the terms of the Gandhi-Irwin Pact or what the Mahatmaji later on termed 'The Provisional Settlement'. They [the people] had thought of and looked at the Gandhi-Irwin negotiations as a ray of hope and means to attain commutation of the death sentences of Bhagat Singh, Sukhdev and Raj Guru. Another hero of theirs—Chandra Shekhar Azad, had been murdered by Lord Irwin's administration. Petitions signed by thousands and lakhs of people were being sent to the Viceroy to grant commutation of the life-sentences of their beloved heroes.

Gandhiji and the Congress headed by Pt. Jawaharlal Nehru were trumpeting the 'Surrender Pact'—called the 'Provisional Settlement' as their great national "achievement".

26

Was Mahatma Gandhi Duty-Bound to Save Bhagat Singh?

One of the most important issues, discussed in almost all books written by various authors on Bhagat Singh, had been Mahatma Gandhi's role in saving the lives of Bhagat Singh and his revolutionary comrades from the gallows. Most of the learned authors have detailed as to how Mahatma Gandhi had tried to prevail upon Lord Irwin, the Viceroy, to suspend and commute the death sentences on the martyrs. There are, however, some other writers who differed with the authors expressing the above views. They observed [the latter ones] that Mahatma Gandhi's efforts were weak and half-hearted and he was not serious and keen to save the country's heroes' lives.

And the controversy goes on. The basic question is, as to how Mahatma Gandhi was concerned with the lives of these martyrs and how he was liable and duty-bound to save them from the hangman's noose? Both Mahatma Gandhi and Bhagat Singh had a diametrically opposite approach on various political issues and, especially, on the path to win the freedom of the country from the yoke of the British Empire. Mahatma Gandhi believed in non-violence as his creed to tackle and solve the problems being faced by the thirty crores of Indian people and this included the freedom of the country. His path was a path of compromise with the aggressor, the oppressor, the exploiter and the coloniser—the British imperialists. Bhagat Singh's path, on the other hand, was a path of revolution and achievement of independence by all means including the violent ones to overthrow the foreign rulers. Their paths were as opposed to each other as chalk and cheese. The primary object of all the movements launched by

Mahatma Gandhi, whether it was the non-cooperation movement or the various civil disobedience movements including 'Satyagraha', was to counter the increasing resurgence of revolutionary fervour due to the actions of the revolutionaries. Other objectives such as the attainment of the dominion status, and the independence of the country, or the acceptance of Gandhiji's Eleven Points as well as the repeal of the Salt Tax, were secondary and some of them were even inconsequential. Mahatma Gandhi hated the concept of revolution envisaged by Bhagat Singh and the Hindustan Socialist Republican Association and the Hindustan Socialist Republican Army constituted by him [Bhagat Singh], Chandra Shekhar Azad and other comrades. Mahatma Gandhi mostly talked of some sort of 'Swaraj' or 'Purna Swaraj'. He would rarely use the word 'Independence'. The resolution of 'Complete Political Independence' was passed to counter and combat the rising 'violent force' [Read Revolution]. It was evident that within a few days after passing 'the Independence Resolution', he [Mahatma Gandhi] enunciated his 'Eleven Points' offering the same to the Viceroy in his letter written on March 2, 1930. On the acceptance of the Eleven Points, Mahatma Gandhi had stated, that he would not think of launching the civil disobedience movement, He drew the Viceroy's attention, in his letter, to the pressing force of violence—stating that his 'Satyagraha' was to counter the same with all his soul force. There was no mention of independence in either his Eleven Points or in the letter to the Viceroy. The civil disobedience movement was actually reduced to the demand for the repeal of the Salt Tax while in the Resolution for the 'Complete National Independence', it was to be launched to attain the complete national independence. Was it, thus, not a betrayal of the trust of the rank and file of the Congress?

So far as the question of saving the lives of Bhagat Singh and his two comrades was concerned, it would have been done, had Mahatma Gandhi launched a civil disobedience movement on the issue of commutation of their sentences. The movement would have taken the form of a tornado from the Khyber Pass to Kanyakumari. The British Government would have been forced to concede this demand. But again the question–why would he do so?

Disregarding the patriotic call of the Ghadr Party to the Indians and particularly the Indian immigrants in America, to avail of the opportunity, provided by the First World War in 1914 and the troubles faced by Great Britain as a result of the same, for organising a revolt against the British rule for the liberation of their motherland, Mahatma Gandhi, on his return from South Africa in 1915, had launched a drive with all his heart and soul for the enlistment of the poor Indians in the British army to defend the British Empire.

The British Empire with the massive aid in men and material extracted from Indians through her Raj [rule] over the country as well as with the support of her loyalists and collaborators led by Mahatma Gandhi, Gokhale and Tilak, was ultimately victorious over her enemies led by Germany. But immediately after that, the British rulers were confronted with another danger—'the internal danger' and 'war' being waged by the Ghadrites and the revolutionaries to overthrow the British imperialist rulers. They, the British rulers, keeping in view the various reports including an earlier one from a former Lt. Governor of Punjab, Sir Denzil Ibbetson, were preparing a legislation known as the Rowlatt Act, necessary to deal with the troublesome problems. The first sentence of the Lt. Governor's report ran as: "Regard the present political situation in Punjab exceedingly serious and exceedingly dangerous and as urgently demanding a remedy". The British were astute rulers as they, heeding another earlier warning in the 1880s from Allan Octavian Hume, a retired senior British civil servant, had formed the Indian National Congress in 1885 as a safety-valve to tackle any danger of revolt by the Indians.

Seeing the British Empire in trouble again—this time from another side, i.e. the Ghadrites and the Revolutionaries, Mahatma Gandhi was not the one to keep quiet. Devising a new strategy, he propounded a new theory of 'Non-Violence', 'Satyagraha and Truth' as his main weapon to counter the Ghadrites and the Revolutionaries. Earlier during the world war years when the Empire needed Indians to fight and rescue her [the Empire] from her defeat in Europe, Mahatma Gandhi had urged the famine-stricken Indians to enlist themselves in the army, learn the use of arms in order to become free from the reproach of being called 'cowards' and 'effeminates' and thus gain 'Swaraj'. He [Mahatma Gandhi] now asked them to inculcate and adopt "non-violence' as their creed. They [Indians] should eschew all form of violence and lay down their arms against the British armed might, he told them. They [people] should show their strength by enduring all suffering in the hands of their enemies. It was entirely an about-face or volt face from Mahatmaji's previous ideology. It showed astuteness in tackling and subduing the increasing influence and strength of the revolutionaries and saving the British rulers.

"I think the growing generation [read revolutionaries] will not be satisfied with petitions, etc. We must give them something effective. Satyagraha is the only way, it seems to me, to stop terrorism". [Read revolutionary actions] [*CWMG*, Vol. 15, p. 120] "Satyagraha certainly is, could have prevented the ambitious and high-spirited youths [read revolutionaries] of the country from seeking questionable activities for want of better..." "By Satyagraha alone could India be rid of violence [read revolutionary actions] and her patient suffering was bound to bend the mightiest power." [*CWMG,* Vol. 15, pp. 126-127].

Still another extract reflects his seriousness to put down the revolutionatry actions in his letter to K. Natrajan, Edition of *Indian Social Reformer*, Bombay, to whom Mahatma Gandhi wrote: "If you do not provide the rising generation with an effective remedy against the excesses of authorities, you will let loose the powers of vengeance and the doctrines of the Little Bengal Cult of violence [read revolutionary actions] will spread with a rapidity which all will deplore." [*CWMG*, Vol. 15, pp. 106]

Freeing the country from the revolutionaries had, thus, become virtually a lifelong commitment for Mahatma Gandhi. What was the need for Mahatma Gandhi to make any effort to save their lives? The answer is the unfortunate coincidence of the impending Congress Session at Karachi and the execution of the martyrs. By the time the Congress Session was nearing to be held in the last week of March 1931, Bhagat Singh's popularity was receiving tremendous publicity.

Mahatma Gandhi first talked about Bhagat Singh to Lord Irwin, the Viceroy at the conclusion of his meeting with him on February 18, 1931. Mahatma Gandhi's version as given on page 155 of his *CWMG*, Vol. 51 is as follows: "These two titbits are not relevant. Now the third (titbit) has no connection with our discussion and it may even be inappropriate on my part to mention it. But if you want to make the present atmosphere more favourable, you should suspend Bhagat Singh's execution."

The Viceroy liked this very much. He said: "I am very grateful to you that you have put this thing before me in this manner. Commutation is a difficult thing, but suspension is certainly worth considering." I (Gandhiji) said about Bhagat Singh: "He is undoubtedly a brave man but I would certainly say that he is not in his right mind. However, this is the evil of capital punishment that it gives no opportunity to such a man to reform himself. I am putting this matter before you as a humanitarian issue and desire suspension of sentence in order that there may not be unnecessary turmoil in the country. I myself would have released him, but I cannot expect any government to do so. I would not take it ill even if you do not give any reply on this issue."

The Viceroy's version as given on page 151 of the *CWMG*, Vol. 51 is as follows: "In conclusion and not connected with the above, he mentioned the case of Bhagat Singh. He did not plead for commutation, although he would, being opposed to all taking of a life, take that course, himself. He also thought, it would have an influence for peace. But he did ask for postponement in the present circumstances ... ".

Mahatma Gandhi spoke to Lord Irwin, the Viceroy, again on March 19, 1931. Lord Irwin states as follows: "As he was leaving, he asked if he might mention the case of Bhagat Singh saying that he had seen in the Press the intimation of his execution for March 24th. This was an unfortunate day, as it coincided with the arrival of the new President of the Congress at Karachi and there would be great popular excitement.

I told him I had considered the case with the most anxious care, but could find no grounds on which I could justify to my conscience commuting the sentence. As to the date, I had considered, the possibility of postponement till after the Congress, but had deliberately rejected it on various grounds. He (Gandhiji) appeared to appreciate the force of these arguments and said no more," said Irwin. [*CWMG*, Vol. 51, p. 272]

Mahatma Gandhi spoke to the Viceroy once again through writing a letter on March 23, 1931 [It was his day of silence].

The letter began saying: "It seems cruel to inflict this letter on you, but the interest of peace demands a final appeal. Though you were frank enough to tell me that there was little hope of your commuting the sentence of death on Bhagat Singh and two others, you said, you would consider my submission of Saturday." Continuing his letter, Mahatma Gandhi also wrote: "Seeing that I am able to inform you that the revolutionary Party has assured me that in the event of these lives being spared, that Party will stay its hands. Suspension of sentence pending cessation of revolutionary murders becomes in my opinion a peremptory duty ..." [Here the Apostle of Truth seems to state something about the revolutionaries which could not be true]. The letter ended urging: "Execution is an irretrievable act. If you think there is the slightest chance of an error of judgment, I would urge you to suspend for further review an act that is beyond recall... [*CWMG*, Vol. 51, p. 290]

How lightly and casually, Mahatma Gandhi spoke to Lord Irwin on February 18, 1931 about the issue of Bhagat Singh mentioning it as another "titbit" and as an after-thought saying: "It may even be inappropriate on my part to mention it and again at the end of his talk, saying, "I would not take it ill even if you do not give any reply on this issue."

On March 19, 1931 Lord Irwin stated how Mahatma Gandhi broached the issue of Bhagat Singh: "As he was leaving, he asked if he might mention the case of Bhagat Singh...," making it aparent that Mahatma Gandhi was not serious in saving the lives of Bhagat Singh and his comrades. He [Gandhiji] never asked for commutation and always urged Lord Irwin to suspend [postpone] the execution, meaning till after the Congress Session at Karachi.

Here is what Alan Campbell Johnson, author of Lord Irwin's biography titled *Viscount Halifax* had, on page 313, reproduced what Sir Herbert Emerson, the Home Member, had recorded: "Sir Herbert Emerson, the Home Member who was called upon to play a prominent role in the Delhi negotiations, records listening with amazement to Lord Irwin and Gandhi, after agreement had been reached by them, that Bhagat Singh must be executed, engage in a prolonged discussion not as between two statesmen on the political implications of terrorism [Read revolutionary actions], but as between two saints on the sanctity of human life."

Alan Campbell Johnson, on page 314 of the said book, writes further: "It is incredible but true that in spite of his refusal to grant the reprieve, Irwin was able to extract a pledge from Gandhi that he would specifically condemn acts of terrorism [read revolutionary actions] at the next meeting of Congress, and that Gandhi for his part kept his word and in all the orgy of tears over the murderer [read Bhagat Singh] roundly denounced political crime. There could be no more compelling evidence of the trust that bound the Viceroy and Mahatma to each other and made their relationship unique in the annals of British India."

They had better be hanged before the Karachi Congress than after: Here is one more. This is from Dr. Pattabhi Sitaramayya's *The History of the Indian National Congress*, Vol. I, p. 442. "Anyway Lord Irwin was unable to help in the matter, but undertook to secure a postponement of the execution till after the Karachi Congress. The Karachi Session was to meet in the last days of March, but Gandhi himself definitely stated to the Viceroy that if the boys should be hanged, they had better be hanged before the Congress than after. The position of affairs in the country would be clear. There would be no false hopes lingering in the breasts of the people. The Gandhi-Irwin Pact would stand or fall on its own merit at the Congress, and on the added fact that the three boys had been executed."

Mr. H.W. Emerson, the Home Secretary, had written a letter to Gandhiji informing him of a meeting of protest in the evening on the day Bhagat Singh, Sukhdev and Rajguru were to be executed. In the letter, he [Emerson] sought Gandhiji's assistance to check the creation of conditions which if uncontrolled, might have serious consequences. The meeting was to be addressed by Subhas Chandra Bose. Gandhiji promptly wrote back giving valuable advice to Mr. Emerson as follows: "I thank you for your letter just received. I knew about the meeting you refer to. I have already taken every precaution possible and hope that nothing untoward will happen. I suggest that there should be no display of police force and no interference at the meeting. Irritation is undoubtedly there. It would be better to allow it to find vent through meetings, etc." [The readers will recall that Mahatma Gandhi had similarly advised Lord Chelmsford in his letter dated May 30, 1919 "to appoint a Committee to soothe the public mind after the Jallianwala Massacre, thus showing his sympathies and support to the British Empire"]

The letter shows how friendly and sympathetically Mahatma Gandhi was advising the British rulers. In his autobiography *Fullness of Days* on page 150, Lord Irwin now Lord Halifax, says that during negotiations on March 19, 1931, Mahatma Gandhi had sought his permission, to say, that he had pleaded for the young men's lives.

Mahatma Gandhi had no concern about the lives of the three youngmen. In his mind he was so apprehensive of the possible demonstrations against him and the other Congress leaders that he, on March 21, 1931, telegraphically instructed the Karachi Congress Reception Committee to cancel all processions and functions to welcome the new Congress President, Mr. Vallabhbhai Patel and he, along with other Congress leaders, got down at Malir, a small railway station, 13 miles from the main Karachi station. But there too, they had to face hostile demonstrators with the black flags shouting "leaders go back", "down with Truce", etc.

At the outset of the Congress Session on March 27, Pt. Jawaharlal Nehru, the retiring President, was asked to move the resolution on Bhagat Singh though it had been drafted by Mahatma Gandhi. The resolution ran: 'The Congress while disassociating itself from and disapproving of political violence in any shape or form, places on record its admiration of the bravery and sacrifice of the late Sardar Bhagat Singh and his comrades, -Sukhdev and Rajguru and mourns, with the bereaved families, the loss of these lives ...' Mr. V.L Shastri moved an amendment for the deletion of the words "disapproval of political violence". He deprecated half-hearted, stinking, grudging compliments to the great men who had been executed. At this stage loudspeakers failed and Mr. Shastri protested that they had been put out of order deliberately and pleaded that a differential treatment should not be meted out to him. The President ruled that the speaker's time was up and that he should finish his speech. Mr. Shastri again protested that he did not have his say and complained that loudspeakers had been put out of order. He stated that Mrs. Kamladevi Chattopadhya, was to have seconded him, had been persuaded not to do so. The President, however, ruled that his time was over.

Mr. Tarachand Lalwani seconded the amendment. He declared that the whole world knew that the creed of the Congress was non-violence. Why, then repeat it over and over again year after year? The world might well say, "friends, you are protesting too much."

Mr. Pandey from Kumaun said the reservation in the original resolution was like putting nails in the coffins of Bhagat Singh and others. The original resolution was put to vote and was passed. [*The Tribune*, March 29, 1931]

There was not a word of condemnation of the cruel British rulers for murdering the county's heroes in the Congress Resolution passed at the Karachi Congress Session.

Bhagat Singh, Sukhdev, Rajguru Memorial Committee

At a meeting of some prominent Congressmen of Punjab, on April, 28, 1931, 'The Bhagat Singh, Sukhdev, Rajguru Memorial Committee was formed. The meeting was presided over by Bawa Nihal Singh. It was attended by Dr. Satya Pal, Sardar Kishan Singh, Mehta Anand Kishore, Lala Pindi Das, Mangal Singh, Lala Ram Saran Das, Lala Munilal, pleader, Ferozepur, Smt. Shanno Devi, Dr. Mohammad Alam, Dr. Dharam Vir, Mr. Abdul Ghani of Ludhiana and others. On the suggestion of Lala Pindi Das, it was decided to collect a sum of Rupees ten lakhs for the memorial. A working committee of the following was constituted. The members were

Pt. Jawaharlal Nehru, Pt. Madan Mohan Malaviya, Maulana Abul Kalam Azad, Dr. M.A. Ansari, Subhas Chandra Bose, Mr. Sen Gupta, Shri Satyamurthi, Mr K.F. Nariman, Smt. Sushila Ghosh, Bawa Nihal Singh, Khan Abdul Ghaffar Khan, Dr. Sayed Mehmud, Dr. Satya Pal, Dr. S. Kitchlew, Babu Purshottam Dass Tandon, Dr. K. Santhanam, Baba Gurdit Singh, Sardar Sardul Singh Kaveeshar, Mehta Anand Kishore, Maulvi Ahmed Din, Smt. Shanno Devi, Lala Pindi Das, Maulana Zaffar Ali Khan, Sardar Mangal Singh, Sardar Kishen Singh, Ch. Kartar Singh, Babu Shiv Prasad Gupta, Mr. Manilal Kothari, Mr. Narain Das Bichar and Dr. Mohammad Alam.

Mehta Anand Kishore was appointed General Secretary and Maulvi Abdul Ghani and Smt. Sushila Ghosh as Secretaries. Bawa Nihal Singh was chosen as the Financial Secretary. The Publicity Committee consisting of S. Gopal Singh Quomi, Lala Pindi Das and Mr. Mani Ram Katia was to be headed by Dr. Satya Pal. The People's Bank and the Punjab National Bank were appointed the bankers. [*The Tribune,* Lahore, April 28, 1931]

Mehta Anand Kishore, General Secretary, wrote to Mahatma Gandhi requesting him to give his blessings and to become the Committee's Patron. Mahatma Gandhi refused to associate himself with the memorial and the Memorial Committee. His letter written on June 20, 1931 is as follows:

"A memorial erected in honour of anybody, undoubtedly, means that the memorialists would copy deeds of those in whose memory they erect the memorial. It is also an invitation to posterity to copy such deeds. I am, therefore, unable to identity myself in any way with the memorial" [*CWMG*, Vol. 46, p. 21].

Mahatma Gandhi, it seemed, had an obsession of Bhagat Singh. Now dead, he [Bhagat Singh] still rankled him in his breast. He [Mahatma Gandhi] felt terrified to imagine Bhagat Singh even in stone. Later, Mahatmaji's refusal to associate himself with the Memorial Committee made it almost defunct. All the prominent Congressmen including Pt. Jawaharlal Nehru, Maulana Azad, Subhas Chandra Bose who were earlier keen, eager and felt honoured to join the Memorial Committee and whose names were included in the Working Committee of the Memorial Forum, developed cold feet. The All India Bhagat Singh, Sukhdev, Rajguru Memorial Committee, thus, fizzled out.

A New Resolution on Bhagat Singh: Within four months, after the resolution, placing on record, its admiration for the bravery and sacrifice of Bhagat Singh, Sukhdev and Rajguru and mourning their loss, with the families of the martyrs, Mahatma Gandhi drafted another resolution, got it approved from the Congress Working Committee and was passed at the meeting of the All India Congress Committee held on August 6, 1931 at Bombay.

The AICC calls upon the Congress organisations to carry on special propaganda against all acts of public violence even where provocation is given for such acts by the British Government. Further the AICC. appeals to the nationalist Press to use all its influence on this behalf." [*The History of the Indian National Congress,* Vol. I, p. 69]

Karachi Congress Resolution on Bhagat Singh: A Mistake

The Karachi Congress Resolution, praising Bhagat Singh and His Comrades, was called a "Mistake" by Mahatma Gandhi, thereby, repudiating it.

Some excerpts from Mahatma Gandhi's long speech delivered while he moved the resolution: "Let me tell you in all humility that there is much more in my heart than is contained in the text of the resolution. It is my own draft and hence I want to make this clear. I would have liked to go even further but the resolution represents the extent to which I was confident that I would carry you with me..."

A Mistake: "When in the past we have condemned acts of violence, we have expressed admiration for courage and sacrifice of the youngmen. In my opinion, the limit was reached when we passed the Bhagat Singh resolution at Karachi. I now feel that it was a mistake. Those who knew Bhagat Singh had told me a good deal about his fine character, his rare courage and sacrifice and I drafted the resolution. But I find that the qualifications of the resolution have been forgotten and the praises have been exploited. I am deeply pained.... I now see clearly that, however, worthy the motive was, the way in which the resolution was worded was a mistake and we have avoided it this time". "Therefore, there is the Congress creed and we have to work it out faithfully."

"And now a word to the national newspapers. They can help a great deal if they will. One often sees glaring headlines in them suggesting of approval of political murders. Let them, therefore, beware of the slightest suggestion of encouragement to violence."

"I am told by young men that if I cannot help them, I should keep quiet, but not hinder them. My answer to them is, if you must kill English officers, why not kill me instead? I plead guilty to the charge of putting an obstacle in your way in my own way. It is my creed. Have no mercy on me and despatch me straightaway. But so long as there is breath in me, I resist you in the manner I know. If you will spare me, do not lay hands on government servants, be they big or small."

[Extracts of Mahatma Gandhi's speech have been taken from, *The Tribune* dated August 18, 1931. The full text is published in *Young India.*]

The resolution passed at the Karachi Congress Session in the last week of March 1931 praising Bhagat Singh, Rajguru and Sukhdev's bravery and sacrifice was drafted by Mahatma Gandhi but introduced by Pt. Jawaharlal Nehru—the outgoing President of the Congress while Sardar Vallabhbhai Patel was presiding. Both Pt. Nehru and Sardar Patel along with the other members of the Congress Working Committee had now approved the new resolution passed at the August 6, 1931 meeting of the Congress Committee at Bombay virtually repudiating, thereby, their earlier statements and the resolution praising the three martyrs' bravery and sacrifice at the Karachi Congress Session, showing their duplicity and doubleness.

It is worth remembering that the valour and sacrifices of earlier revolutionaries including those of Bengal and Punjab, the Babbar Akalis, Ghadrite heroes, etc. had never been acknowledged and praised by the Congress leadership. Gandhiji's concept of 'Truth' did not apply in their cases and God according to Mahatmaji disapproved their actions–valorousness, and sacrifices.

27

Bhagat Singh Was a True Marxist

What was Shaheed Bhagat Singh's social and political ideology? In a display of crass opportunism, all kinds of political groups and individuals have attempted to adopt Bhagat Singh and co-opt his fame to further their own nefarious causes. It seems that there is a concerted effort going on to de-ideologise Bhagat Singh, and turn him into a benign and fictional hero. From the Khalistani sympathisers making a quick buck from selling T-shirts 'adorned' with his pictures next to Bhindranwale, to the present-day BJP/RSS followers who would reduce him to a mere martyr without an ideology; Bhagat Singh has become an enigma for the new generation. The tag of a 'terrorist' may even scare the poorly informed amongst them. Innumerable books have been written on Bhagat Singh, and almost every author has developed a separate chapter in his or her book on this issue. The difference of opinion on his ideology is widespread.

Bhagat Singh: An Insatiable Reader and Prolific Writer

Fortunately, Bhagat Singh was an avid reader and a writer; and despite the young age at the time of his martyrdom, he left a legacy in the form of numerous pamphlets, articles and in-court statements to leave no doubts regarding his ideology. Bhagat Singh was his own best spokesman, and some of the relevant articles are reproduced. However, it is also important to understand him from the perspective of the considerable scholarship and myth-making that have evolved around him from across the political and ideological spectrum.

The controversy over, "Was Bhagat Singh a Marxist?" is unnecessary. It arose when one of the co-accused in the Lahore Conspiracy Case, after profusely praising him, stated, "It will be an exaggeration to say that Bhagat Singh was a Marxist". The above comments triggered a stream of writings by prominent political figures, scholars and writers evaluating and measuring Bhagat Singh's understanding and belief in Marxism. Most of the views expressed on Bhagat Singh being a Marxist and if so, how much, reflected the extent of the viewer's own limited knowledge and grasp of Marxism.

Lenin, gave his famous definition of a Marxist as follows: "Only he is a Marxist who extends the recognition of the class struggle to the recognition of the Dictatorship of the Proletariat. This is what constitutes the most profound distinction between the Marxist and the ordinary petty bourgeois. This is the touchstone on which the real understanding and recognition of Marxism should be tested" ... ['The State and Revolution']. Bhagat Singh, clearly was true to this touchstone, or definition of a Marxist. In his article, 'The Philosophy of the Bomb', written as a rebuttal to Mahatma Gandhi's criticism of revolutionary actions in 'The Cult of the Bomb', Bhagat Singh wrote:

> The revolutionaries believe that the deliverance of their country will come through revolution. The revolution, they are constantly working and hoping for, will not only express itself in the form of an armed conflict between the foreign government and its supporters and the people. It will also usher in a new social order. The revolution will bring the death-knell of capitalism, class distinctions and privileges. It will bring joy and prosperity to the starving millions who are seething today under the terrible yoke of both foreign and Indian exploitation. It will bring the nation into its own. It will give birth to a new state, a new social order. Above all, it will establish the 'Dictatorship of the Proletariat' and will forever banish social parasites from the seat of political power. ['Bhagat Singh and Lenin's Touchstone of a Marxist' has been further explained in later pages.]

In his Statement in the Sessions Court, Bhagat Singh's belief in the 'Dictatorship of the Proletariat' is well articulated. Explaining the definition of 'Revolution', he stated "by Revolution, we mean the ultimate establishment of an order of the society... in which the sovereignty of the proletariat should be recognised... we have given a fair and loud enough warning. If, however, it [warning] goes unheeded... a grim struggle will ensure involving the overthrow of all obstacles, and the establishment of the 'Dictatorship of the Proletariat' to pave the way for the consummation of the ideal of revolution."

Efforts have been made to delink Bhagat Singh from his Marxist ideology ever since he forthrightly articulated it through his statement during his trial in the Sessions Court on June 6, 1929. Pt. Jawaharlal Nehru, who initially highlighted Bhagat Singh's statements in the *Congress Bulletin*, later expressed regrets after being reproached by Mahatma Gandhi. Subsequently, in his *An Autobiography*, Pt. Nehru chose to omit Bhagat Singh's Marxist ideology and attributed his nationwide popularity to the daring act of avenging the death of Lala Lajpat Rai.

Professor Chaman Lal, a renowned research scholar and an eminent writer comes nearest to the recognition of Bhagat Singh as a Marxist. In his 15-page introduction to *Bhagat Singh: The Jail Note Book and Other Writings* published by 'Left Word' in 2007, he stated with slight reticence on Bhagat Singh's full grasp of Marxism. On page 20 he writes. "As is evident, Bhagat Singh was clearly very close to a Marxist understanding of society and change." The views of Soviet scholars such as Mitrokhin and A.V. Raikov, about Bhagat Singh's ideological legacy, have also been quoted. They too had only placed him [Bhagat Singh] within the Marxist tradition. In his latest book titled *Understanding Bhagat Singh*, published by Aakar books in 2013, Professor Chaman Lal, on page 15 expressed Bhagat Singh's ideology stating: "And since they were asked in the lower court what he meant by the word 'revolution', he explains the concept of 'revolution' almost in Marxist terminology, thereby, qualifying it by prefixing it with "almost"".

Professor Bipan Chandra, an eminent historian, in his books described Bhagat Singh as "also a Marxist thinker in the making". In the earlier editions of his books, he mentioned Bhagat Singh as a terrorist though in the later editions he has been called a revolutionary nationalist.

Many distinguished Marxist scholars and thinkers, each one of them presuming himself to be an authority on Marxism, have also measured Bhagat Singh's knowledge of Marxism by qualifying phrases such as "Bhagat Singh was making his way towards acceptance of Marxism as a guide". "It is more than evident that Bhagat Singh was steadily evolving from a revolutionary terrorist to be a Marxist." "Bhagat Singh and his comrades were nationalist revolutionaries to the core who wanted to drive out the British rulers, gain independence and establish socialism". "They were in fact impatient patriots who detested any wait-and-see or go slow policy". "Bhagat Singh accepted socialism as a goal in 1928, but hangovers from the past still remained". "Bhagat Singh was a pioneer among revolutionaries moving towards socialism, but it did not mean that Bhagat Singh had comprehended all aspects of Marxism". "It was Bhagat Singh and his comrades alone who were inexorably moving ideologically towards the third current of Marxian Socialism and the Communist Party". "A certain amount of confusion still prevailed in the Manifesto [of HSRA] about the role of terrorism," etc.

Chander Pal Singh, who in his book titled, *Bhagat Singh Revisited* published in 2011, has contended that Bhagat Singh was no ideologue. He has stated:

"There cannot be an iota of doubt that if there was any continuity in his thought process, it was intense patriotism; if there was a persistent dream, it was the freedom of the motherland and if there was one passion which seized him throughout his short life, it was to embrace martyrdom."

> Chander Pal Singh, further asserted; "Masses of this nation worship Bhagat Singh as a patriot and martyr only, and not as an ideologue ...".

Professor V.N. Datta is another prominent scholar who wrote *Gandhi and Bhagat Singh*, and has tried to belittle Bhagat Singh's precocious scholarship and knowledge gained from extensive study. He has written:

> Bhagat Singh had a disrupted education. He could not complete his school education. He moved from one place to another. It is true that

> he had read voraciously during his prison days. Statements issued by him in the court were amended by Asaf Ali, which is understandable. Of course, he had access to the Dwarkadass Library from where he obtained books on various subjects for his self-study. It raises doubts how a person of his disrupted educational background could at the age of twenty-three or so write such commendable literary and scholarly pieces reflecting a maturity of thought, a wide sweep of history, and a mastery of the English language. The original documents including his letters are not available. The authorship of the articles attributed to him still remains a mystery.

Such disparaging remarks about Bhagat Singh from these 'learned' authors, reflect their own poverty of scholarship, or worse an ill-advised but concerted effort to belittle his vast knowledge and undermine his (Bhagat Singh) reputation as an inspiration for those who struggle for social and economic progress.

There are, on the other hand, Harpal Brar, Hans Raj Rehbar, Omesh Saigal, Manmath Nath Gupta and Satyam who have affirmed that no one better articulated the Marxist ideals than Bhagat Singh did in India. Satyam, a prominent writer on Bhagat Singh has asserted that Bhagat Singh was a Marxist. Writing a foreword of about 18 pages for his book in Hindi titled *Bhagat Singh Aur Uske Sathion Ke Sampooran Uplabhad Dastawaize*, Satyam, by citing references and quotations from his [Bhagat Singh] writings and giving a short review of the evolution of Bhagat Singh's thought process, has clearly shown that Bhagat Singh had fully grasped all the features of Marxism and he was a Marxist.

Harpal Brar, a reputed intellectual and author of many outstanding works, in his book, *Inquilab Zindabad: India's Liberation Struggle,* has stated that the real advance made by the national revolutionaries towards the acceptance of Socialism only came in 1928, at the initiative of Bhagat Singh and formation of 'The Hindustan Socialist Republican Association':

> "Bhagat Singh and his comrades were the products of their time and circumstances—a time when the economic and political developments in the domestic and international arena were thrusting the masses

into the whirlpool of revolutionary policies, radicalising the petty bourgeoisie and obliging the latter to adopt Marxism as the only weapon for the liberation of the masses from subjugation, oppression, misery, squalor and hunger. No one better symbolised this process than Bhagat Singh; no one better articulated the new socialist ideals than he did. Precisely for that reason he emerged as the most representative spokesman of this new vision of society, and, in the process, from being a mere youthful individual, he became a phenomenon."

In a similar vein, **Hansraj Rehbar** in his book, *Bhagat Singh and Ignited History*, wrote:

"The nationalised [Indian] version of Marxism and Leninism, which was established by Bhagat Singh, is, in fact, the ideology of Bhagat Singh. Bhagat Singh, and not the Communist Party of India, was the real representative of Marxism in India...Bhagat Singh's comrades, who after their release from the jails, had joined the Communist Party, made a mistake and as the proverb goes, turned into salt in the salt mine... They, thus, not only let Bhagat Singh down but also abandoned the ideals for which the Hindustan Socialist Republican Association had been formed. They should rather have taken up Bhagat Singh's baton and revived 'The Hindustan Socialist Republican Association' and carried on his task on the basis of the guidelines given in his 'An Address to the Young Political Workers' and other writings." Hansraj Rehbar further adds" 'Thereafter (After the martyrdom of Chandra Shekhar Azad, Bhagat Singh, Sukhdev and Rajguru), the leadership of the Party came into the hands of those who were weak or of dubious character. As a result of this, Yashpal usurped the post of the Commander and, later on, went to jail by getting himself dramatically arrested. Consequently, the Party disintegrated for lack of a suitable leadership'.

Omesh Saigal, IAS [Rtd.] and a former Chief Secretary of Delhi Administration, has been another distinguished intellectual and author of many books. In his book, *Shaheed Bhagat Singh: Unique Martyr in the Freedom Movement*, he has unreservedly acknowledged Bhagat Singh to be a true Marxist-Leninist:

"Sardar Bhagat Singh didn't put on Scientific Socialism on a shirt worn only on the platform like our communists. He remained true to dialectical materialism, which is as much a part of Socialist

Philosophy as the head is a part of the body... Whether one likes it or not, Bhagat Singh has become the epitome of the fight for Socialism more than any person or party has... Bhagat Singh was more than a symbol. He was a visionary with a dream, the madness of a Spinoza, the halo of a superhuman." [Baruch Spinoza (November 24, 1632 to February 21, 1677) was a Dutch philosopher. His magnum opus, the posthumous 'Ethics' has earned him recognition as one of the most important Western thinkers. Hegel said, "you are either a Spinozist or not a philosopher at all. He was named the 'Prince of Philosophers'."

Omesh Saigal also wrote about Gandhism, stating:

> "Mahatma Gandhi's Ahimsa and Satyagraha was an ideological shield for the British rulers, as well as for the Indian bourgeoisie to confront the revolutionaries led by Bhagat Singh and their ideology of Scientific Socialism. The definition of 'Swaraj' was deliberately kept vague. Mahatma Gandhi was mortally afraid of revolution."

Manmath Nath Gupta, in his book *Bhagat Singh and His Times,* has testified the services of Bhagat Singh to the cause of Marxism in the following words:

> "Bhagat Singh was not a fanatic. His mind was a mammoth 'blotter' which absorbed and retained fragments of the best revolutionary minds. His attitude towards life and death was that of a born fighter, but he was singularly free from the symptoms of a traditional terrorist leader. His services to Socialism are greater than that of any Indian. He has become the symbol of fight for Socialism more than any person or party has. His martyrdom constitutes a challenge not only to the enemies of Socialism, but is also a warning to those 'Leftists' who indulge in frothy talk of revolution and Marxism but are wedded to parliamentarianism and are addicts of a soft life".

Bhagat Singh: An Unquenchable Reader and Prolific Writer: 'The Hindustan Socialist Republican Association' was a Party that strictly observed its rules and regulations and its members fully abided by its discipline. Bhagat Singh was the General Secretary and Bhagwati Charan Vohra, the Propaganda Secretary while Chandra Shekhar Azad was the Party's overall incharge as well as the Commander-in-Chief of its armed wing called 'The Hindustan Socialist Republican Army'. They could not openly see and consult each other but surreptitiously maintained some contacts. Bhagat Singh would be planning and drafting all the documents of the Party including the Manifestoes of 'The Naujawan Bharat Sabha' and 'The Hindustan Socialist Republican Association', 'The Philosophy of The Bomb' and various letters, notices and other documents. This had been corroborated by Jitendra Nath Sanyal on page 108 of his book captioned *Bhagat Singh: A Biography*. These were clandestinely smuggled out by Bhagat Singh from his prison walls to Bhagwati Charan Vohra for getting the same typed, printed, published and issued. Many of these writings were brought out in the name of 'Balraj' or 'Kartar Singh', fictitious names. He did not mention his own name on most of the documents written by him. These were being written secretly. Obviously, they could not be circulated to other co-accused colleagues. This precaution was necessary to prevent the documents falling into the hands of the British authorities. In this respect, comrade Ajay Ghosh, comrade Shiv Verma and other co-accused comrades who were lodged in Borstal Jail, while Bhagat Singh was in the Central Jail, Lahore, could not have knowledge of such writings. They, therefore, were not well-conversant with what Bhagat Singh read, thought and wrote including the extent of his knowledge of Marxist philosophy. They, it seemed, simply saw him with his pockets full of books and reading them, whenever and wherever he found time. What Shiv Verma had written, stating Bhagwati Charan Vohra as an author of *The Philosophy of the Bomb*, was not correct and was only Shiv Verma's conjecture. Yashpal was a police informer, according to some authors of the books on Bhagat Singh.

Lenin's Touchstone of a Marxist and Bhagat Singh

Lenin gave his famous definition of a Marxist as follows: "Only he is a Marxist who extends the recognition of the class struggle to the recognition of the Dictatorship of the Proletariat. This is what constitutes the most profound distinction between the Marxist and the ordinary petty [as well as big] bourgeois. This is the touchstone on which the real understanding and recognition of Marxism should be tested"... "Opportunism does not extend the recognition of the class struggle precisely to what is most important to the period of transition from capitalism to communism, to the period of the overthrow and the complete abolition of the bourgeoisie. In reality, this period inevitably is a period of an unprecedently fierce class struggle in unprecedentedly acute forms and, consequently, during this period, the state must inevitally be a state that is democratic in a new way for the proletariat and the propertyless in general, and dictatorial in a new way against the bourgeoisie. To proceed, the essence of Marx's teaching on the state, has been mastered only by those who understand that 'Dictatorship of a Single Class' [Proletariat] is necessary, not only for every class society in general, not only for the proletariat, which has overthrown the bourgeoisie, but also for the entire historical period which separates capitalism from classless society, i.e. from communism". [and that has become all the more clear after the restoration of capitalism in USSR, after the death of Stalin and in China after the demise of Mao] ... the forms of bourgeois states are extremely varied, but their essence is the same, all these states whatever their form, in the final analysis are inevitably the dictatorship of the bourgeoisie. The transition from Capitalism to Communism certainly cannot but yield a tremendous abundance and variety of political forms, but the essence will inevitably be the same, the Dictatorship of the Proletariat" [The State and Revolution by Lenin].

Marxism is a complex philosophy and science not easy to comprehend and much more difficult to apply it accurately. Had it not been so, the Marxist Government in Chile (South America) headed by Salvador Allende would not have been overthrown in 1973 and millions of communists in that country would not have been butchered. The mistaken belief in the 'Peaceful Competition And Peaceful Transformation of Capitalism to Socialism' was the main culprit. It is a simple logic. Why would the ruling bourgeoisie allow the proletariat to dig their (bourgeoisie) own grave through the use of their instrument, i.e. the bourgeois democracy?

Bhagat Singh was true to the touchstone of a Marxist. In the statement made before the Sesssions Court on June 6, 1929, Bhagat Singh had prophetically foretold of the establishment of the 'Dictatorship of the Proletariat' to pave the way for the consummation of the ideal of revolution.

Further, in his pamphlet, *The Philosophy of the Bomb,* Bhagat Singh had prophesied that the revolution "will give birth to a new state, a new social order. Above all it will establish the 'Dictatorship of the Proletariat' and will forever banish social parasites from the seat of political power".

There is a vast treasure of literature on Marxism. One life, it seems, is not enough to go through the whole of it. And Bhagat Singh had been allowed to live less than just one third of a human being's normal span of life. He, therefore, had a limited time and yet could go through the vast literary material on Marxism but was accorded no time to give a practical shape to his Marxist knowledge. It is not, however, just study of a large number of books that makes one knowledgeable of the science or philosophy of Marxism. It is one's comprehension, perception and mental grasp that would make one, an erudite Marxist person. Nature had blessed Bhagat Singh with all the qualities and abilities to grasp and imbibe the essence of Marxism. He was fortunate to have learned teachers in the National College, Lahore, such as Professor Jayachandra Vidyalankar, Bhai Parmanand, and Principal Chhabildas from whom and with whose guidance he learnt and with whom he used to discuss Marxism. Another great institution of learning for Bhagat Singh was Dwarka Das Library, whose Librarian, Raja Ram Shastri would procure books and magazines for Bhagat Singh, not only from the well-known bookshop in Lahore called Rama Krishna & Sons but from all the other bookshops in Lahore, as well as other cities. Raja Ram Shastri himself had become inbued with and devoted to Marxism. These two institutions proved to be like the Marxist Universities for Bhagat Singh. He was known to be a voracious reader and it was said, his shirt and trouser pockets remained filled with books. He would be seen reading not only during travelling but anywhere he would find time to. It was here at these two then great institutions that he grasped and imbibed the essence of Marxism. He was, thus, a self-taught and self-educated Marxist. He was not only a voracious reader but also a prolific writer. His vast knowledge of the many other currents of thoughts including Anarchism and Nihilism prevalent in Europe and Russia could be judged from the four articles he wrote for a journal known as *Kirti*. [Worker] *Kirti* readers as well as its editor, Comrade Sohan Singh Josh must have learnt a lot from Bhagat Singh and articles written by him (Bhagat Singh). Bhagat Singh wrote three articles on 'Anarchism' and one article on 'Russian Nihilists' and he also wanted to write on 'Communism'. He must have written on Communism and Socialism also and there is a possibility we may find his articles written on these subjects some time in future.

Jitendera Nath Sanyal, a co-accused of Bhagat Singh, in his book titled *Bhagat Singh: A Biography*, has stated: Bhagat Singh was an extremely well-read man and his special sphere of study was Socialism. The batch of young men who figured in the Lahore Conspiracy Case was essentially an intellectual one. But even in this group Bhagat Singh predominated for his intellectual ascendancy. Though Socialism was his special subject, he had deeply studied the history of the Russian revolutionary movement from its beginning in the early 19th century to the October Revolution of 1917. It is generally believed that very few in India could be compared to him in the knowledge of this special subject. The economic experiment in Russia under the Bolshevik regime also greatly interested him.

Pritam Singh, Professor of Economics, Oxford Brookes University, UK, had, in an article published in *The Tribune*, stated that with Bhagat Singh in the leadership position of the Indian Socialist tradition, he would have become the rallying force against the Gandhi and Nehru-led Congress's pro-capitalist vision. It is worth imagining that the polarisation in the country would not have been Congress versus Muslim League, Hindu versus Muslim and Gandhi versus Jinnah but would have been Gandhi versus Bhagat Singh, Capitalism versus Socialism and mere transfer of power versus Socio-Economic revolution. Of the many possibilities open in the

1930s in India, one was the large-scale migration of the Congress Cadre to the fold of the Bhagat Singh-led radical alternative. That possibility died with the hanging of Bhagat Singh. Had Bhagat Singh not been hanged in 1931, there would have been a serious contest between the Gandhi and Nehru-led Congress vision and the Bhagat Singh-led Socialist vision. Bhagat Singh had the advantage over the Indian Communists that his radicalism was popularly seen as home-grown and rooted.

Bhagat Singh, according to Raja Ram Shastri, was a clear-headed and strong-willed personality. He would not, let his left hand know, what his right hand was doing. It was here that he planned to set up three organisations to prepare the country's youth, labourers and farmers for preparing the country for a Socialist Revolution. The organisations were 'Naujawan Bharat Sabha' to work openly and legally. It was meant to recruit whole-time professional revolutionaries from amongst the members of the Sabha. The other two organisations were 'The Hindustan Socialist Republican Association' and 'The Hindustan Socialist Republican Army'. These two were to work underground.

As repeatedly emphasised by the great Marxist Masters—Karl Marx, F. Engels, V.I. Lenin, J.V. Stalin, Mao and Fidel Castro, that Marxism was not a dogma. Bhagat Singh too did not believe it to be so. He planned to practise Marxism according to the concrete socio-political situation in India. His definition of the concept of 'Terrorism' and the importance of its role in bringing about revolution is a marvellous contribution to Marxist literature. He knew that it was difficult for the workers and peasants themselves to take the initiative to educate themselves about Marxism and revolution. He, therefore, had urged the educated youth, the professional revolutionaries, to live and spend their days and nights with the workers in their slums as well as with the farmers in their fields and hovels in villages to educate them. In his 'An Address to the Young Political Workers' [considered to be his behest to the youth of the country] written on February 2, 1931, he made it clear that "The programme requires at least twenty years for its fulfilment...it requires neither the emotion nor the death, but the life of constant struggle, suffering and sacrifice. Crush your individuality first. Shake off the dreams of personal comfort. Then start to work. Inch by inch you shall have to proceed ..."

Bhagat Singh has not yet been recognised as a martyr and is described as a terrorist. In order to dispel Bhagat Singh's image as a young and handsome revolutionary martyr and Marxist ideologue, his statue has been erected in the Parliamentary Complex, New Delhi by the Government of India that has no connection with Bhagat Singh. The revolutionary Bhagat Singh in European clothes and a felt hat was called "ridiculous" by those bureaucratic-minded ones entrusted with the task of guiding and supervising the erection of the statue. They did not realise and understand that by wearing those clothes, he had defeated, the then CID of the mightiest British Empire not once but twice. They also did not realise that the First Prime Minister of Independent India used to adorn himself in European attire while attending the conferences of the Prime Ministers of the British Commonwealth in London and visiting other foreign countries.

28

Terrorism: A Necessary and an Inevitable Phase of Revolution

The role of terrorism in fighting the British imperialism, in the revolution and the establishment of Socialism has been aptly and superbly explained in the Manifesto of the HSRA as well as in *The Philosophy of the Bomb*, authored by Bhagat Singh, the General Secretary of the Party and typed, printed, published, and issued by Bhagwati Charan Vohra as the Party's Propaganda Secretary. These were issued in the name of Kartar Singh, a fictitious name to save the documents from falling into the hands of the British Jail authorities. Had comrade Lenin been then alive, he would have hailed the description of the role of terrorism given by Bhagat Singh.

> "We have been taken to task for our terroristic policy. Our answer is that terrorism is never the object of revolutionaries, nor do they believe that terrorism alone can bring independence. Undoubtedly, the revolutionaries think, and rightly, that it is only by resorting to terrorism alone that they can find a most effective means of retaliation. The British Government exists, because the British have been successful in terrorising the whole of India. How are we to meet this official terrorism? Only counter-terrorism on the part of the revolutionaries can checkmate effectively this bureaucratic bullying. A feeling of utter helplessness pervades in the society. How can we overcome this fatal despondency? It is only by infusing a real spirit of sacrifice that lost self-confidence can be restored." [Manifesto of the Hindustan Socialist Republican Association]
>
> "It [terrorism] is a phase, a necessary, an inevitable phase of the revolution. Terrorism is not the complete revolution and the revolution is not complete without terrorism. This thesis can be supported by an analysis of any and every revolution in history. Terrorism instils fear in

the hearts of the oppressors. It brings hopes of revenge and redemption to the oppressed masses. It gives courage and self-confidence to the wavering. It shatters the spell of the superiority of the ruling class and raises the status of the subject race in the eyes of the world, because it is the most convincing proof of a nation's hunger for freedom. Here in India, as in other countries in the past, terrorism will develop into the revolution and the revolution into independence, social, political and economic". [From *The Philosophy of the Bomb*].

Sadly, in every country when the oppressed and exploited masses resisted and rose against injustice and exploitation, they were and are called terrorists and anarchists. It is a convenient way to denounce them and dismiss their voice by the bourgeoisie in every country.

"How Beautiful is Terrorism?"

Here are a few lines from a poem by a Syrian poet Nizar Qubbani, a former Syrian diplomat:

We are accused of terrorism
if we refuse to die
with Israel's bulldozers
tearing our land tearing our history...
Are accused of terrorism
if we refuse to be effaced;
If we throw a stone
At the glass of the Security Council
After the Caesar of Caesars
grabbed it for his own ;
We are accused of terrorism
if we refuse to negotiate with the wolf;
We are accused of terrorism
if we defended our land
and the honour of dust;
if we revolted against
the rape of people, our rape ;
If we defended the ...
Last stars in our sky ...
If this was sin
how beautiful is terrorism?
I am with terrorism.
As long as the new world order
Wants to slaughter my offspring
And send them to the dogs
For all this I raise my voice high:
I am with terrorism...

[A clarification: Revolutionary terrorism targeted only the agents of the British or world imperialism. The revolutionaries never intended to harm the innocent British and Indians. The Taliban terrorists, on the other hand, killed innocent people, professing religious faith or belonging to ethnic groups, other than that of the Taliban terrorists.]

29

How Britain Had to Transfer Power to India

What the British rulers thought of Indian political leadership and what the transfer of power to the Indian leaders could mean to the Indian masses had been excellently stated by Mr. C.R. Attlee on p. 246 of his book written in 1931 and titled *The Labour Party in Perspective.*

Mr. Attlee wrote: "India for the Indians" is a simple slogan, but it is necessary to see what it means in terms of human life. There is no particular gain in handing over the peasants and workers of India to be exploited by their own capitalists and landlords."

> "Nationalism is a creed that may be sustained with great self-sacrifice and idealism, but may shelter class domination and intolerance of minorities as well as economic exploitation."... "Throughout all the enquiries into the constitutional position of India, Labour members have always realised that nationalism was not enough. They have recognised frankly that it is unlikely that a poor and illiterate population will escape exploitation at the hands of the rich, the privileged and the educated class..." to conclude, the Labour Party, "having to deal with the actual existence of the British Empire and Commonwealth, will seek to apply in that sphere, as in all others, the principles of Socialism."

Ironically, Mr. Attlee handed over the peasants and workers of India to be exploited by their own [Indian] capitalists and landlords in 1947, when his Labour Party was in power and Mr. Attlee was the Prime Minister of Great Britain. The Labour Party headed by Mr. Attlee had come to power in 1945 after the end of the Second World War but, sadly, they did not take any step to apply the principles of Socialism in India, as claimed by Mr. Attlee in his book. That is how the fake socialists talk but would not act. This is what Bhagat Singh had predicted and warned of in his writings.

By the end of the Second World War, Great Britain had weakened, both militarily and financially. Her manpower had also depleted. She was no longer sure of the loyalty of the Indian services and was rather frightened of the possible revolution in case she continued to keep her hold over her colonial possessions including India. The question as to whether to continue to rule over India or to share power with the Indian leadership or to leave, was being discussed from time to time since 1942 within the British Cabinet and with the then Viceroys as well as with the Indian political leaders.

After the British Labour Party came to power, the overwhelming view was to hand over power to the Indians. The following paragraphs give a glimpse of the minds of the decision-makers and the reason and circumstances which led them to take a decision to finally hand over power on a platter to their Indian political collaborators. [The Congress and the Muslim League leadership]

Almost before the Labour Administration was fully formed, the Prime Minister, [Mr. C.R. Attlee] had on his desk, a secret memorandum from Lord J.M. Keynes, [the famous economist], warning that Britain faces a financial 'Dunkrik'. "The war had been fought with complete disregard for the financial consequences". And wrote Keynes, "Britain was virtually bankrupt. We have not a hope of escaping what might be described without exaggeration, and without implying that we should not eventually recover from it, a financial 'Dunkrik'. The war had been fought with complete disregard for the financial consequences"; and wrote Keynes, "Britain was virtually bankrupt. This", said Keynes, "must either lead to an enforced and humiliating withdrawal from overseas obligations, or a reduced standard of living at home with an even greater austerity than in war times. The conclusion argued Keynes, "was inescapable. Britain would have to ask the United States for money. In the event, the Americans would drive a hard bargain." [*Britain's Declining Power* by Ronald Hayan, p. 130]

'What happened in the international sphere after the Second

World War, gradually but decisively reinforced the sense that a global Empire was not only beyond Britain's means, but was now also threatening her prestige and reputation and becoming a liability. The Cold War determined the main outlines of British policy. Because of it, Britain had to satisfy the nationalists, side with the USA, strengthen the Commonwealth and square the United Nations. Because of it, the whole thrust of decolonisation was to proceed in such a way as to encourage the emergence of pro-Western nationalist states.'

'Strong, well-disposed interior regimes were considered essential geo-politically. A power vacuum must be avoided at all costs. The Chief of Staff thought, Russia would at least try to influence independent India, and if Britain was at war with Russia, India could easily be run-over by Russia ... India was the lynchpin of Commonwealth air communications, the strategic protecting flank for Persian Gulf oil supplies, and it had important deposits of Thorium in Travancore *[Thorium was needed to make atomic bombs]. The great game cast a long shadow.'* (Ibid., p. 114)

'Field Marshal Lord Wavell [the Viceroy] and the Commander-in-Chief, General Auchinleck, were advising that "there was a real threat in 1946 of large-scale anti-British disorders amounting to even a well-organised uprising aiming to expel the British by paralysing the administration. The Royal Indian Naval Ratings in February was the trigger. This could be very serious, and disaffection might spread to Indian troops in the Middle East with alarming repercussions."

In a note by Field Marshall Viscount Wavell to the Prime Minister, on the Services, on June 29, 1946, as stated in Vol. 7, p. 1087 of the *Transfer of Power Series for India* [*TOPI*] in twelve volumes, he wrote that during the war, the cadre of the ICS had proved insufficient for the task imposed on it, and many of the older men were tired and had lost heart. Even among the younger men there were many, who, finding their conditions of service distasteful and thinking that there was no future for them in India, wished to retire as soon as possible. Conditions were similar in the Indian Police and there had been no British recruitment since the war began.

In November 1946, Attlee set out with typically trenchancy his reasons to transfer power to Indians: (a) In view of our commitments all over the world, we had not the military force to hold India against widespread guerrilla movement or to conquer India. If we had, public opinion especially in our Party, would not stand for it. (b) It was very doubtful if our own troops would be prepared to act. (c) We would have world opinion against us and be placed in an impossible position at UNO (d). We had not now the administrative machinery, either the British or Indian to carry out such a policy.

Mr. Clement Attlee wrote to Bevin in a private and confidential communication that it has been a common ground with all of us who have had to study the Indian problem that there are millions of Indians who do not really wish for a change of government, but they are passive. The active elements in the population, including all the educated classes, have become indoctrinated to a greater or lesser extent with nationalism. This was largely true even at the time of the Simon Commission (1928). Since then the pace has accelerated. We have always governed Indians through the Indians. Without the tens and thousands of lesser functionaries, we could not carry on. In a typical district of one or two million population it is quite common for there to be only one or two white officials..Under the regime of constitutional governments, which have now been in existence with some intervals for a number of years, the loyalty of Indian officials is increasingly directed towards the Indian governments and not the British Raj: With the knowledge that the termination of British rule in India is not far off, how can you expect them not to look to the former. It would be quite impossible even if you could find a few hundred British to administer against the active opposition of the entire politically minded of the population.

C.R. Attlee, in his book *As it Happened*, further writes that 'Communism, which has little appeal to people enjoying a comparatively high standard of life, appears to many of the people of Asia as a liberating force. An attempt to maintain the old colonialism would, I am sure, have immensely aided the communist attack on Asia.

There was no mention of Mahatma Gandhi's non-co-operation

and civil disobedience or Satyagraha movements by the decision-makers in Great Britain. The 'Quit India Movement' in 1942 had been discussed by the then Viceroy, Lord Linlithgow in his reports to Mr. Amery, the Secretary of State for India and those were mostly of the acts of murders of policemen, burning of police stations and other acts of violence in various parts of the country, with the remark in a report stating that these diabolical acts are a comment on non-violence as understood by the proletariat.

Ronald Hyam on p. 66 of his book did write about Mahatma Gandhi and it was as a gesture of gratitude for his creed of non-violence that saved the British Empire in India from bloodshed (that is revolution). He stated: "It was his [Gandhi] preaching of non-violence more than any other single factor that stood between India and bloodshed [revolution] on a frightful scale." The British imperialists had adorned him with an honorific-like title calling him their 'Best Policeman' in India.

Reginald Massey, in his book *Shaheed Bhagat Singh and the Forgotten Indian Martyrs* has given an excellent account of the mutiny of the Royal Indian Naval Ratings in February 1946. He has also given an account of the then Acting Governor of West Bengal, Justice Phani Bhushan Chakraborty's conversation with C.R. Attlee, while he was on a visit to Calcutta in 1956, with regard to the events leading to the British decision to quit India in 1947. Chakraborty recorded as follows: "I asked Lord Attlee about the extent to which the British decision was influenced by Gandhi's activities. On hearing this question, Attlee's lips widened slowly, putting emphasis on every single letter, "Mi—Ni—Mal".

The sudden decision of transferring power to the Indian political leaders after the end of the Second World War was primarily due to Great Britain's own compulsions. They had felt terrified because of the acts of violence on a large scale against the British and Indian officials during Mahatma Gandhi's 'Quit India Movement' as the Indian freedom-fighters including the rank and file of the Congress did not bother about the creed of non-violence during the Movement. They [the British rulers] had become so weakened economically and militarily that they could not gather enough manpower and financial resources to maintain their control over India as well as over their other colonial possessions.

So, they decided to exercise their rule by other means, instead of the direct rule. They handed over their power to the collaborationist leaders of the colonies and it was a policy followed by other European imperialist powers also such as Holland and Belgium in Indonesia in Asia and Congo in Africa respectively. France felt reluctant to do so and had to suffer humiliating defeats in Indo-China (Vietnam) in Asia and Algeria in Africa. Great Britain also gracefully allowed herself to be subordinated to American imperialism and her multilateral corporations and by accepting herself to be a junior partner so much so that a few years back, Britain was called America's "puppy" by the media.

America had taken over the role of a world policeman to look after the economic interests of Capitalism and Imperialism.

In July 1947, the Indian Independence Bill was passed by the British Parliament. On August 15, 1947, India became free and a member of the British Commonwealth of Nations. Lord Mountbatten, the last British Viceroy of India, was given an unprecedented reception and strangely at the request of the Indian leaders, especially, Pt. Nehru, he became the first Governor-General of India. Not only he, many other British officers were retained by Prime Minister Pt. Nehru on some of the key positions. Field Marshal Auchinleck was appointed the Supreme Commander of India and Pakistan while General Lockhart was made the Commander-in-Chief of the Indian Army. Air Marshal Elmhirst was appointed the Commander-in-Chief of the Indian Air Force. The British Governors of Bengal, Madras and Bombay were also retained on their respective posts. It was quite natural that these officers owed their primary loyalty to their King in England than to India.

As Governor-General of India, Lord Mountbatten was not only a constitutional figurehead, he was also appointed chairman of the Cabinet Defence Committee investing him with real executive authority, thereby, permitting him to interfere in military affairs.

He exercised this authority by ensuring that India did not extend her military operations upto the Pakistan border in 1947-48. Pakistan had then invaded Kashmir and India was waging a war to expel the invaders from the territory of Jammu and Kashmir. Lord Mountbatten stopped Indian military operations from clearing the invaders from the whole of Kashmir and thereby, allowed Pakistan to occupy a part of Kashmir territory which is now called 'Pakistan Occupied Kashmir'. He also prevailed upon Pt. Nehru to take the Kashmir issue to the UNO, a body dominated by imperialist powers such as UK, USA and France.

India, under Pt. Jawaharlal Nehru's Prime Ministership, had decided to join the British Commonwealth which was presided over by the Queen of England.

Mr. C.R. Attlee, Premier of Great Britain in 1947, on p. 186 in his book, *As it Happened*, had acknowledged his gratitude to Pt. Jawaharlal Nehru for his "high statesmanship whereby in respect of India, the British Monarch was recognised as Head of the Commonwealth. He (Pt. Nehru) had to face the critics in his own rank who had strong theoretical views on independence and republicanism."

It showed, how India had, under the Prime Ministership of Pt. Jawaharlal Nehru, integrated herself with the erstwhile coloniser, the imperialist Great Britain.

30

After the Transfer of Power

The National Planning Commission set up in March 1950 under the chairmanship of Prime Minister, Pt. Jawaharlal Nehru, had drafted India's First Five Year Plan 1951-56 for the country's reconstruction. Its declared goal was to restore more or less the pre-war availability of consumer goods taking into consideration the increase in the population.The Plan was to improve agricultural production and to get over the stagnation in the agricultural sector aggravated by the Partition of the country. The topmost priority was, therefore, given to irrigation, fertilisers, provision of technical knowledge and equipment for improving efficiency. The Plan, being primarily an agricultural plan, was, therefore, not a plan for the industrialisation of the country. There was no attempt to build a sizeable base for heavy industry which might at least lead the country to rapid industrialisation after five years. There was provision for the expansion of light and consumer goods but the rate of development was so slow that it was only in 1955 that the pre-war amount of essential consumer goods could be available to the people. The country's dependence on foreign industries—a backward feature of the economy, was to remain undisturbed. Even after five years, the country would be importing 3 million tons of foodgrains providing a consumption level of 14.5 ounces per adult per day. There was no provision for land reforms that could have triggered the expansion of both the demand and supply position in the rural areas.

The Eastern Economist had commented thus: "The pressure of population and poverty on the land cannot be reduced significantly by agricultural measures being conceived. The attack on rural poverty should be made, paradoxically by giving industry, and not agriculture, a prominent place. It is a profound error to take away the dynamic element from industry in Indian planning, for the net effect would, then, be to abolish a high rate of economic progress which is the prime purpose of the Plan."

"That we should be thinking of producing only 4,500 million yards of cloth in textile mills after 5 years, when we produced 4,800 million yards in 1943-44, is an example of economic myopia which can hardly be excused."The situation with regard to the sources of financing was seen to be uncertain and depressing and that meant low targets set in the Plan.

In spite of such an ill-devised and inexpertly prepared First Five Year Plan, Prime Minister Pt. Nehru thought in a big way as would be evident from what he had written [as follows] in a letter to the Chief Ministers after his return from China in 1954.

> "Many countries today are planning their development and seeking to make rapid progress. We have to keep pace with others and even try to go ahead of them. Ultimately every country will be judged by the results it shows in human well-being and national progress. Every other consideration will be secondary". "...We are not going to have a hundred years in order to make good. [with Western countries] Our problems, therefore, are essentially similar to those of other under-developed countries in Asia. It was for this reason that I was particularly interested in what was happening in China and I said that the most exciting countries for me today were India and China. We differ, of course, in our political and economic structures, yet the problems we face are essentially the same. The future will show which country and which structure of government yields greater results in every way."
> *[From a letter to The Chief Ministers, November 15, 1954]*

There was another comment on India's First Five Year Plan in *The Eastern Economist*: "Accepting defeat on resources, the rate of economic progress stipulated in the Plan is designed only to restore the pre-war availability of essential consumer goods by the end of 1955-56. This Plan had been made realistic by accepting the impossibility of large-scale planning without large domestic capital resources."

At this difficult economic and financial situation faced by India, the USA's financial and military resources were totally devoted to the reconstruction of the West European countries and Japan, devastated by the Second World War and save them from Communism which was knocking at their doors. The USA, therefore, could not afford to extend the necessary financial assistance to India in spite of all the overt and covert efforts of the Prime Minister Pt. Jawaharlal Nehru.

One wonders as to how the author of a number of chapters on Marxism and the titanic Five Year Plans of the then Soviet Union in his *Glimpses of World History*, could have approved of such a paltry and inconsequential Five Year Plan for his own country. A few lines on the Five Year Plans of the Soviet Union written by Pt. Jawaharlal Nehru in his book would show how he viewed the Soviet Planning.

> The Soviet Government looked far ahead and decided to concentrate on heavy industries in the Five Year Plans. In this way the foundations of industrialism would be firmly laid, and it would be easy to have the light industries afterwards. The heavy industries would also make Russia less dependent on foreign countries for machinery.
>
> Many prominent Bolsheviks thought that the strain and suffering caused by the agricultural programme were too great and there should be a relaxation. But not so Stalin. Grimly and silently he held on. He was no talker; he hardly spoke in public. He seemed to be the iron image of an inevitable fate going ahead to the predestined goal. And something of his courage and determination spread among the Communist Party's members and other workers in Russia.
>
> That the Five Year Plans had completely changed the face of Russia. From a feudal country, it had suddenly become an advanced industrial country. There had been an amazing cultural advance, and in the social services. The system of social health and accident insurance were the most inclusive and advanced in the world. In spite of privation and want, the terrible fear of unemployment and starvation which hung over workers in other countries, had gone. There had been a new sense of economic security among the people.
>
> "It had never happened yet in the world", J.V. Stalin pointed out, "that a huge backward agrarian land should be turned into an industrial country without plundering colonies, without robbing

> foreign countries or without big loans and long-term credit from the outside" ... "we have been able to organise the industrialisation of our country with our own forces." [*Glimpses of World History* by Pt. Jawaharlal Nehru, pp. 885-887]

Fortunately for India, Mr. M.N.V. Novikov, the then Russian Ambassador in India declared that the Soviet Union was prepared to supply all capital equipment and machinery and technical assistance to India on payment of Indian currency or against Indian goods. He had also pleaded for the strengthening of the trade relations between the two countries. Besides the Soviet Union, some other communist countries such as Czechoslovakia and Hungary in Eastern Europe also expressed their readiness to supply India her needs for her development programme.

But India could not accept any assistance from the then Soviet Union. She [India] feared any tilt towards the Soviet Union could have not only given a stimulus to Communism in India but would have also been a reason to antagonise the USA. India was totally against having any sort of alliance with the then Soviet Union, and in private assured the USA that she (India) would side with the USA in case there was a war between her (USA) and the Soviet Union.

Pt. Jawaharlal Nehru, in a letter to the Chief Ministers on July 15,1950 had warned and then expressed his views: "We face today a vast and powerful Soviet group of nations which tends to become a monolithic bloc, not only pursuing a similar internal economic policy but a common foreign policy. That policy is an expansionist one and, thus, there is a tendency for it to come into conflict with others. It is expansionist not only in the normal political sense but also in encouraging internal trouble in other countries. That internal trouble would not go far, if economic conditions were more or less satisfactory. We do not like this expansionist policy, external or internal. At the same time, we realise that there are certain factors which help it and unless those internal factors are changed, we cannot effectively meet that challenge." [*Selected Works of Jawaharlal Nehru*, Vol. 14, April 8 to July 1950, p. 492]

Earlier on February 8, 1950, Pt. Jawaharlal Nehru had also

written in a confidential note: "If there is a world war, there is no possibility of India lining up with the Soviet Union, whatever else she may do. It is obvious that our relations with the United Kingdom (India's former conquerer and subjugator) in political and economic matters are far more close than with the Soviet Union, nor is it likely that they will develop to any great extent for obvious reasons." [A.G. Noorani's article in *Frontline*, November 9, 2001, p. 77]

In the above issue of *Frontline* on page 76 in Noorani's article, there is something that is surprising: "He [kux] has overlooked the archival material published by Professor M.S. Venkataramani in *Frontline*, April 9 and 23 and May 7 and 21, 1999 which revealed how, in 1948, bypassing the Indian Ambassador, Nehru not only sought arms but a long-term military collaboration between the USA and India, that is a military alliance." [Note by Mr. Pai, Principal Private Secretary of Pt. Jawaharlal Nehru on his [Pt. Jawaharlal Nehru] remarks in his talks with Loy Henderson, USA's then Ambassador on February 8, 1950, *Jawaharlal Nehru Collection,* Vol. 13]

Concept of Mixed Economy

Realising the financial weakness as well as the lack of technological capabilities of the Indian industrialists such as the Tatas and Birlas, Pt. Nehru had devised the concept of 'Mixed Economy'. Under this concept, the State undertook the task of setting up the heavy and the large-scale industries. The economy was divided into the Public Sector and the Private Sector. Heavy industries relating to the steel, electronics, petroleum, chemical, heavy engineering such as the Bhilai Steel Plant, Bokaro Steel Factory, Gujarat Refinery, Bharat Heavy Electricals, etc. were set up in the Public Sector, mostly with the financial and technical help of the Soviet Union. Pt. Nehru's views of the Soviet Union had changed after Stalin's death and when she, led by Nikita Khrushchev, had gradually started transferring the Soviet economy from the socialist to the capitalist mode of production. By this time, the Indian communists too had started supporting some of Pt. Nehru's policies. In the meantime, the Soviet Union's relations with China had soured due to the ideological differences and she had become more and more friendly with India and began helping India in her economic development. Many of the heavy industrial projects were set up with the massive help of the then Soviet Union.

The Private Sector moved into the consumer goods and light industries, the machinery for which was provided by the country's steel and engineering mills in the Public Sector at much lower costs than would have been provided by the foreign countries.

Pt. Nehru took no interest in the school education of the children of the millions of poor people whose education continued to be disregarded. The children of the upper-dogs were able to get quality education in the costly private schools such as Sanawar School, Sanawar (Himachal Pradesh) and elsewhere. With a view to providing well-trained managerial, technological and engineering personnel to the Private and the Public Sectors, Pt. Nehru had set up a number of Indian Institutes of Technology and Management in the country.

In spite of the emphasis on the improvement and development of agriculture in her First Five Year Plan, India could not substantially increase her food production. She had to feed her people through heavy food imports under PL 480 from the USA. Similarly, the scale of development in the industrial sector, despite appreciable help from the Soviet Union, remained inconsiderable as compared to the impressive advancements made by Communist China as well as in an earlier period by Communist Russia under J.V. Stalin.

China, under the leadership of Mao Tse Tung, had, within approximately ten years, made remarkable strides in reconstructing her economy and raising the standard of living of her people and, thus, had set an example. The development had the potentiality of persuading the people of the Southeast Asian countries to follow the path of Communist China. In Indonesia, there was already one of the largest Communist Parties of the world. Powerful communist insurgencies were going on in Malaysia and Burma. The Viet Cong Communists of Ho Chi Minh of Indo-China were waging a relentless war against the colonial power of France and her local so-called democratic regime. Some other small countries such as

Laos and Cambodia were leaning towards China. It was a worrying situation for the USA. Mr. J.F. Kennedy, then an influential leader in the US Senate felt prompted to stop this drift against the democratic world and thought of strengthening India's development efforts. The result was a 'Conference on India and the United States' convoked at Washington DC on May 4, 1959.

Conference on India and the United States in 1959—J.F. Kennedy's Speech

Pointing out the struggle and the opportunity to demonstrate whose way of life is better, Mr. J.F. Kennedy made a strong plea at the Conference, to chalk out a long-range programme of long-term loans to India to overtake the challenge of Communist China. The following is a part version of Mr. Kennedy's speech. [A copy of the speech exists in the Senate Speech file of the John F. Kennedy Pre-Presidential Papers at the John F. Kennedy Library, USA.]

Speech Titled: India and China

"No struggle in the world today deserves more of our time and attention than which now grips the attention of all Asia. I am not referring to the unhappy tide of events in Tibet, where the world is being shown once again, that man's eternal desire to be free, can never be suppressed. Nor am I referring to the intermittent hostilities that endanger the Formosan Strait, or the truce lines in Korea and Indochina. I am referring to another struggle equally fierce but less obvious—less in the headlines but far more significant in the long run".

And that is the struggle between India and China for leadership of the East, for the respect of all Asia, for the opportunity to demonstrate whose way of life is better.

The battle may be more subtle than loud—it may not even be admitted by either side—but it is a very real battle nonetheless. For it is these two countries that have the greatest magnetic attraction to the uncommitted and underdeveloped world. It is these two countries which offer a potential route of transition from economic stagnation to economic growth. India follows a route in keeping with human dignity and individual freedom, with only haphazard assistance from this country. Red China represents the route of regimented controls and ruthless denial of human rights, with considerable aid from the USSR.

It should be obvious that the outcome of this competition will vitally affect the security and standing of this nation. But do we fully realise how it is coming out? Both China and India began their development efforts at about the same time—1950. They started with similar economic structures, similar standards of living and similar problems of skilled labour and natural resources. Actually India had some advantages—in transportation and trained personnel, for example.

But the harsh facts of the matter are that in the last decade China has surged ahead of India in most sectors of its economy. Its gross national output has expanded about three times as fast. In terms of industrial capacity, investment, education and even household consumption, China has slowly pulled up and now moved ahead. Its food production has nearly doubled, while India's has increased by less than 50 per cent. By the most authoritative estimates, at present levels of agricultural growth, India will have by 1965 a food production deficit of over 25 million tons—a gap which cannot be filled by any foreign aid or domestic rationing programme.

In steel production, China has moved from a position of inferiority to marked superiority. In 1950 China produced as much steel as Great Britain did in 1880. By 1958 China had moved to a point of productive superiority in steel to modern Great Britain today—and is making equal growth in coal and other major ingredients of national strength. Chou En-lai declared at the Party Congress this month: "It took us only six years to achieve in steel production what took Britain more than 50 years".

Since 1952 China has tripled the number of engineers and technicians in its industries and added four million workers to its skilled labour force.

Last year, China's rate of economic growth was at least three times as high as India's. Perhaps her official figures which claim to have doubled both agricultural and steel production may be discounted—but the fact remains that they are based on a hard record of fact compared to the sagging performance in India—and this is the record which has great appeal to those nations, uncertain of which route they should follow.

Within the last year the Chinese have produced their first automobile. Within the next year they may have launched their first earth satellite. Even more seriously, they may well begin to take their place among the select company of nuclear powers. And perhaps equally significant for the future is the fact that China has become a major trading nation not only in Southeast Asia, where she is gradually supplanting Japan, but also in the growing trade movements to Europe and Africa. Indian primary products such as manganese ore and oil seeds, for example. now suffer heavily as a result of China's price competition. Red China is now able to repay its loans from the communist bloc, while India is not only in need of considerable further assistance, but has been forced to drastically reduce its foreign exchange reserves to meet its investment gap.

For the first time in modern history, a government appears to have found a way–however brutal its human defects¬which appears to solve the problems of large peasant under-employed and labour surplus. The mobilisation of the unemployed mass of Chinese rural workers through economic communes, cottage industry, small pig-iron schemes and all the rest is an achievement whose political and intellectual impact in less developed areas is bound to be immense.

For, the ambitious goals and growth of both the Russians and Chinese are major political influences throughout the newly awakened world. The sturdy confidence of the Red Chinese is measured against the uncertainties of the Indian Government. The Chinese leader, moreover, boasts that within the next year China will make still further leaps into the future. He promises that the total value of agricultural and industrial output will rise by as much as 40 per cent in one year. He hopes, for example, to raise coal output by 110 million tons in 1959 alone.

Even if these hopes cannot be fulfilled, in India—by contrast—targets are wavering. Hopes are set upon maintaining a real rate of growth of only 2 to 3 per cent. This year the Indian population will rise. Increased agricultural output may not even feed the nearly 8 million new mouths of India's exploding population this year. It is in this setting that we consider this challenge—not by playing down and depreciating the very real physical achievements of China, but rather by determining to match these achievements in India by a real record of performance consistent with our ideals and democratic methods.

For the struggle is not over and the potentialities for gain in India are still great. In the Chinese language, the word "crisis" is composed of two characters—one representing danger, and one representing opportunity. The danger now is clear. But let us also make the most of our opportunities. For if they are lost now, they may never come again.

So let there be no mistake about the nature of the crisis, both the danger and the opportunity. And let there be no mistake about the urgency of our participation in this struggle. It is not enough that we participate for temporary relief. We must be willing to join with other Western nations in a serious long-range programme of long-term loans, backed up by technical and agricultural assistance designed to enable India to overtake the challenge of Communist China. The tool for this programme can well be the Development Loan Fund.I have joined with Senator Fulbright in proposing that the operations of the Development Loan Fund be stabilised and its scale increased by placing it on a 5-year basis with authority to loan up to $1.5 billion a year.

"This is the critical year for India when the Second Five Year Plan will prove to be either fruitful or futile. This is also the year when the Third Plan beginning in 1961 will be designed. This is the year, in short, when India must appraise her future and her relations with the rest of the world."

500 Million Dollar Military Package Planned

The J.F. Kennedy administration had also planned a 500 million dollar military package for India including help to increase arms production and creation of six mountain divisions. This had been decided following intense negotiations between New Delhi and Washington.

But this planned military package as well as J.F. Kennedy's previous proposal to create the Development Loan Fund, made at the Conference on India and the United States, could not fructify due to the assassination of President Kennedy. President Lyndon Johnson, his successor, neither followed the proposal for the military aid package nor the one concerning the Development Loan Fund.

India's faulty military policy decision of forward deployment of Indian troops on the India-China border and helping the Dalai Lama faction of Tibetans to free Tibet from the Chinese occupation and, later on, giving asylum to the Dalai Lama in 1959 were some of the reasons which resulted in the India-China War in 1962.

During the India-China War in 1962, Prime Minister Pt. Nehru had turned to President Kennedy for urgent military support. He had written two secret letters within a few hours of each other on November 19, 1962 for the US air force to defend India from China. But before the President could act, the Chinese announced their decision to make a unilateral withdrawal from the Indian territory.

Seeking military aid from the US even in the face of advancing Chinese troops, was a highly risky proposition. Had the Chinese not made the unilateral announcement to withdraw and the US air force had stepped in to defend the Indian territory, there might have been the Korean war-like situation, resulting in a huge devastation and thousands of innocent deaths. Was it an appropriate decision, especially keeping in view the reluctance felt by B.K. Nehru, a cousin of the Prime Minister and then India's Ambassador to the US, to deliver the letters to the US President? These letters had remained a secret till the veteran journalist the late Inder Malhotra got them published in *The Indian Express* in November, 2010 after obtaining the same from the J.F. Kennedy Library, USA.

There were certain laws such as the law of Sedition [Section 124A of the Indian Penal Code] which it was expected, Prime Minister Pt. Jawaharlal Nehru would either abrogate or suitably amend. The repeal of Section 124-A was one of the Eleven Points of Mahatma Gandhi and Pt. Jawaharlal Nehru [Pt. Nehru was then the President of the Congress], for the acceptance of which, the civil disobedience movement of 1930 had been launched.

'Junk Sedition Law'. It leads itself to easy abuse,' were the captions of an editorial of *The Times of India*, a leading daily of the country. The editorial [dated February 18, 2016] stated: "India's archaic sedition law—which Mahatma Gandhi had described as "prince among political sections of the Indian Penal Code, designed to suppress the liberty of the citizen"—unfortunately remained on its statute books even a century later.' 'Such anti-democratic laws must be scrapped forthwith. It was high time free India rid itself of this relic of British colonialism".

Regretfully, this as well as some other vestiges of the colonial period, such as the law of contempt, had not been dispensed with by Pt. Nehru during his 17-year long Prime Ministership. Rather a draconian and obnoxious (as described by an Ex-Home Minister of free India) Armed Forces Special Powers Act [AFSPA] was enacted in 1958 by him.

In spite of the three Five Year Plans [1951-56, 1956-61, 1961-1966] drafted and executed under the guidance and supervision of Prime Minister Pt. Jawaharlal Nehru, the food situation in the country remained very gloomy. The shortfall in food production was expected to be seven to eight million tonnes in 1965-66, then Food Minister Mr. C. Subramanian revealed in the Lok Sabha on December 1, 1965. He hoped that some stable arrangements for the supply of PL 480 wheat from the USA would have to be made. Due to the difficult foreign exchange situation, it would not be possible to import food from any other country than America. *[The Hindu,* December 2, 1965].

The statement of the country's Food Minister showed what a fiasco India's planned development was! Yet India didn't learn any lesson from the Soviet planning or from China's planning: "Last year China's rate of growth was at least three times as high as of India", the then US Senator and the future US President, J.F. Kennedy had revealed in his May 4, 1959 speech. China had made grand strides in almost all fields of development including the production of food-grains within ten years of her liberation in 1948.

Mr. Felix Green, a renowned American author on a visit to India, had pertinently asked Pt. Nehru as to why he did not make use of Indian millionaires' and billionaires' huge wealth for the well-being of India's poor millions? Pt. Nehru's reply was: "It would mean struggle and even violence". Pt. Nehru was afraid of the struggle and the opposition from the vested interests and let the poor semi-starved multitudinous Indians suffer.

A democratically-elected government headed by Pt. Jawaharlal Nehru as its Prime Minister had been established in the country. By January 1950, India had got her Constitution. But the economy and, therefore, all levers of power and that means political power, remained under the control of the landlords and capitalists.

Prime Minister Pt. Jawaharlal Nehru, like a true social democrat and a bourgeois leader did often talk of Socialism and other Marxist phrases but took care to appoint all his Finance Ministers from Sir Shanmukham Chetty, T.T. Krishnamchari, C.D. Deshmukh to Morarji Desai, etc, who enjoyed the trust of the Indian bourgeoisie as well as of the International Monetary Fund [IMF] and the World Bank and of the US leadership. Prime Minister Pt. Jawaharlal Nehru was ingenious enough to understand that in the post-Second World War international political situation, it was difficult for a third world ruler to survive without having the goodwill of the newly emerged hegemonic imperialist American superpower.

31

Salient Features of Bhagat Singh's Ideology

- Revolution is Law; Revolution is order; and Revolution is the Truth. [Bhagat Singh in the Manifesto of The Hindustan Socialist Republican Association]
- The youths of our nation have realised this truth. They have learnt painfully the lesson that without revolution, there is no possibility of enthroning order, law and love, in place of chaos and legal vandalism and hatred which are reigning supreme today. [Ibid]
- Revolution is a phenomenon which nature loves and without which there can be no progress either in nature or in human affairs. [Ibid]
- Revolution is not a philosophy of despair or a creed of desperadoes. [Ibid]
- Revolution may be anti-god but is certainly not anti-man. It is a vital living force which is indicative of eternal conflict between the old and the new, between life and living death, between light and darkness. [Ibid]
- There is no concord, no symphony, no rhythm without revolution. [Ibid]
- The music of the spheres of which poets have sung, would remain an unreality, if a ceaseless revolution were to be eliminated from the space. [Ibid]
- Revolution is certainly not an unthinking brutal campaign of murder and incendiarism; it is not a few bombs thrown here and a few shots fired there; neither is it a movement to destroy all the remnants of civilisation and blow to pieces time-honoured principles of justice and equality. [Ibid]

- Human nature, with all its prejudices and conservatism, has a sort of instinctive dread of revolution. Upheavals have always been a terror to holders of power and privilege. [Ibid]
- The spirit of revolution should always permeate the soul of humanity so that the reactionary forces may not accumulate [strength] to check its eternal onward march. [Ibid]
- The old order should change, always and ever, yielding place to new, so that one "good" order may not corrupt the world. It is in this sense that we raise the shout, "Long Live The Revolution" [On the Slogan of Long Live the Revolution-Edit in the *Modern Review*].
- The sense in which the word 'Revolution' is used in that phrase [Long Live the Revolution] is the spirit, the longing to change for the better. [Bhagat Singh-Rejoinder to the Edit in the *Modern Review].*
- One should not interpret the word "Revolution" in its literal sense. Various meanings and significances are attributed to this word, according to the interests of those who use or misuse it. For the established agencies of exploitation it conjures up a feeling of blood-stained horror. To the revolutionaries it is a sacred phrase. [On the Slogan of 'Long Live the Revolution']
- By revolution we mean that the present order of things, which is based on manifest injustice must change. Producers or labourers, in spite of being the most necessary element of society, are robbed by their exploiters, of the fruits of their labour, and deprived of their elementary rights. The peasant who grows corn for all, starves with his family; the weaver who supplies the world market with textile fabrics, has not enough to cover his own and his children's bodies; masons, smiths and carpenters who raise magnificent palaces, live like pariahs in the slums. The capitalists and exploiters, the parasites of society squander millions on their whims. These terrible inequalities and forced disparity of chances are bound to lead to chaos. [Statement in the Sessions Court].
- By revolution, we mean the ultimate establishment of an order

of society in which sovereignty of the proletariat should be recognised and a world federation should redeem humanity from the bondage of capitalism and misery of imperial wars. [Ibid]

- Revolution is an inalienable right of mankind. [Ibid]
- The revolutionaries believe that deliverance of their country will come through revolution. The revolution, they are constantly working and hoping for, will not only express itself in the form of an armed conflict between the foreign government and its supporters and the people, it will also usher in a new social order. [*The Philosophy of the Bomb*].
- The revolution will ring the death knell of capitalism and class distinctions and privileges. It will bring joy and prosperity to the starving millions, who are seething today under the terrible yoke of both foreign and Indian exploitation. It will bring the nation into its own. It will give birth to a new state, a new social order. Above all, it will establish the Dictatorship of the Proletariat and will forever banish social parasites from the seat of political power. [Ibid]
- The political revolution does not mean the transfer of the state [or more crudely, the power] from the hands of the British to the Indians, but to those Indians who are at one with us as to the final goal, or to be more precise, the power to be transferred to the revolutionary Party through popular support. After that, to proceed in right earnest is to organise the reconstruction of the whole society on the Socialist basis. If you do not mean this revolution, then please have mercy. Stop shouting 'Long Live The Revolution'. The term revolution is so sacred, at least to us, that it cannot be so lightly used or misused. [Bhagat Singh in 'An Address to the Young Political Workers']
- We want a Socialist revolution, the indispensable preliminary to which is the political power. That is what we want. [Ibid].
- Revolution did not necessarily involve sanguinary strife. It was not a cult of bomb and pistol. They may sometimes be mere means for its achievement. Undoubtedly, they play a prominent

part in some movements, but they do not—for that very reason—become one and the same thing. A rebellion is not a revolution. It may ultimately lead to that end. [Rejoinder to an Edit in the *Modern Review*]

- "The sword of revolution is sharpened on the whetting-stone of ideas". [Bhagat Singh in 'Statement Before the Lahore High Court Bench'.]
- You cry 'Long Live the Revolution'. Let me assume that you really mean it. According to our statement in the Assesmbly Bomb Case, Revolution means the complete overthrow of the existing social order and its replacement with the Socialist Order. For that purpose our immediate aim is the achievement of power. As a matter of fact, the state, the government machinery is just a weapon in the hands of the ruling class to further and safeguard its interest. We want to snatch and handle it to use it for the consummation of our ideal, that is, social reconstruction on new that is Marxist basis. For this purpose we are fighting to handle the government machinery. All along we have to educate the masses and to create a favourable atmosphere for our social programme. It is in struggles that we can best train and educate them. ['An Address to the Young Political Workers']
- You [The Young Political Workers] must know that revolution means action. It means a change brought about deliberately by an organised and systematic work, as opposed to sudden and unorganised or spontaneous change or breakdown. ['An Address to the Young Political Workers']
- As regards the methods, peaceful or otherwise to be adopted for the consummation of the revolutionary ideal, let us declare that the choice rests with those who hold power. Revolutionaries, by virtue of their altruistic principles, are lovers of peace—a genuine and permanent peace based on justice and equality, not the illusory peace resulting from cowardice and maintained at the point of bayonets. If the revolutionaries take to bombs and pistols, it is only as a measure of terrible necessity, as a last recourse. [Statement of the Undefended Accused]

- The revolutionary armies shall march to other lands not to rule down from their thrones but stop their blood-sucking exploitation and thus liberate the toiling masses. But, there shall not be the primitive national or racial hatred to goad our men to fight. [Bhagat Singh in 'Introduction to Dreamland']
- Compromises are dreaded because the conservatives try to disband the revolutionary forces after the compromise. But able and bold revolutionary leaders can save the movement from such pitfalls. We must be very careful at such junctures to avoid any sort of confusion of the real issues, especially, the goal. The British Labour leaders betrayed their real struggle and have been reduced to mere hypocrite imperialists. In my opinion the diehard conservatives are better to us than these polished imperialist Labour leaders. About the tactics and strategy one should study the life-work of Lenin. His definite views on the subject of compromise will be found in "Left Wing Communism." ['An Address to the Young Political Workers']
- For us, compromise never means surrender, but a step forward and some rest. That is all and nothing else. [Ibid]
- If you [The Young Political Workers] say that you will approach the peasants and labourers to enlist their active support, let me tell you that they are not going to be fooled by any sentimental talk. They ask you quite candidly what they are going to gain by your revolution for which you demand their sacrifice. ['An Address to the Young Political Workers']
- What difference does it make to them [labourers and peasants] whether Lord Reading is the head of the Indian Government or Sir Purshotamdas Thakurdas? What difference will there be for a peasant if Sir Tej Bahadur Sapru replaces Lord Irwin! It is useless to appeal to his [peasant or labourer] national sentiment. You can not use him for your purpose; you will have to mean seriously and make him understand that the revolution is going to be for his good. The Revolution of the Proletariat and for the Proletariat. [Ibid]
- **A Remarkable Marxist Postulation**: The Party had formulated

a remarkable Marxist postulation that if today the present British Government was handed over to the Congress and the system of administration remained just the same, The Hindustan Socialist Republican Association would be as much against the Congress Rule as against the British Government at present. If during the regime of the Congress Government as described above, the British [Great Britain] Government would establish a parallel Government in India, based on socialist principles, the Party would help the British Government and not the Government of the Congress in the country. [*The Tribune*, April 11, 1931]

- The real revolutionary armies are in the villages and in factories—the peasantry and the labourers. But our bourgeois leaders do not and cannot dare to tackle them. The sleeping lion once awakened from its slumber will become irresistible even after the achievement of what our leaders aim at. [Ibid]
- They [The young men] have to awaken crores of slum-dwellers of the industrial areas and villagers living in worn-out cottages, so that we will be independent and the exploitation of man by man will become an impossibility. ['Message to the Punjab Students' Conference']
- And to prepare the masses and organise the forces for the revolution is a very difficult task. And that requires a very great sacrifice on the part of the revolutionary workers. It is beyond the power of any man to make a revolution. Neither can it be brought about on any appointed date. It is brought about by a special environment, social and economic. The function of an organised party is to use any such opportunity by these circumstances. [An Address to the Young Political Workers]
- Along with the advent of the 20th century, the British bureaucracy has adopted quite a new policy towards India. They are drawing our bourgeoisie and petty bourgeoisie into their fold by adopting the policy of concessions. Their cause is being made common. The progressive movement of British capital in India will inevitably lead to that end. In the very near future we will find that class and their great leaders having thrown

their lot with the foreign rulers. Some round-table conference or any such body will end in a compromise between the two. [*Manife*sto of the Naujawan Bharat Sabha]

- The position of the Indian proletariat is, today, extremely critical. It has a double danger to face. It has to bear the onslaught of foreign capital, on the one hand, and the treacherous attack of Indian capital, on the other. The latter is showing a progressive tendency to join forces with the former. [Manifesto of the HSRA].
- Indian capital is preparing to betray the masses into the hands of foreign capital and receive as a price of this betrayal, a small share in the government of the country. [Ibid]
- Non-violence may be a noble ideal, but is a thing of the morrow. We can, situated as we are, never hope to win our freedom by mere non-violence. The world is armed to the very teeth. And the world is too much with us. All talk of peace may be sincere, but is false ideology. What logic, we ask, is there in asking the country to traverse a non-violent path when the world atmosphere is surcharged with violence and exploitation of the weak? [Ibid]
- We believe in violence, not as an end itself but as a means to a noble end. And the votaries of non-violence, as also the advocates of caution and circumspection, will readily grant this much at least that we know how to suffer for and to act upto our convictions. Shall we here recount all those sacrifices which our comrades have offered at the altar of our common Mother? Many a heart-rending and soul-stirring scene has been enacted inside the four walls of His Majesty's prison. [Ibid]
- Force when aggressively applied is "violence" and is, therefore, morally unjustifiable, but when it is used in the furtherance of a legitimate cause, it has its moral justification. The elimination of force at all costs is Utopian, and the new movement which has arisen in the country, and of that dawn we have given a warning, is inspired by the ideal which guided Guru Gobind Singh and Shivaji, Kamal Pasha and Riza Khan, Washington

and Garibaldi, Lafayette and Lenin. ['Statement in the Sessions Court']

- If, however, it [warning] goes unheeded and the present system of government continues to be an impediment in the way of the natural forces that are swelling up, a grim struggle will ensure involving the overthrow of all obstacles, and the establishment of the 'Dictatorship of the Proletariat' to pave the way for the consummation of the ideal of revolution. [Ibid]
- We want to emphasise the lesson often repeated by history, that it is easy to kill individuals but you cannot kill ideas. Great empires crumbled while ideas survived. The Bourbons and Czars fell, while the revolution marched ahead triumphantly. [*To Make the Deaf Hear*]
- Destruction is not only essential but indispensable for construction. The revolutionaries have to adopt it as a necessary item of their programme... Lenin said to Gorky once that he could not bear music which upset his whole nervous system, and used to feel a desire to pat the heads of the artists. "But," added he, "this is not the time to pat the heads. The hands descend now to smash the skulls, though our ultimate aim is the elimination of all sorts of violence." This is truly how the revolutionaries feel when they have to resort to violent means as a terrible necessity. [Bhagat Singh in 'Introduction to Dreamland']
- The author [Ram Saran Das] suggests education as the only weapon to be employed. But, everybody can easily realise that the present government here, or, as a matter of fact, all the capitalist governments are not only going to help any such effort, but on the contrary, suppress it mercilessly. [Ibid]
- We must make it clear that revolution does not merely mean an upheaval or a sanguinary strife. Revolution necessarily implies the programme of systematic reconstruction of society on a new and better adapted basis, after complete destruction of the existing state of affairs [i.e. regime] [Ibid]
- We have been taken to task for a terroristic policy. Our answer is

that terrorism is never the object of revolutionaries, nor do they believe that terrorism alone can bring independence. No doubt, the revolutionaries think, and rightly, that it is only by resorting to terrorism alone that they can find a most effective means of retaliation. The British Government exists, because the British have been successful in terrorising the whole of India. How are we to meet this official terrorism? Only counter-terrorism on the part of revolutionaries can checkmate effectively this bureaucratic bullying. [Manifesto of the Hindustan Socialist Republican Association]

- It [terrorism] is a phase, a necessary, an inevitable phase of the revolution. Terrorism is not the complete revolution and the revolution is not complete without terrorism. This thesis can be supported by an analysis of any and every revolution in history. Terrorism instils fear in the hearts of the oppressors. It brings hope of revenge and redemption to the oppressed masses. It gives courage and self-confidence to the wavering. It shatters the spell of the superiority of the ruling class.. Here in India as in other countries in the past, terrorism will develop into the revolution and the revolution into independence, social, political and economic. [Ibid]
- A revolutionary believes in reason more than anything. It is to reason, and to reason alone, that he bows. No amount of abuse and condemnation, even if it emanates from the highest of the high can turn him from his set purpose. To think that a revolutionary will give up his ideas, if public support and appreciation is withdrawn from him, is the highest folly. Many a revolutionary has, ere, then or now, stepped on the scaffold and laid his life down for the cause, regardless of the curses that the constitutionalist agitators rained plentifully upon him. If you [Gandhiji] will have the revolutionaries suspend their activities, reason with them squarely. That is the one and the only way. For the rest let there be no doubt in anybody's mind. A revolutionary is the last person on earth to submit to bullying. [*The Philosophy of the Bomb*]

- In spite of all the denunciations and condemnations by their own kith and kin, and ruthless repression and persecution by the alien government, the party of young men will ever live to teach a lesson to the haughty rulers. They will be so bold as to cry even amidst the raging storm of opposition and repression, even on the scaffold: "Long Live the Revolution" [Bhagat Singh in 'Beware, Ye Bureaucracy']
- Let no one, in this blessed land of ours, run with the idea that the youths are irresponsible. They know where they stand. No one knows better than these youths, that their path is not strewn with roses. From time to time they have paid a fairly decent price, for their ideals. It does not, therefore, lie in the mouth of anybody to say that youthful impetuousity has feasted upon platitudes. [Bhagat Singh in Manifesto of 'The Hindustan Socialist Republican Association']
- And no one can do justice to anybody without taking his motive into consideration. If we ignore the motive, the biggest generals of the world will appear like ordinary murderers; revenue officers will look like thieves and cheats. Even judges will be accused of murder. This way, the entire social system and the civilisation will be reduced to murders, thefts and cheatings. If we ignore the motive, the government will have no right to expect sacrifices from its people and its officials. Ignore the motive and every religious preacher will be dubbed as a preacher of falsehoods, and every prophet will be charged of misguiding crores of simple and ignorant people. [Bhagat Singh; 'Statement Before the Lahore High Court Bench']
- If we set aside the motive, then Jesus Christ will appear to be a man responsible for creating disturbances, breaking peace and preaching revolt, and will be considered to be a "dangerous personality" in the language of the law. But we worship him. He commands great respect in our hearts and his image creates vibrations of spiritualism amongst us. Why? Because, the inspiration behind his actions was that of a high ideal. The rulers of that age could not recognise that high idealism. They

only saw his outward actions. Nineteen centuries have passed since then. Have we not progressed during this period? Shall we repeat that mistake again? If that be so, then we will have to admit that all the sacrifices of mankind and all the efforts of the great martyrs, were useless and it would appear, as if we are still at the same place where we stood twenty centuries ago. [Ibid]

- The end of law is not to abolish or restrain but to preserve and enlarge freedom. The legitimate power is required to govern by promulgated laws established for the common good alone and resting ultimately on the consent and the authority of the people, from which law no one is exempted—not even the legislators. [Statement of the Undefended Accused]
- The sanctity of law can be maintained only so long as it is the expression of the will of the people. When it becomes a mere instrument in the hands of an oppressing class, it loses its sanctity and significance, for the fundamental preliminary condition for administration of justice is the elimination of every interest. As soon as the law ceases to correspond to the popular social needs, it becomes the means for perpetration of injustice and tyranny. The maintaining of such a law is nothing but a hypocritical assertion of a special interest against the common interest [Ibid].
- The laws of the present government exist for the interest of the oppressing rulers, against the interest of our people, and as such, they have no moral binding whatsoever. It is, therefore, the incumbent duty of all Indians to defy and disobey these laws. The law courts, as part and parcel of the machinery of exploitation, cannot administer justice, especially in political cases where there is a clash between the interests of the government and the people. We know that these courts are nothing but the stages for the performance of the mockery of justice. [Ibid]
- We believe and do hereby declare that man being the source of all the authority, no individual or government can be entitled to any authority and unless and until it is directly derived from the people. [Ibid]

- Bhagat Singh did not believe in the existence of God. He was an atheist. He asked, if there is an almighty, omnipresent,omniscient and omnipotent God, who created the earth or world, please let me know why did He [God] create it? This world of woes and miseries, a veritable, external combination of numberless tragedies: not a single soul being perfectly satisfied. ['Why I Am An Atheist']
- Why does He [God] not infuse the altruistic enthusiasm in the hearts of all capitalists to forego their rights of personal possessions of the means of production and thus redeem the whole labouring community—nay the whole human society from the bondage of capitalism. [Ibid]
- Bhagat Singh asked why omnipotent God does not stop everyman when he is committing any sin or offence? He [God] can do it quite easily. Why did He[God] not kill war lords or kill the fury of war in them and thus avoid the catastrophe hurled down on the head of humanity by the Great War? [Ibid]
- Religious superstitions and bigotry are a great hindrance in progress. They have proved an obstacle in our way and we must do away with them. The thing that cannot bear free thought must perish. [Manifesto of the Naujawan Bharat Sabha].
- As regards the moral status of love, I may say that it in itself is nothing, but passion, not an animal passion but a human one, and very sweet too. Love in itself can never be an animal passion. Love always elevates the character of man. It never lowers him, provided love be love. ['Letter to Sukhdev']
- The true love cannot be created. It comes of its own accord, nobody can say when. It is but natural. [Ibid]
- Charity cannot solve the problems of hunger and disease in India and for that matter in any country. [Ibid]
- Charity: [From the pages of 'Bhagat Singh's Jail Diary'] Philanthropy has been fashionable in every age. Charity takes the insurrectionary edge off of poverty. Therefore, the philanthropic rich man is a benefactor to his fellow magnates, and is made to feel their gratitude. He [Jesus] denied the legitimacy of alms-

giving as a plaster for the deep-lying sore in social tissue... Philanthropy as a substitute for justice, he [Jesus] would have none of it..

- Charity is twice cursed. It hardens him that gives and softens him that takes. It does more harm to the poor than exploitation, because it makes them willing to be exploited. It breeds slavishness which is moral suicide. The only thing, Jesus would permit, a swollen fortune to do, was to give itself to revolutionary propaganda, in order that swollen fortunes might be, forever after, impossible...[*Bouck White*, Clergyman, born 1874, USA] [Bhagat Singh's Jail Diary]
- To stop our people fighting each other, we have to arouse class consciousness among them. The poor workers and the peasants and those belonging to the middle classes should be told that their real enemy being the capitalists (and landlords) they should beware of them. They should not be helped. All the poor people in the world, irrespective of their religion, race or nation, have the same rights. It is in their interest that they forget their distinctions of religion, race and nation and unite and try to snatch power from the (capitalists) rulers. They would not lose anything but their chains in such struggles. They will be economically well off and free. [Bhagat Singh on 'Communal Problem and its Solution']
- The young men, in whose hands the reins of this country are going to be given, are being educated in an unsatisfactory manner. What could be the result of such endeavours is not difficult to guess. We agree that the main concern of a student is to pursue his studies and he should devote all his time and energy to them. But shouldn't the development of ability to understand the conditions of our country and the ways and means to improve them be a part of his studies? If that is not there, then I consider that education (which, is being given) is simply useless. There is no fun of having it if it can equip us to be clerks only. What is the need of such education? [Bhagat Singh on 'Students and Politics']

- A student was reading a book, *Appeal to the Young by* Prince Kropotkin. A professor enquired as to what that book was? It seemed to have been the work of some Bengali. The boy replied: Prince Kropotkin is a famous name. He was an authority on Economics. It is necessary for every professor to be aware of this name. The boy, laughing at the 'ability' of his professor, also added: And he was a Russian gentleman. The word 'Russian' was like a thunderbolt and the professor said: "You are a Bolshevik because you are reading political books."
  What an able Professor he was! What can that poor student learn from him? [Bhagat Singh on 'Students and Politics']
- You (Scheduled Castes) are the real working class. Organise yourself. You lose nothing but your chains of slavery. Rise and revolt against the present order. The slow reforms will yield nothing. Bring about revolution through a social movement and gird your loins for political and economic revolution. You are the real support of this country. You are its power. O, sleeping lions, rise and blare the bugle of revolt! [Bhagat Singh on 'The Problem of Untouchability]
- This Association [The Hindustan Socialist Republican Association] [HSRA] stands for revolution in India in order to liberate her from foreign domination by means of organised armed rebellion .Open rebellion by a subject people must always, in the nature of things, be preceded by secret propaganda and secret preparations. [Manifesto of The Hindustan Socialist Republican Association]
- The future programme of preparing the masses will begin with the motto: "Revolution by the masses and for the masses." In other words, 'Swaraj' not only attained by the masses, but also for the masses, for the 90 per cent. [Manifesto of the Naujawan Bharat Sabha]
- To proceed systematically, what you need the most is a Party with workers of the type with clear-cut ideas and keen perception and ability of initiative and quick decision. The Party will have iron discipline. That will create a number of workers who will

be forced to lead an underground life. They should continue the work with the same zeal. And it is this group of workers that will produce worthy leaders for the real opportunity [An Address to the Young Political Workers].

- The Party requires workers who can be recruited only through the youth movement. Hence we find the youth movement as the starting point of our programme. The youth movement should organise study circles, class lectures and publication of leaflets, pamphlets, books and periodicals. This is the best recruiting and training ground for political workers [Ibid].
- Those young men who may have matured their ideas and may find themselves ready to devote their life to the cause, may be transferred to the Party. The Party workers should always guide and control the work of the youth movement as well. The Party should start with the work of mass propaganda [Ibid].
- And in order to create political consciousness, not only of national politics but class politics as well, the Party should organise a big publishing campaign. Subjects on all problems englightening the masses of the socialist theory should be within easy reach and distributed widely. The writing should be simple and clear. [Ibid]
- The military department of the Party should always keep ready all the war-material it can command for any emergency. It should back the political work of the Party. It cannot and should not work independently. [Ibid]
- If you start the work on these lines, you will have to be very sober. The programme requires at least twenty years for its fulfilment. Cast aside the youthful dreams of a revolution within ten years or Gandhi's utopian promises of Swaraj in one year. It requires neither the emotion nor the death, but the life of constant struggle, suffering and sacrifice. Crush your individuality first. Shake off the dreams of personal comfort. Then start to work. No failure and betrayals shall dishearten you. No travails imposed upon you shall snuff out the revolutionary will in you. Through the ordeal of suffering and sacrifice you will come out

victorious. [Ibid]

- We want people who may be prepared to fight without hope, without fear and without hesitation, and who may be willing to die unhonoured, unwept and unsung. Without that spirit, we will not be able to fight the great twofold battle that lies before us, twofold because of the internal foe, on the one hand, and a foreign enemy, on the other. Our real battle is against our own disabilities which are exploited by the enemy and some of our own people for their selfish motives. [Manifesto of the Naujawan Bharat Sabha]
- Without going into details, we can safely say that to achieve our object, thousands of our most brilliant young men, like Russian youth, will have to spend their precious lives in villages and slums and make the people understand what the Indian revolution would really mean. They must be made to realise that the revolution which is to come, will mean more than a change of masters. [Ibid]
- They [young men] must organise themselves free from any influence and refuse to be exploited any more by the hypocrites and insincere people who have nothing in common with them and who always desert the cause at the critical juncture. In all seriousness and sincerity, let them make the triple motto of "service, suffering, sacrifice" their sole guide. This is not the work of a day or a year. Decades of matchless self-sacrifice will prepare the masses for the accomplishment of that great work and only the revolutionary young men will be able to do that. [Ibid]
- We take this opportunity to appeal to our countrymen –to the youth, to the workers and peasants, to the revolutionary intelligentsia—to come forward and join us in carrying aloft the banner of freedom. Let us establish a new order of society in which political and economic exploitation will be an impossibility. The sovereignty of the proletariat shall be recognised. We count the advent of such revolution. Long Live The Revolution. [*The Philosophy of the Bomb*]

- The days of capitalist and imperialist exploitation are numbered. The war neither began with us nor is it going to end with our lives. It is the inevitable consequence of the historic events and the existing environment. ['No Hanging, Please Shoot Us']
- Let us declare that the state of war does exist and shall exist so long as the Indian toiling masses and the natural resources are being exploited by a handful of parasites. They may be purely British capitalist or mixed British and Indian or even purely Indian. They may be carrying on their insidious exploitation through mixed or even on purely Indian bureaucratic apparatus...It shall be waged ever with new vigour, greater audacity and unflinching determination till the socialist republic is established and the present social order is completely replaced by a new social order, based on social prosperity and thus every sort of exploitation is ended and humanity is ushered into the era of genuine and permanent peace. [Bhagat Singh in 'No Hanging, Please Shoot Us']
- We believe that imperialism is nothing but a vast conspiracy organised with predatory motives. Imperialism is the last stage of development of insidious exploitation of man by man and of nation by nation. The imperialists, with a view to further their piratical designs, not only commit judicial murders through their law courts but also organise general massacres, devastations and other horrible crimes like war. They feel no hesitation in shooting down innocent and unarmed people who refuse to yield to their depredatory demands or to acquiesce in their ruinous and abominable designs. Under the garb of custodians of 'law and order', they break peace, create disorder, kill people and commit all conceivable crimes. [Statement of the Undefended Accused]
- Imperialist designs shall no more actuate our dreamland people to wage wars. There shall be no more war trophies. The revolutionary armies shall march to other lands not to rule or loot the people, but to pull the parasitic rulers down from their thrones and stop their blood-sucking exploitation and thus to

liberate the toiling masses. [Introduction to Ram Saran Das's Book *The Dreamland*]

- We believe all capitalist governments, and particularly this British Government thrust upon the helpless but unwilling Indian nation, to be no better than an organised gang of robbers, and a pack of exploiters equipped with all the means of carnage and devastation. In the name of 'law and order', they crush all those who dare to expose or oppose them. [Statement of the Undefended Accused]
- There is no crime that Britain has not committed in India. Deliberate misrule has reduced us to paupers, has "bled us white". As a race and a people we stand dishonoured and outraged. Do people still expect us to forget and forgive? We shall have our revenge—a people's righteous revenge on the tyrant. Let cowards fall back and cringe for compromise and peace. We ask not for mercy and we give no quarter. Ours is a war to the end—to Victory or Death. Long Live the Revolution [*The Philosophy of the Bomb*]

32

From Shaheed-e-Azam Bhagat Singh's Perspective

"What is freedom of expression? Without the freedom to offend, it ceases to exist". *–Anonymous*

"Speech is really free only when it hurts" *–Anonymous*

"The world owes much to rebels who would dare to argue in the face of Pontiff and insist that he is not infallible".

—Dr. Baba Saheb B.R. Ambedkar

"Dissent is the highest form of patriotism".*—Howard Zinn*

"Freedom is hammered out on the anvil of discussion, dissent and debate". *—Hubert H. Humphrey*

"There should be freedom for the thought we hate. Freedom of speech has no meaning if there is no freedom after speech."*–Sanjay Kishan Kaul*, then Chief Justice of the Madras High Court and now Honourable Judge of the Supreme Court of India

"Silence is complicity. Speak now or surrender your ground".

—Michelle Malkin

"Growth for the sake of growth is the ideology of the cancer cell".*—Edward Abbey*

"Agitate! Agitate! Ought to be the motto of every reformer. It is the opposite of stagnation: the one is life, the other death".

—Ernestine Rose. This is Shaheed-e-Azam Bhagat Singh's message.

Bhagat Singh

- Bhagat Singh had boundless and titanic intellectual and physical faculties which had not been duly realised and acknowledged.

His capacity to write his documents is being doubted. His available documents have been taken in casually. It is, therefore, no wonder that not only his political adversaries, even eminent historians called him a terrorist or revolutionary terrorist in their history books.

- Bhagat Singh was one of the rare Marxist philosophers, India had produced. He was just 20 years old when he had gone through the volumes of *Capital* by Karl Marx. Not many communists understood the essence of Marxism as he did. Only a few days before his execution, he had written his famous essay, 'An Address to the Young Political Workers' which is a guide on how to bring about revolution. According to Omesh Saigal, a former Chief Secretary of the Delhi Administration, who had also authored a book on Bhagat Singh, "Bhagat Singh has become the epitome of the fight for Socialism more than any person or a Party has. He was a visionary with a dream, the madness of a Spinoza, the halo of a superhuman".
- Many of Bhagat Singh's colleagues, after their release from prisons on the completion of their Jail terms, had joined the Communist Party instead of reviving their own Party (The Hindustan Socialist Republican Association). They, thus, not only let Bhagat Singh down but also abandoned the ideals for which the Hindustan Socialist Republican Association had been formed. The political views of his colleagues, such as Shiv Verma, Ajoy Ghosh and their assessment of Bhagat Singh's political thoughts reflected the ideology of the Communist Party they had joined after their release from the prisons. Bhagat Singh had never approved the policies of the Communist Party. During his two meetings with Comrade Sohan Singh Josh, Bhagat Singh had made his differences clear. Had he considered the then already in existence Communist Party qualified to bring about a Socialist Revolution, he in his 'An Address to the Young Political Workers', would not have written "What you need is a Party with workers [professional revolutionary workers] of the type discussed above..."

- Bhagat Singh wanted to completely smash and destroy the prevailing exploitative, oppressive, unjust bourgeois state machine and in its place, through a Socialist Revolution, establish a system based on Scientific Socialism.
- He had a firm belief that during the transitional period from Socialism to Communism, there would be a period of the Dictatorship of the Proletariat.
- For Bhagat Singh, the British capitalists were not the only sinners. He held the Indian capitalists equally responsible for the exploitation of the Indian masses as well as India's natural resources. In all his writings, he stressed on the two foes — the British Capital and the Indian Capital. He repeatedly emphasised the necessity of replacing the present colonial social order by a new social order based on the Scientific Socialist ideology.
- Bhagat Singh's foreboding had proved to be true when in 1947, the British bourgeoisie led by Vincent Attlee, then Prime Minister of Great Britain, had transferred, on a platter, power from the British Landlord-Capitalist class to their Indian collaborators representing the Indian Landlord-Capitalist class. India's multitudinous hoi-polloi have-nots did not gain anything while Bhagat Singh's Socialist Revolution had aimed at mainly benefiting them
- Bhagat Singh was not infallible. No one is. His and his party's decision to kill J.A. Scott that resulted in the killing of J.P. Saunders to avenge Lala Lajpat Rai and the nation's humiliation was a mild denouncement and a soft impeachment of the British imperialist rulers, for they [Scott and Saunders] were just like hired assassins. The real culprits were the British Imperialist rulers. The tragic incident of Lala Lajpat Rai's death should have motivated the leadership of The Hindustan Socialist Republican Association and its rank and file to have themselves spread into as many villages and industrial slums as possible, making the tin-sheds and mud-hut-hovels as their new abodes, educating the peasants and workers about what the

Socialist Revolution would mean to them and, thereby, making them battle-ready for the revolution. They would, of course, be doing it incognito. They were young and within the next twenty or thirty years, they would have educated and prepared a huge number of workers and peasants who would be politically class conscious professional revolutionaries and a part of the Hindustan Socialist Republican Army. A programme of action, on the lines given by Bhagat Singh in his pamphlet entitled, 'An Address to the Young Political Workers', would have served as a useful guide for action.

- Similarly offering themselves for arrest after the Assembly bomb explosions meant the end of any more actions. The two "actions" did arouse the revolutionary political consciousness of the people but there was no one left to channelise the same to bring about the actual revolution. Their execution and the long-term imprisonment of their comrades in Andamans and in the jails elsewhere had put an end to much of the revolutionary activity, resulting in the revolution bypassing India.
- Posing a pertinent question, Dr. Shalley K. Gupta, who had helped the author in proof reading and editing the draft of the book, had asked: Would Bhagat Singh have remained a believer in Socialist Revolution even after 1947, or would he have actually been accommodated in the ruling setup? If he had chosen either option, how successful would his leadership be?

The answer to the question could be found in Bhagat Singh's *Letter to the Governor of Punjab* written a day before his execution and in his article, *'An Address to the Young Political Workers'* as well as in many of his other documents.

In his letter to the Governor, Bhagat Singh stated that *"the state of war shall continue to exist so long as the Indian toiling masses and the country's resources are being exploited by the British (Foreign) and Indian capitalists and landlords. The war will continue till the present oppressive, unjust and exploitative social order is completely replaced by a new social order based on Scientific Socialism and the Dictatorship of the Proletariat."*

- Bhagat Singh had the potentialities of emerging as India's Lenin, Mao, Ho Chi Minh or Fidel Castro. This is corroborated by the assessment of his teacher, Professor Jayachandra Vidyalankar. The assessment of Bhagat Singh made by Professor Vidyalankar, with whom he had often discussed political matters, was probably the best, is reproduced:

  "The young man, [Bhagat Singh] who was suspected to be the murderer of Saunders could have easily committed, had he wished, many such actions by remaining underground, beyond the reach of the authorities, and that could have caused a sort of terror in the hearts of the enemies of the country and given solace and strength to the sufferers at their hands. I don't know, how far it was correct for such a young man to have got himself arrested for doing such a small job. [throwing bombs in the Assembly]. But as far as I am concerned, I wouldn't have been happy even seeing Bhagat Singh doing the former job—that is leading a band of some 10 to 20 guerrillas and doing daring deeds [to frighten the rulers and encouraging his countrymen]—*for I have always visualised a different Bhagat Singh. He had infinite potential to be one who could, after receiving proper education in warfare, lead, at an appropriate moment, the armies for the liberation of India and be an arbiter to decide the fate of the battles fought for changing her history. That Bhagat Singh had the capacity and capabilities to play such roles would not be known to the persons who are full of him only after seeing a small part played by him."*

Mahatma Gandhi

Mahatma Gandhi's personality as an icon from Bhagat Singh's perspective could be summed up as follows:

- Mahatma Gandhi was a friend, admirer and well wisher of the British Empire. He did not wish India to completely sever her relationship with Great Britain.
- On his return from South Africa in 1915, Mahatma Gandhi took up the task of raising recruits for the British Indian army to serve and save the Empire during the First World War.
- Disregarding his creed of non-violence, Mahatmaji implored the poor Indians to learn the use of arms and prove that they

were not cowardly and effeminate and assured them that was the straightest way to win 'Swaraj'. He had also offered to train them how to use the arms.

- In the drive to raise recruits, besides Mahatma Gandhi, other nationalist leaders such as Gopal Krishna Gokhale, Bal Gangadhar Tilak, Pt. Motilal Nehru and Sardar Vallabhbhai Patel had also campaigned for the enlistment of recruits for the British Indian army.
- The drive to raise the recruits was a counter-blow to the Ghadrites who were secretly endeavouring to arouse the Indian soldiers in the cantonments to rise in revolt against the British rulers.
- Mahatma Gandhi, Pt. Motilal Nehru, Pt. Jawaharlal Nehru, Sardar Vallabhbhai Patel and other such leaders remained oblivious to and gave the cold shoulder to the death sentences and life-long incarcerations awarded to thousands of Ghadrites by the British rulers.
- After the end of the First World War, there was no need to campaign for the recruits for the army. Now the British Empire faced the danger from the Ghadrites and revolutionaries. So Mahatma Gandhi set in motion his creed of non-violence as a counter measure against them. He forgot how he had implored the poor Indians to learn the use of arms to kill and get killed during the First World War.
- The non-cooperation and civil disobedience movements were meant to be safety-valves against the rising tide of revolutionary fervour and the revolutionaries' actions led by Bhagat Singh and his Party as well as the valorous Ghadrites.
- Mahatma Gandhi did not say a word in condolence on Jatindra Nath Das's martyrdom after his 63 days of hunger strike. He, however, drafted a resolution deploring the revolutionaries' attempt to blow up the Viceroy's Special and congratulating him (The Viceroy Lord Irwin) on his miraculous escape and got it passed at the Lahore Congress Session while Pt. Jawaharlal Nehru was the Congress President.

- In a letter to the then Viceroy of India after the Jallianwala Bagh Massacre, Mahatma Gandhi wrote that "I was not prepared to condemn Martial Law as such; I was unwilling to do anything calculated needlessly to irritate the local authority; and lastly I was not prepared to infer from Sir Michael O'Dwyer's reported severe administration during the peace period that Martial Law measures would be unduly hard."
- "Mahatma Gandhi also suggested to the Viceroy that a committee comprising both officials and non-officials may be appointed. It would calm the public mind to restore confidence [much shaken by the Jallianwala Massacre and other events in Punjab] in the good intentions of the government ..." –M.K. Gandhi [*CWMG*, Vol. 15, pp. 334-335]
- In a letter to Mr. V.S. Srinivasa Sastri on June 6, 1919, Mahatma Gandhi commented on the poet's letter [Rabindranath Tagore] to the Viceroy renouncing his Knighthood and expressed his disapproval. "The Punjab horrors have produced a burning letter from the poet. I personally think it is premature." –M.K. Gandhi [*CWMG*, Vol. 15, pp. 345-346]
- Mahatma Gandhi himself had been awarded by the British, a Boer Medal, a Zullu Medal besides the Kaiser-e-Hind Medal for his services to them. These, he did not renounce as a protest against the Jallianwala Massacre by the British imperialists as the poet Rabindranath Tagore had done.]
- Following the assassination of Sir Michael O'Dwyer at the hands of Udham Singh, Mahatma Gandhi told reporters: "The news of the death of Sir Michael O'Dwyer and the injuries to Lord Zetland, Lord Lamington and Sir Louis Dane, has caused me deep pain. I regard this act as one of insanity."
- When questioned by the President of the 'Disorders Inquiry Committee' on January 9, 1920 about the objects of the Rowlatt Bills, "if he [Mahatma Gandhi] had any doubts that the objects were to put down revolutionary and anarchical crimes."Mahatma Gandhi replied, "he had no doubt that the objects were laudable" [*CWMG*, Vol. 16, p. 378].

- After the execution of Bhagat Singh, his two revolutionary comrades and the killing of Chandra Shekhar Azad, Mahatma Gandhi and Pt. Jawaharlal Nehru were successful in their mission of thwarting the Socialist Revolution.
- The British were grateful to Mahatma Gandhi for saving them from the bloodshed [Read Revolution]. 'It was Mahatmaji's preaching of non-violence, more than any other single factor that had stood between India and bloodshed [Read Revolution] on a frightful scale according to the British politicians'.
- The British imperialists acknowledged and appreciated the valuable services rendered to the British Empire by Mahatma Gandhi when Ellen Wilkinson, then a Member of the British Parliament and later on, a Minister in Winston Churchill's Cabinet and C.R. Attlee's Cabinet, praised Mahatmaji, after her official visit to India in 1932, stating that 'he was the best policeman the British had in India'.
- The British handed over power to the leadership of the Indian National Congress and the Muslim League due to their fear of revolution and in order to thwart the same as well as due to the bankruptcy of their own financial resources and the paucity of their manpower. It is a myth that India got independence due to the civil disobedience and 'Satyagraha' movements.
- On socio-economic issues, Mahatma Gandhi had a regressive and feudal outlook. These are best detailed in Mahatma Gandhi's own book captioned 'Hind Swaraj'. Pt. Jawaharlal Nehru had described these unworkable and reactionary views in the chapter titled 'Paradoxes' on p. 515 of his *An Autobiography.*
- Mahatmaji's sage-like figure and his moral phrases had a rhetorical influence on the people, who bestowed on him the honorific title of 'Mahatma'. He was a par excellent politician.

Jawaharlal Nehru

Pt. Jawaharlal Nehru's personality as an icon from Bhagat Singh's prismo is summed up as follows: The views expressed may be read through the lens of Bhagat Singh:

- Pt. Jawaharlal Nehru was a social democrat, an astute and a mature bourgeois politician.
- He, like Mahatma Gandhi, was a staunch opponent of Communism, Socialist Revolution and the revolutionaries, not withstanding, his sometimes expressing soft verbiage for them.
- He, in his *An Autobiography* repeatedly referred to the revolutionaries as terrorists and revolutionary actions were dubbed as acts of terrorism.
- On p. 262 of his *An Autobiography*, damning the revolutionaries, after Chandra Shekhar Azad had met him at his residence at Allahabad in February 1931, Pt. Nehru stated "many of them, it seemed to me, have definitely the fascist mentality".
- Much of what Pt. Jawaharlal Nehru had professed about as well as had written against imperialism in general and British imperialism in particular, it seemed, was forgotten after he became Prime Minister.
- Practising Keynesianism, masking it 'Democratic Socialism' and using Marxian phrases in his writings, Pt. Jawaharlal Nehru had created an impression that he was a Socialist and even a Marxist.
- In 1931, after Pt. Jawaharlal Nehru's approval and endorsement of the Gandhi-Irwin Pact, the League Against Imperialism became exceedingly angry with him, and ex-communicated him with bell, book and candle by a resolution. Pt. Nehru had earlier attended its conference held at Brussels [Europe] in 1927 [*An Autobiography,* p. 164]. It may be added that Mr. Virendra Chattopadhya, an Indian [Mrs. Sarojini Naidu's brother] was one of the Secretaries of the League.
- Pt. Jawaharlal Nehru as Prime Minister skirted and neglected to bring about imperative and demanding high priority social reforms. The Congress Party under his leadership and the government under his Prime Ministership continued to pander to the clergy and to the retrograde elements in the religious communities who were strong opponents of any reform in their religious and faith-based and custom-based laws. He, however, pushed forward some social reforms in the case of Hindus

including the granting of property rights to Hindu women in spite of the strong opposition from the conservative and reactionary elements within the Congress Party and the country. There was even a forceful opposition by the then President of India, Shri Rajendra Prasad.

- The way the term 'Secularism' was explained and defined by Pt. Jawaharlal Nehru was fallacious. According to him, the State would accord equal respect to all the religions. That was a subtle measure not to curb but to promote communalism of every variety in an indirect way. All the never-ending rituals, customs, traditions, superstitions, caste divisions, gender discriminations practised by the religious communities continued, thereby, keeping the people backward. Religion should have been kept separate from the State and treated as one's personal matter to be practised by the people within the four walls of their homes.
- Except setting up a few Indian Institutes of Technology and Business Administration for the benefit of the big industrialists in managing their business affairs, Pt. Nehru grossly neglected the education sector, including the school education. The children of the elite classes could get quality education in privately well-managed schools and in the Cambridge and Oxford Universities in England which millions of children of the poor classes could not afford.
- There was no improvement in the treatment meted out to the poitical prisoners as promised by him as well as by Shri Lal Bahadur Shastri before independence. The conditions of the prisoners continued to be as bad, if not worse, as those were during the British Rule.
- **The Law of Sedition:** the abrogation of Section 124 A, which was one of the items of Mahatma Gandhi's Eleven Points sent to Lord Irwin, the Viceroy, for acceptance, and which Pt. Nehru himself had been declaring that the same would be repealed after India became independent, continued. He, on the other hand, passed the draconian Armed Forces Special Powers Act [AFSPA] in 1958.

- He was a master rhetorician as his ability for rhetorical diction was unsurpassable.
- He practised State Capitalism calling it Democratic Socialism, thereby, giving Scientific Socialism an unsavoury reputation.
- He was farsighted in realising that after the Second World War, it was difficult for any head of a Third World country to survive without having an understanding with the USA. He had, therefore, during his initial years of attaining power, secretly assured the USA that in case of a Third World War, India would side with the USA.
- Pt. Jawaharlal Nehru was handed over power on a platter by the British rulers, thereby, blunting the threat of Socialist Revolution. He earned the sobriquet of 'Maker of Modern India'.

It is only with the establishment of a social order based on Scientific Socialism that there would be jobs for all and there would be no unemployement; that free quality education and the free quality health services would be available to the have–nots; that the gulf between the rich and the poor and the chasm between the high and low castes would vanish and that those belonging to all religions and communities would be treated equally.

Neither Keynesianism (a sort of welfareism propounded by the famous economist, Lord J.M. Keynes) nor the Democratic Socialism of Pt. Nehru, that in fact was State Capitalism, can provide jobs, quality education and quality health services to one and all, nor the prevailing system of Globalisation, Neoliberalism, Privatism (Market Economy), can solve the problems of the people. All these socio-political systems mean the 'Billionaires Raj' (Rule) (as it happened last year when 73 per cent wealth of India went to the 1 per cent wealthiest ones).

33

An Address to the Young Political Workers

February 2, 1931

To
The Young Political Workers,

Dear Comrades

Our movement is passing through a very important phase at present. After a year's fierce struggle some definite proposals regarding the constitutional reforms have been formulated by the Round Table Conference and the Congress leaders have been invited to give their opinion on them and to explore the possibility whether they would call off their movement in the present circumstances. Whether they decide in favour or against, is a matter of little importance to us. The present movement is bound to end in some sort of compromise. The compromise may be effected sooner or later. And compromise is not such ignoble and deplorable a thing as we generally think. It is rather an indispensable factor in the political strategy. Any nation that rises against the oppressors is bound to fail in the beginning, and to gain partial reforms during the medieval period of its struggle, it has to pass through compromises. And it is only at the last stage—having fully organised all the forces and resources of the nation—that it can possibly strike the final blow in which it might succeed to shatter the ruler's government. But even then it might fail, which makes some sort of compromise inevitable. This can be best illustrated by the Russian example.

In 1905 a revolutionary movement broke out in Russia. All the leaders were very hopeful. Lenin had returned from the foreign countries where he had taken refuge. He was conducting the struggle. People came to tell him that a dozen landlords were killed and a score of their mansions were burnt. Lenin responded by telling them to return and to kill twelve hundred landlords and burn as many of their palaces. In his opinion that would have meant something if revolution failed. The Duma was introduced. The same Lenin advocated the view of participating in the Duma. This is what happened in 1907. In 1906 he was opposed to the participation in the first Duma which had granted more scope of work than the second one whose rights had been curtailed. This was due to the changed circumstances. Reaction was gaining the upper hand and Lenin wanted to use the floor of the Duma as a platform to discuss socialist ideas.

Again, after the 1917 revolution, when the Bolsheviks were forced to sign the Brest-Litovsk Treaty, everyone except Lenin, was opposed to it. But Lenin said: "Peace". "Peace and again peace: peace at any cost—even at the cost of many of the Russian provinces to be yielded to German War Lords". When some anti-Bolshevik people condemned Lenin for this treaty, he declared frankly that the Bolsheviks were not in a position to face the German onslaught and they preferred the treaty to the complete annihilation of the Bolshevik Government.

What I wanted to point out was that compromise is an essential weapon which has to be wielded every now and then as the struggle develops. But what we must always keep before us, is the idea of the movement. We must always maintain a clear notion as to the aim for the achievement of which we are fighting. That helps us to verify the successes and failures of our movements and we can easily formulate the future programme. Tilak's policy, quite apart from the ideal, i.e. his strategy, was the best. You are fighting to get sixteen annas from your enemy, you get only one 'anna'. Pocket it and fight for the rest. What we note in the moderates is their ideal. They start to achieve one 'anna' and they cannot get it. The revolutionaries must always bear in mind that they are striving for a complete revolution. Complete mastery of power in their hands. Compromises are dreaded because the conservatives try to disband the revolutionary forces after the compromise. But able and bold revolutionary leaders can save the movement from such pitfalls. We must be very careful at such junctures to avoid any sort of confusion of the real issues, especially the goal. The British Labour leaders betrayed their real struggle and have been reduced to mere hypocrite imperialists. In my opinion the diehard conservatives are better to us than these polished imperialist Labour leaders. About the tactics and strategy one should study Lenin's life-work. His definite views on the subject of compromise will be found in 'Left-Wing Communism'.

I have said that the present movement, i.e. the present struggle, is bound to end in some sort of compromise or complete failure.

I said that, because in my opinion, this time the real revolutionary forces have not been invited into the arena. This is a struggle dependent on the middle class shopkeepers and a few capitalists. Both these, and particularly the latter, can never dare to risk their property or possessions in any struggle. The real revolutionary armies are in the villages and in factories, the peasantry and the labourers. But our bourgeois leaders do not and cannot dare to tackle them. The sleeping lion once awakened from its slumber will become irresistible even after the achievement of what our leaders aim at. After his first experience with the Ahmedabad labourers in 1920, Mahatma Gandhi declared: "We must not tamper with the labourers. It is dangerous to make political use of the factory proletariat" (*The Times*, May 1921). Since then, they never dared to approach them. There remains the peasantry. The Bardoli resolution of 1922 clearly defines the horror the leaders felt when they saw the gigantic peasant class rising to shake off not only the domination of an alien nation but also the yoke of the landlords.

It is there that our leaders prefer a surrender to the British than to the peasantry. Leave alone Pt. Jawaharlal Nehru. Can you point out any effort to organise the peasants or the labourers? No, they will not run the risk. There they lack. That is why I say they never meant a complete revolution. Through economic and administrative pressure they hoped to get a few more reforms, a few more concessions for the Indian capitalists. That is why I say that this movement is doomed to die, may be after some sort of compromise or even without. The young workers who in all sincerity raise the cry "Long Live the Revolution", are not well organised and strong enough to carry the movement themselves. As a matter of fact, even our great leaders, with the exception of perhaps Pt. Motilal Nehru, do not dare to take any responsibility on their shoulders, that is why every now and then they surrender unconditionally before Gandhi. In spite of their differences, they never oppose him seriously and the resolutions have to be carried for the Mahatma.

In these circumstances, let me warn the sincere young workers who seriously mean a revolution, that harder times are coming. Let them beware lest they should get confused or disheartened. After the experience made through two struggles of the Great Gandhi, we are in a better position to form a clear idea of our present position and the future programme.

Now allow me to state the case in the simplest manner. You cry "Long Live the Revolution." Let me assume that you really mean it. According to our definition of the term, as stated in our statement in the Assembly Bomb Case, revolution means the complete overthrow of the existing social order and its replacement with the socialist order. For that purpose our immediate aim is the achievement of power. As a matter of fact, the State, the government machinery is just a weapon in the hands of the ruling class to further and safeguard its interest. We want to snatch and handle it to use it for the consummation of our ideal, i.e. social reconstruction on the new, i.e. Marxist basis. For this purpose we are fighting to handle the government machinery. All along we have to educate the masses and to create a favourable atmosphere for our social programme. In the struggles we can best train and educate them.

With these things clear before us, i.e. our immediate and ultimate object having been clearly put, we can now proceed with the examination of the present situation. We must always be very candid and quite business-like while analysing any situation.

We know that since a hue and cry was raised about the Indians' participation in and share in the responsibility of the Indian government, the Minto-Morley Reforms were introduced, which formed the Viceroy's Council with consultation rights only. During the Great War, when the Indian help was needed the most, promises about self-government were made and the existing reforms were introduced. Limited legislative powers have been entrusted to the Assembly but subject to the goodwill of the Viceroy. Now is the third stage.

Now reforms are being discussed and are to be introduced in the near future. How can our young men judge them? This is a question; I do not know by what standard the Congress leaders are going to judge them. But for us, the revolutionaries, we can have the following criteria:

1. Extent of responsibility transferred to the shoulders of the Indians.
2. Form of the government institutions that are going to be introduced and the extent of the right of participation given to the masses.
3. Future prospects and the safeguards.

These might require a little further elucidation. In the first place, we can easily judge the extent of responsibility given to our people by the control our representatives will have on the Executive. Till now, the Executive was never made responsible to the Legislative Assembly and the Viceroy had the veto power, which rendered all the efforts of the elected members futile. Thanks to the efforts of the Swaraj Party, the Viceroy was forced every now and then to use these extraordinary powers to shamelessly trample the solemn decisions of the national representatives under foot. It is already too well known to need further discussion.

Now in the first place we must see the method of the Executive formation: Whether the Executive is to be elected by the members of a popular assembly or is to be imposed from above as before, and further, whether it shall be responsible to the House or shall absolutely affront it as in the past?

Regarding the second item, we can judge it through the scope of franchise. The property qualifications making a man eligible to vote should be altogether abolished and universal suffrage be introduced instead. Every adult, both male and female, should have the right to vote. At present, we can simply see how far the franchise has been extended.

I may here make a mention about provincial autonomy. But from whatever I have heard, I can only say that the Governor imposed from above, equipped with extraordinary powers, higher and above the legislature, shall prove to be no less than a despot. Let us call it the "provincial tyranny" instead of "autonomy." This is a strange type of democratisation of the state institutions.

The third item is quite clear. During the last two years the British politicians have been trying to undo Montague's promise for another dole of reforms to be bestowed every ten years till the British Treasury is exhausted.

We can see what they have decided about the future.

Let me make it clear that we do not analyse these things to rejoice over the achievement, but to form a clear idea about our situation, so that we may enlighten the masses and prepare them for further struggle. For us, compromise never means surrender, but a step forward and some rest. That is all and nothing else.

Having discussed the present situation, let us proceed to discuss the future programme and the line of action we ought to adopt.

As I have already stated, for any revolutionary party a definite programme is very essential. For, you must know that revolution means action. It means a change brought about deliberately by an organised and systematic work, as opposed to sudden and unorganised or spontaneous change or breakdown. And for the formulation of a programme, one must necessarily study:

1. The goal.

2. The premises from where we are to start, i.e. the existing conditions.

3. The course of action, i.e. the means and methods.

Unless one has a clear notion about these three factors, one cannot discuss anything about the programme.

We have discussed the present situation to some extent. The goal also has been slightly touched. We want a socialist revolution, the indispensable preliminary to which is the political revolution. That is what we want. The political revolution does not mean the transfer of the state (or more crudely, the power) from the hands of the British to the Indian, but to those Indians who are at one with us as to the final goal, or to be more precise, the power to be transferred to the revolutionary party through popular support. After that, to proceed in right earnest is to organise the reconstruction of the whole society on the Socialist basis. If you do not mean this revolution, then please have mercy. Stop shouting "*Long Live the Revolution.*" The term revolution is too sacred, at least to us, to be so lightly used or misused. But if you say you are for the national revolution and the aims of your struggle is an Indian republic of the type of the United State of America, then I ask you to please let me know on what forces you rely that will help you bring about that revolution. The only forces on which you can rely to bring about any revolution whether national or the socialist, are the peasantry and the labour. Congress leaders do not dare to organise those forces. You have seen it in this movement. They know it better than anybody else that without these forces they are absolutely helpless. When they passed the resolution of complete independence—that really meant a revolution—they did not mean it. They had to do it under pressure of the younger element, and then they wanted to use it as a threat to achieve their hearts' desire—Dominion Status. You can easily judge it by studying the resolutions of the last three sessions of the Congress. I mean Madras, Calcutta and Lahore. At Calcutta, they passed a resolution asking for Dominion Status within twelve months, otherwise they would be forced to adopt complete independence as their object, and in all solemnity waited for some such gift till midnight after December 31, 1929. Then they found themselves "honour bound" to adopt the Independence resolution, otherwise they did not mean it. But even then Mahatmaji made no secret of the fact that the door (for compromise) was open. That was the real spirit. At the very outset they knew that their movement could not but end in some compromise. It is this half-heartedness that we hate, not the compromise at a particular stage in the struggle.

Anyway, we were discussing the forces on which you can depend for a revolution. But if you say that you will approach the peasants and labourers to enlist their active support, let me tell you that they are not going to be fooled by any sentimental talk. They ask you quite candidly: what are they going to gain by your revolution for which you demand their sacrifices, what difference does it make to them whether Lord Reading is the head of the Indian government or Sir Purshotamdas Thakurdas? What difference for a peasant if Sir Tej Bahadur Sapru replaces Lord Irwin? It is useless to appeal to his national sentiment. You can't "use" him for your purpose; you will have to be serious and make him understand that the revolution is going to be for his good. The revolution of the proletariat and for the proletariat.

When you have formulated this clear-cut idea about your goals you can proceed in right earnest to organise your forces for such an action. Now there are two different phases through which you will have to pass. First, the preparation; second, the action.

After the present movement ends, you will find disgust and some disappointment amongst the sincere revolutionary workers. But you need not worry. Leave sentimentalism aside. Be prepared to face the facts. Revolution is a very difficult task. It is beyond the power of any man to make a revolution. Neither can it be brought about on any appointed date. It is brought about by special environments, social and economic. The function of an organised party is to use any such opportunity offered by these circumstances. And to prepare the masses and organise the forces for the revolution is a very difficult task. And that requires a very great sacrifice on the part of the revolutionary workers. Let me make it clear that if you are a businessman or an established worldly or family man, please do not play with fire. As a leader you are of no use to the Party. We have already very many such leaders who spare some evening hours to deliver speeches. They are useless. We require—to use the term so dear to Lenin—the "professional revolutionaries". The full-time workers who have no other ambitions or life-work except the revolution. The greater the number of such workers organised into a party, the greater the chances of your success.

To proceed systematically, what you need the most is a party with workers of the type discussed above with clear-cut ideas and keen perception and the ability of initiative and quick decisions. The Party will have iron discipline. The policy of voluntarily going to jail should altogether be abandoned. That will create a number of workers who will be forced to lead an underground life. They should undertake the work with the same zeal. And it is this group of workers that will produce worthy leaders for the real opportunity.

The Party requires workers who can be recruited only through the youth movement. Hence we find the youth movement as the starting point of our programme. The youth movement should organise study circles, class lectures and publication of leaflets, pamphlets, books and periodicals. This is the best recruiting and training ground for political workers.

Those young men who may have mature ideas and may find themselves ready to devote their lives to the cause, may be transferred to the Party. The Party workers will always guide and control the work of the youth movement as well. The Party should start with the work of mass propaganda. It is very essential. One of the fundamental causes of the failure of the efforts of the Ghadar Party (1914-15) was the ignorance, apathy and sometimes active opposition of the masses. And apart from that, it is essential for gaining the active sympathy of and organising the peasants and workers. The name of the Party or rather...* a communist Party. This Party of political workers, bound by strict discipline, should handle all other movements. It will have to organise the peasants' and workers' parties, labour unions, and kindred political bodies, and in order to create political consciousness, not only of national politics but class politics as well. The Party should organise a big publishing campaign, publishing material on all socio-political issues as well as on subjects relating to Scientific Socialism enlightening the masses of the socialist theory which should be within easy reach and distributed widely. The writings should be simple and clear.

There are certain people in the labour movement who enlist some absurd ideas about the economic liberty of the peasants and workers without political freedom. They are demagogues or muddle-headed people. Such ideas are unimaginable and preposterous. We mean the economic liberty of the masses, and for that very purpose we are striving to win the political power. Undoubtedly in the beginning, we will have to fight for small economic demands and privileges of such classes. But these struggles are the best means for educating them for a final struggle to conquer political power.

Apart from these, there will necessarily be organised a military department. This is very important. At times its need is felt very badly. But at that time you cannot start and formulate such a group with substantial means to act effectively. Perhaps this is the topic that needs a careful explanation. There is a great probability of my being misunderstood on this subject. Apparently I have acted like a terrorist. But I am not a terrorist. I am a revolutionary who has got such definite ideas of a lengthy programme as is being discussed here. My "comrades in arms" might accuse me, like Ram Prasad Bismil, for having been subjected to a certain sort of reaction in the condemned cell, which is not true. I have got the same ideas, same convictions, same zeal and same spirit as I used to have outside, perhaps—even, decidedly — better. Hence I warn my readers to be careful while reading my words. They should not try to read anything between the lines. Let me announce with all the strength at my command, that I am not a terrorist and I never was, except perhaps at the beginning of my revolutionary career. And I am convinced that we cannot gain anything through those methods. One can easily judge it from the history of The Hindustan Socialist Republican Association. All our activities were directed towards an aim, i.e. identifying ourselves with the great movement as its military wing. If anybody has misunderstood me, let him amend his ideas. I do not mean that bombs and pistols are useless, rather the contrary. But I mean to say that mere bomb-throwing is not only useless but sometimes harmful. The military department of the Party should always keep ready all the war-material it can command for any emergency. It should back the political work of the Party. It cannot and should not work independently.

On these lines indicated above, the Party should proceed with its work. Through periodical meetings and conferences they should go on educating and enlightening their workers on all topics.

If you start the work on these lines, you will have to be very sober. The programme requires at least twenty years for its fulfilment. Cast aside the youthful dreams of a revolution within ten years or Gandhi's utopian promises of Swaraj in one year. It requires neither the emotion nor the death, but the life of constant struggle, suffering and sacrifice. Crush your individuality first. Shake off the dreams of personal comfort. Then start to work. Inch by inch you will have to proceed. It needs courage, perseverance and very strong determination. No difficulties and no hardships should discourage you. No failure and betrayals should dishearten you. No travails imposed upon you should snuff out the revolutionary will in you. Through the ordeal of sufferings and sacrifice you will emerge victorious. And these individual victories will be the valuable assets of the revolution.

—Bhagat Singh

Long Live the Revolution.*

*Some words are missing here.

*An abridged version of this letter is found in *The Abhyudaya*. Allahabad, May 8, 1931 and *The People*, Lahore, July 29, 1931. The fuller version is found in a CID officer C.E.S. Fairweather's *A Note on the Progress of the Agitation of the Joint Morcha in Bengal,* 1936.

34

The Philosophy of the Bomb

[In 1929, a bomb exploded under the Viceroy Irwin's special train, from which he, however, escaped. Gandhiji thanked God for the Viceroy's narrow escape and condemned, in his article 'The Cult of the Bomb', the revolutionaries for the act. It was, in reply to Gandhiji's article, that this outstanding document was written by Bhagat Singh, General Secretary of the HSRA. It was clandestinely smuggled out to Bhagwati Charan Vohra from the Central Jail, Lahore, where Bhagat Singh was lodged. Being the Propaganda Secretary of The Hindustan Socialist Republican Association, Mr. Vohra typed, got printed and issued it. The document was issued in the name of Kartar Singh, a fictitious name]

Introductory

Recent events, particularly, the Congress resolution, on the attempt to blow up the Viceregal Special on the December 23, 1929, and Gandhi's subsequent writings in *Young India*, clearly show that the Indian National Congress, in conjunction with Gandhi, has launched a crusade against the revolutionaries. A great amount of public criticism, both from the press and the platform, has been made against them. It is a pity that they have, all along, been, either deliberately or due to sheer ignorance, misrepresented and misunderstood. The revolutionaries do not shun criticism and public scrutiny of their ideals or actions. They rather welcome these as chances of making those, who have a genuine desire to do so, understand the basic principles of the revolutionary movement and the high and noble ideals that are a perennial source of inspiration and strength to it. It is hoped, that this article will help the general public to know the revolutionaries as they are and will prevent mistaking them for what interested and ignorant persons would have it believe them to be.

Violence or Non-Violence

Let us, first of all, take up the question of violence and non-violence. We think that the use of these terms in itself, is a grave injustice to either party, for they express the ideals of neither of them correctly. Violence is physical force when applied for committing injustice, and that is certainly not what the revolutionaries stand for. On the other hand, what generally goes by the name of non-violence, is in reality the theory of soul-force, as applied to the attainment of personal and national rights through courting suffering and hoping thus to finally convert your opponent to your point of view. When a revolutionary believes certain things to be his right, he asks for them, pleads for them, argues for them, wills to attain them with all the soul-force at his command, stands the greatest amount of suffering for them, and is always prepared to make the highest sacrifice for their attainment. He also backs his efforts with all the physical force he is capable of. You may coin what other word you like to describe his methods, but you cannot call it violence, because that would constitute an outrage on the dictionary meaning of that word. Satyagraha is insistence upon truth. Why press, for the acceptance of truth, by soul-force alone? Why not add physical force also to it? While the revolutionaries stand for winning independence by all forces, physical as well as moral, at their command, the advocates of soul-force would like to ban the use of physical force. The question really, therefore, is not whether you will have violence, but whether you will have soul-force plus physical force or soul-force alone. The revolutionaries believe that the deliverance of their country will come through revolution. The revolution, they are constantly working and hoping for, will not only express itself in the form of an armed conflict between the foreign government and its supporters and the people, it will also usher in a new social order. The revolution will ring the death knell of capitalism and class distinctions and privileges. It will bring joy and prosperity to the starving millions who are seething today under the terrible yoke of both foreign and Indian exploitation. It will bring the nation into its own. It will give birth to a new state, a new social order. Above all, it will establish the Dictatorship of the Proletariat and will forever banish social parasites from the seat of political power.

Terrorism

The revolutionaries already see the advent of the revolution in the restlessness of the youth, in its desire to break free from the mental bondage and religious superstition that hold them. As the youth will get more and more saturated with the psychology of revolution, it will come to have a clearer realisation of national bondage and a growing, intense, unquenchable thirst for freedom. As it will grow, this feeling of bondage, this infuriated youth will begin to kill the oppressors. Thus has terrorism been born in the country. It is a phase, a necessary, an inevitable phase of the revolution. Terrorism is not the complete revolution and the revolution is not complete without terrorism. This thesis can be supported by an analysis of any and every revolution in history. Terrorism instils fear in the hearts of the oppressors. It brings hopes of revenge and redemption to the oppressed masses. It gives courage and self-confidence to the wavering. It shatters the shell of the superiority of the ruling class and raises the status of the subject race in the eyes of the world, because it is the most convincing proof of a nation's hunger for freedom. Here in India, as in other countries in the past, terrorism will develop into the revolution and the revolution into independence, social, political and economic.

Revolutionary Methods

This then is what the revolutionaries believe in, that is what they hope to accomplish for their country. They are doing it both openly and secretly, and in their own way. The experience of a century-long and world-wide struggle, between the masses and the governing class, is their guide to their goal, and the methods they follow have never been known to fail.

The Congress and the Revolutionaries

Meanwhile, what has the Congress been doing? It has changed its creed from Swaraj to complete independence. As a logical sequence to this, one would expect it to declare a war on the British government. Instead, we find, it has declared war against the revolutionaries. The first offensive of the Congress came in the form of a resolution deploring the attempt made on December 23, 1929, to blow up the Viceroy's Special. It was drafted by Gandhi and, he fought tooth and nail for it, with the result that it was passed by a trifling majority of 81 in a house of 1,713. Was even this bare majority a result of honest political convictions? Let us quote the opinion of Sarla Devi Chaudhrani who has been a devotee of the Congress all her life. In reply she says: "I discovered in the course of my conversations with many of the Mahatma's followers that it was only their sense of personal loyalty to him that was keeping them back from expression of the independent views and preventing them from voting against any resolution whatsoever that was fathered by Mahatmaji." As to Gandhi's arguments in favour of the proposition, we will deal with them later, when we discuss his article 'The Cult of the Bomb' which is more or less an amplification of his speech in the Congress. There is one fact about this deplorable resolution which we must not lose sight of, and that is this. In spite of the fact, that the Congress is pledged to non-violence and has been actively engaged in carrying on propaganda in its favour for the last ten years, and in spite of the fact also that the supporters of the resolution indulged in abuse, called the revolutionaries 'cowards' and described their actions as 'dastardly' and one of them even threateningly remarked that if they wanted to be led by Gandhi, they should pass this resolution, could only be adopted by a dangerously narrow majority. That demonstrates, beyond the shadow of a doubt, how solidly the country is backing the revolutionaries. In a way Gandhi deserved our thanks for having brought the question up for discussion and thus having shown to the world at large that even the Congress, the strong-hold of non-violence, is at least as much, if not more, with the revolutionaries as with him.

Gandhi on the War Path

Having achieved a victory which cost him more than a defeat, Gandhi has returned to the attack in his article 'The Cult of the Bomb'. We will give it our closest attention before proceeding further. That article consists of three things—his faith, his opinion and his arguments. We will not discuss what is a matter of faith with him because reason has little in common with faith. Let us then take such of his opinions as are backed by arguments and his arguments, proper, against what he calls violence and discuss them one by one.

Do the Masses Believe in Non-Violence?

He thinks that on the basis of his experience during his latest tour in the country, he is right in believing that the large masses of Indian humanity are yet untouched by the spirit of violence and that non-violence has come to stay as a political weapon. Let him not delude himself on the experiences of his latest tour in the country. Though it is true, that the average leader confines his tours to places where only the mail train can conveniently land him, while Gandhi has extended his tour limit to where a car can take him, the practice of staying only with the richest people in the places visited, of spending most of his time on being complimented by his devotees in private and public, and of granting 'Darshan', now and then to the illiterate masses whom he claims to understand so well, disqualifies him from claiming to know the mind of the masses. No man can claim to know a people's mind by seeing them from the public platform and giving them 'Darshan' and 'Updesh'. He can, at the most, claim to have told the masses what he thinks about things. Has Gandhi, during recent years, mixed in the social life of the masses? Has he sat with the peasant round the evening fire and tried to know what he thinks? Has he spent a single evening in the company of a factory labourer and shared with him his woes? We have, and therefore, we claim to know what the masses think. We assure Gandhi that the average Indian, like the average human being, understands little of the fine theological niceties about 'Ahimsa' and loving one's enemy. The way of the world is like this. You have a friend you love him, sometimes so much that you even die for him. You have an enemy whom you shun, you fight against him and, if possible, kill him. The gospel of the revolutionaries is simple and straight. It is what has been since the days of Adam and Eve, and no man has any difficulty about understanding it. We affirm that the masses of India are solidly with us because we know it from personal experience. The day is not far, when they will flock in their thousands to work the will of the Revolution.

The Gospel of Love

Gandhi declares, that his faith in the efficacy of non-violence has increased. That is to say, he believes more and more, that through his gospel of love, and self-imposed suffering, he hopes some day to convert the foreign rulers to his way of thinking. Now, he has devoted his whole life to the preaching of his wonderful gospel and has practised it with unwavering consistency, as few others have done. Will he let the world know how many enemies of India he has been able to turn into friends? How many O'Dwyers, Readings and Irwins has he, been able to convert into friends of India? If none, how can India be expected to share his 'growing faith' that he will be able to persuade or compel England to agree to Indian independence through the practice of non-violence?

What would have happened if the bomb, that burst under the Viceroy's Special, had exploded properly? One of the two things suggested by Gandhi would have surely happened. The Viceroy would have either been badly injured or killed. Under such circumstances there certainly would have been no meeting between the leaders of political parties and the Viceroy. The uncalled for and undignified attempt on the part of these individuals, to lower the national prestige by knocking at the gates of the government house with the beggar's bowl in their hands and dominion status on their lips, in spite of the clear terms of the Calcutta Ultimatum, would have been checkmated and the nation would have been powerful enough to kill the Viceroy. One more enemy of India would have met a well-deserved doom. The author of the Meerut prosecutions and the Lahore and Bhusawal prosecutions can appear as a friend of

India only to the enemies of her freedom. In spite of Gandhi and Nehru and their claims to political sagacity and statesmanship, Irwin has succeeded in shattering the unity between different political parties in the country that had resulted from the boycott of the Simon Commission. Even the Congress today is a house divided against itself. Who else, except the Viceroy and his olive tongue, have we to thank for our grave misfortunes? And yet, there exist people in our country who proclaim him 'a Friend of India'.

The Future of the Congress

There might be those who have no regard for the Congress and hope nothing from it. If Gandhi thinks that the revolutionaries belong to this category, he wrongs them grievously. They fully realise the part played by the Congress in awakening in the ignorant masses a keen desire for freedom. They expect great things of it in the future. Though they hold firmly to their opinion, that so long as people like Sen Gupta whose wonderful intelligence compels him to discern the hand of the CID in the late attempt to blow up the Viceroy's Special, and those like Ansari, who think abuse the better part of argument and know so little of politics as to make the ridiculous and fallacious assertion that no nation had achieved freedom by the bomb, have a determining voice in the affairs of the Congress, the country can hope the minimum from them. They are hopefully looking forward to the day, when the mania of non-violence would have passed away from the Congress, and it would march arm in arm with the revolutionaries to their common goal of complete independence. This year it has accepted the ideal which the revolutionaries have preached and lived up to more than a quarter of a century. Let us hope the next year will see it endorses their methods also.

Violence and Military Expenditure: Gandhi is of the opinion that as often as violence has been practised in the country, it has resulted in an increase of military expenditure. If his reference is to revolutionary activities during the last twenty-five years we dispute the accuracy of his statement and challenge him to prove his statement with facts and figures. If, on the other hand, he had the wars that have taken place in India since the British came here, in mind, our reply is that even his modest experiment in 'Ahimsa' and 'Satyagraha' which had little to compare in them with the wars for independence, produced its effect on the finances of the bureaucracy. Mass action, whether violent or non-violent, whether successful or unsuccessful, is bound to produce the same kind of repercussion on the finances of a state.

The Reforms

Why should Gandhi mix the demands of the revolutionaries with the various constitutional reforms granted by the government? They never cared or worked for the Morley-Minto Reforms, Montague Reforms and the like. These the British government threw before the constitutionalist agitators to lure them away from the right path. This was the bribe paid to them for their support to the government in its policy of crushing and uprooting the revolutionaries. These toys—as Gandhi calls them—were sent to India for the benefit of those, who, from time to time, raised the cry of 'Home Rule', 'Self-Government', 'Responsible', 'Full Responsible Government', 'Dominion Status' and such other constitutional names for slavery. The revolutionaries never claim the reforms as their achievement. They raised the standard of independence long ago and have lived for it. They have ungrudgingly laid their lives down for the sake of this ideal and claim that their sacrifices have produced a tremendous change in the mentality of the people. That their efforts have advanced the country a long way on the road to independence is granted by even those who do not see eye to eye with them in politics.

The Way of Progress

As for Gandhi's contention, that violence impedes the march of progress and thus directly postpones the day of freedom, we can refer him to so many contemporary instances where violence has led to the social progress and political freedom of the people who practised it. Take the case of Russia and Turkey, for example. In both countries the party of progress took over the state organisation through an armed revolution. Yet social progress and political freedom have not been impeded. Legislation, backed by force, has made the masses go 'double march' on the road of progress. The solitary example of Afghanistan cannot establish a political formula. It is rather the exception that proves the rule.

Failure of Non-Cooperation

Gandhi is of the opinion that the great awakening in the people, during the days of non-cooperation, was a result of the preaching of non-violence. It is wrong to assign to non-violence the widespread awakening of the masses which, in fact, is manifested wherever a programme of direct action is adopted. In Russia, for instance, there came about widespread awakening in the peasants and workers when the communists launched forth their great programme of Militant Mass Action, though nobody preached non-violence to them. We will even go further and state that it was mainly the mania for non-violence and Gandhi's compromise mentality that brought about the disruption of the forces that had come together at the call of Mass Action. It is claimed that non-violence can be used as a weapon for righting political wrongs. To say the least, it is a novel idea, yet untried. It failed to achieve what were considered to be the just rights of Indians in South Africa. It failed to bring 'Swaraj within a year' to the Indian masses in spite of the untiring labours of an army of national workers and one and a quarter crores of rupees. More recently, it failed to win for the Bardoli peasants what the leaders of the,'Satyagraha' movement had promised—'the famous irreducible minimum of Gandhi and Patel'. We know of all the other trials of non-violence which have been blessed with one result—failure. No wonder, then, that the country refuses to give it another trial. In fact 'Satyagraha' as preached by Gandhi is a form of agitation—a protest, leading up invariably, as has already been seen, to a compromise. It can hardly be of any use to a nation striving for national independence which can never come as a result of a compromise. The sooner we recognise, that there can be no compromise between independence and slavery, the better.

Is It A New Era?

'We are entering upon a new era', thinks Gandhi. The mere act of defining Swaraj as complete independence, this technical change in the Congress constitution, can hardly constitute a new era. It will be a great day indeed when the Congress will decide upon a country-wide Programme of Mass Action, based on well recognised revolutionary principles. Till then the unfurling of the flag of Independence is a mockery and we concur with the following remarks of Sarla Devi Chaudhrani which she recently made in a press interview. "The unfurling of the Flag of Independence", she says, "at just one minute after midnight of December 31, 1929, was too stagy for words—just as the GOC and the assistant GOC and others in gaudy uniforms were cardboard grand officers commanding". "The fact that the unfurling of the flag of independence lay hanging in the balance till midnight of that date, and that the scales might have been turned at even the eleventh hour fifty-ninth minute, had a message from the Viceroy or the Secretary of State come to the Congress granting Dominion Status, proves, that independence was not a heart-hunger of the leaders but that the declaration of it was only like a petulant child's retort. It would have been a worthy action of the Indian National Congress if independence was achieved first and declared afterwards." It is true that the Congress orators will henceforth harangue the masses on complete independence instead of Dominion Status. They will call upon the people to prepare for a struggle in which one party is to deliver blows and the other is simply to receive them, till beaten and demoralised beyond hope of recovery. Can such a thing be named a struggle and can it ever lead the country to complete independence? It was all very well to hold fast to the highest ideal worthy of a nation, but it was nonetheless necessary to adopt the best, the most efficacious and tried means to achieve it, before you become the laughing stock of the whole world.

No Bullying Please

Gandhi has called upon all those who are not past reason to withdraw their support from the revolutionaries and condemn their actions so that "our deluded patriots may, for want of nourishment to their violent spirit, realise the futility of violence and the great harm that violent activities have every time done". How easy and convenient it is to call people deluded, to declare them to be past reason, to call upon the public to withdraw its support and condemn them so that they may get isolated and be forced to suspend their activities, specially when a man holds the confidence of an influential section of the public.

It is a pity that Gandhi does not and will not understand revolutionary psychology in spite of the lifelong experience of public life. Life is a precious thing. It is dear to everyone. If a man becomes a revolutionary, if he goes about with his life in the hollow of his hand ready to sacrifice it at any moment, he does not do so merely for the fun of it. He does not risk his life merely because sometimes, when the crowd is in a sympathetic mood, it cries 'Bravo' in appreciation. He does it because his reason forces him to take that course, because his conscience dictates it. A revolutionary believes in reason more than anything. It is to reason, and to reason alone, that he bows. No amount of abuse and condemnation, even if it emanates from the highest of the high, can turn him from his set purpose. To think that a revolutionary will give up his ideas if public support and appreciation is withdrawn from him, is the highest folly. Many a revolutionary has, ere now, stepped on the scaffold and laid his life down for the cause, regardless of the curses that the constitutionalist agitators rained plentifully upon him. If you will have the revolutionaries suspend their activities, reason with them squarely. That is the one and the only way. For the rest let there be no doubt in anybody's mind. A revolutionary is the last person on earth to submit to bullying.

An Appeal

We take this opportunity to appeal to our countrymen—to the youth, to the workers and peasants, to the revolutionary intelligentsia to come forward and join us in carrying aloft the banner of freedom. Let us establish a new order of society in which political and economic exploitation will be an impossibility. In the name of those gallant men and women who willingly accepted death so that we, their descendants, may lead a happier life, who toiled ceaselessly and perished for the poor, the famished, and exploited millions of India, we call upon every patriot to take up the fight in all seriousness. Let nobody toy 'with the nation's freedom' which is her very life, by making psychological experiments in non-violence and such other novelties. Our slavery is our shame. When shall we have courage and wisdom enough to be able to shake ourselves free of it? What is our great heritage of civilisation and culture worth if we have not enough self-respect left in us to prevent us from bowing in surveillance to the commands of foreigners and paying homage to their flag and king?

Victory or Death

There is no crime that Britain has not committed in India. Deliberate misrule has reduced us to paupers, has "bled us white". As a race and a people we stand dishonoured and outraged. Do people still expect us to forget and forgive? We shall have our revenge—a people's righteous revenge on the tyrant. Let cowards fall back and cringe for compromise and peace. We ask not for mercy and 'we give no quarter'. Ours is a war to the end—to Victory or Death. Long Live the Revolution!

—Kartar Singh, President,
The Hindustan Socialist Republican Association

35

Sukhdev's Letter to Mahatma Gandhi

[Gandhiji was negotiating with the government for the release of political prisoners not convicted of violence. He was also appealing to the revolutionaries to stop their movement. It was in this context that Sukhdev wrote this letter. It was published in *Young India*, April 23, 1931, after the execution of Bhagat Singh, Raj Guru and Sukhdev.]

Most Gracious Mahatmaji

Recent reports since your compromise you have called off your movement and consequently all your prisoners have been released. But, what about the revolutionary prisoners? Dozens of Ghadar Party prisoners imprisoned since 1915 are still rotting in jails, in spite of having undergone the full terms of their imprisonments. Scores of martial law prisoners are still buried in these living tombs, and so are dozens of Babbar Akali prisoners. Deogarh, Kakori, Machhua Bazar and Lahore Conspiracy Case prisoners are amongst those numerous still locked behind bars. More than half a dozen conspiracy trials are going on at Lahore, Delhi, Chittagong, Bombay, Calcutta and elsewhere. Dozens of revolutionaries are absconding and amongst them are many females. More than half a dozen prisoners are actually waiting for their executions. What about all these people? The three Lahore Conspiracy Case condemned prisoners, who have luckily come into prominence and who have acquired enormous public sympathy, do not form the bulk of the Revolutionary Party. Their fate is not the only consideration before the Party. As a matter of fact their executions are expected to do greater good than the commutation of their sentences.

But, in spite of all this, you are making public appeals, asking them to call off their movement. Why should they do so? You have not mentioned any very definite things.

In these circumstances your appeal means you are joining hands with bureaucracy to crush that movement, and your appeals amount to preaching treachery, desertion and betrayal amongst them. If that were not the case, then the best thing for you would have been to approach some of the prominent revolutionaries and talk over the whole matter with them. You ought to have tried to convince them to call off their movement. I do not think you also share the general conservative notion that the revolutionaries are devoid of reason, rejoicing in destruction and devastation.

Let us inform you that in reality the case is quite the contrary. They always consider the pros and cons of every step they take and they fully realise the responsibility which they thus incur and they attach greater importance to the constructive phase of the revolutionary programme than to any other, though in the present circumstances, they cannot but occupy themselves with the destructive part of their programme.

The present policy of the government towards them is to deprive them of the sympathy and support of the masses which they have won in their movement, and then crush them. In isolation they can be easily hunted down. In face of that fact any sentimental appeal to cause demoralisation amongst their ranks would be utterly unwise and counter-revolutionary. It would be rendering direct assistance to the government to crush them.

Therefore, we request you either to talk to some revolutionary leaders—they are so many in jails—and come to terms with them or to stop these appeals. Please, for goodness sake, pursue one of these two alternative courses and pursue it wholeheartedly. If you cannot help them, then please have mercy on them. Leave them alone; they can take care of themselves. They know that the hegemony of the revolutionary party in the future political struggle is assured. Masses are rallying around them and the day is not far off when they will be leading the masses under their banner towards their noble and lofty ideal—the Socialist Republic.

Or, if you seriously mean to help them, then talk to them to understand their point of view, and discuss the problem in detail.

Hope you will kindly consider the above request and let your view be known publicly.

Yours

—One of the Many

36

Statement of the Undefended Accused

[For propaganda purposes the Lahore Conspiracy Case accused had divided themselves into three groups. The first group consisted of comrades who were represented through a lawyer. This was a small group of comrades against whom there was not much evidence and who had chances of getting acquitted. The second group consisted of the unrepresented accused. Bhagat Singh belonged to this group. Comrades of this group were generally vocal in the court. They cross-examined the prosecution witnesses, challenged the prosecution, challenged the rulings of the court, delivered political speeches, and made every effort to prolong the proceedings. The third group consisted of the undefended accused. They were to challenge the bona fides of the court and the government. It consisted of five comrades. On the very first day, they submitted a written statement before the Tribunal, saying that they did not recognise the alien government and the court appointed by it, and that they did not expect any justice from the enemy court. The statement was prepared by Bhagat Singh and was read in the court by Jitendra Nath Sanyal. The other four signatories were Mahabir Singh, Gaya Prasad Katiyar, Kundan Lal and Batukeshwar Dutt. The Tribunal declared it as seditious, banned it and refused to record it as part of the proceedings.] The following is the historic statement of the undefended accused:

To
The Commissioner,
The Special Tribunal
Lahore Conspiracy Case, Lahore

Sirs,

On behalf of my five comrades, including myself, I feel it necessary to make the following statement at the very commencement of the trial and wish that it be retained on the record.

We do not propose to take any part in the proceedings of this case because we do not recognise this government which is said to be based on so-called justice or established by law.

We believe and do hereby declare that man being the source of all the authority, no individual or government can be entitled to any authority and unless and until it is directly derived from the people.

Since this government is an utter negative of these principles, its very existence is not justifiable. Such governments, which are organised to exploit the oppressed nations, have no right to exist except by the right of the sword (i.e. brute force) with which they try to curb all the ideas of liberty and freedom and the legitimate aspirations of the people.

We believe all such governments, and particularly the British Government thrust upon the helpless but unwilling Indian nation, to be no better than an organised gang of robbers, and a pack of exploiters equipped with all the means of carnage and devastation. In the name of 'law and order', they crush all those who dare to expose or oppose them.

We believe that imperialism is nothing but a vast conspiracy organised with predatory motives. Imperialism is the last stage of development of insidious exploitation of man by man and of nation by nation. The imperialists, with a view to further their piratical designs, not only commit judicial murders through their law courts but also organise general massacres, devastations and other horrible crimes like war. They feel no hesitation in shooting down innocent and unarmed people who refuse to yield to their depredatory demands or to acquiesce in their ruinous and abominable designs. Under the garb of custodians of 'law and order', they break peace, create disorder, kill people and commit all conceivable crimes.

We believe that freedom is an undeniable birthright of all people, that every man has the inalienable right of enjoying the fruits of his labour, and that every nation is indisputably the master of its resources. If any government deprives them of these primary rights, it is the right of the people—nay, it is their duty—to destroy that government. Since the British Government is a negation of these principles for which we stand, it is our firm conviction that every effort made, every method adopted to bring about a revolution and to destroy this government is morally justified.

We stand for a change, radical change in the existing order of affairs in social, political and economic spheres, and the complete replacement of the existing order by a new one rendering the exploitation of man by man impossible and thus guaranteeing full liberty to all the people in all the spheres. We feel that unless the social order is changed and socialist society is established, the whole world is in danger of a disastrous catastrophe.

Regarding the methods, peaceful or otherwise, to be adopted for the consummation of the revolutionary ideal, let us declare that the choice rests with those who hold power. Revolutionaries, by virtue of their altruistic principles, are lovers of peace—a genuine and permanent peace based on justice and equality, not the illusory peace resulting from cowardice and maintained at the point of bayonets. If the revolutionaries take to bombs and pistols, it is only as a measure of terrible necessity, as a last recourse. We believe that "Law and Order is for man and not man for Law and Order."

> As the Supreme Juris [SIC; Original transcription is unclear—MIA transcriber] Council of Revolutionary France has well expressed:
>
> "The end of the law is not to abolish or restrain but to preserve and enlarge the freedom. The legitimate power is required to govern by promulgated laws established for the common good alone and resting ultimately on the consent and the authority of the people, from which law no one is exempted—not even the legislators."

The sanctity of law can be maintained only so long as it is the expression of the will of the people. When it becomes a mere instrument in the hands of an oppressing class, it loses its sanctity and significance, for the fundamental preliminary condition for administration of justice is the elimination of every interest. As soon as the law ceases to correspond to the popular social needs, it becomes the means for perpetration of injustice and tyranny. The maintaining of such a law is nothing but a hypocritical assertion of special interest against the common interest.

The laws of the present government exist for the interest of the alien rulers, against the interest of our people, and as such they have no moral binding whatsoever. It is therefore the incumbent duty of all the Indians to defy and disobey these laws. These law courts, as part and parcel of the machinery of exploitation, cannot administer justice—especially in political cases where there is a clash between the interests of the government and the people. We know that these courts are nothing but the stages for the performance of mockery of justice.

For these reasons we decline to be a party to this farcical show and, henceforth, we shall not take any part in the proceedings of the case.

Yours,
— Bhagat Singh

May 5, 1930

J.N. Sanyal, B.K. Dutt, Dr. Gaya Prasad,
Kundan Lal, Mahabir Singh

37

Ramanand Chatterjee's Editorial on 'Long Live the Revolution'

According to a 'Free Press' message, at a meeting of the Naujawan Bharat Sabha (Young men's Bharat League) of Gujranwala in the Punjab, a resolution was passed protesting against the arrest of students on the ground of their shouting "Long Live the Revolution" and "Down with Imperialism", before the Court of the Special Magistrate at Lahore. The resolution states that everyone has the right to utter these cries. It is difficult for a layman to say what cries are legal or are not legal, when even High Court judges have differed in their interpretation of the law of sedition. But young enthusiasts will pardon an old cynical journalist for confessing that the cry of "Long Live the Revolution" has sometimes appeared to him to be somewhat funny.

A revolution may now and then have been a necessity in world history, and we shall personally like an early non-violent social, economic and political revolution in India. But, what is the exact meaning of "Long Live the Revolution"? To be at work is a sign of life. When a desire is expressed for revolution to live long, is it desired that the revolutionary process should be at work every hour, day, week, month and year of our lives? In other words, are we to have a revolution as often as possible? Such ceaseless revolution may make for change, but scarcely for progress, improvement and enlightenment. What one revolution offered must have time to settle down and take root and bear fruit. A ceaseless revolutionary process would make India like what James Russell Lowell called "the Catherine-Wheel Republics of South America", of his day. Undoubtedly, no revolution can produce a final state of improvement; there must be changes even after a revolution. But these should be brought about by evolution. There may again be a revolution after several generations, if not centuries. But this is not what is implied in the slogan "Long Live the Revolution".

On the Slogan of *"Long Live the Revolution"*

[Shri Ramanand Chatterjee, the Editor of *Modern Review*, ridiculed the slogan of "Long Live the Revolution" through his editorial note and gave an entirely wrong interpretation. Bhagat Singh wrote a reply to the note and handed it over to the trying magistrate to be sent to *Modern Review*. This was published in *The Tribune* of December 24, 1929.]

To
The Editor, *Modern Review*

You have in the December 1929 issue of your esteemed magazine, written a note under the caption "Long Live the Revolution" and have pointed out the meaninglessness of this phrase. It would be impertinent on our part to try to refute or contradict the statement of such an old, experienced and renowned journalist as your noble self, for whom every enlightened Indian has profound admiration. Still we feel it our duty to explain what we desire to convey by the said phrase, as in a way it fell to our lot to give these "cries" a publicity in this country at this stage.

We are not the originators of this cry. The same cry had been used in the Russian revolutionary movement. Upton Sinclair, the well known socialist writer, has, in his recent novel *Boston and Oil,* used this cry through some of the anarchist revolutionary characters. The phrase never means that the sanguinary strife should ever continue, or that nothing should ever be stationary even for a short while. By long usage this cry achieves a significance which may not be quite justifiable from the grammatical or the etymological point of view, but nevertheless we cannot abstract from that the association of ideas connected with that.

All such shouts denote a general sense which is partly acquired and partly inherent in them. For instance, when we shout, "Long Live Jatin Das", we cannot and do not mean thereby that Das should physically be alive. What we mean by that shout is that the noble ideal of his life, the indomitable spirit which enabled that great martyr to bear such untold suffering and to make the extreme sacrifice for that we may show the same unfailing courage in pursuance of our ideal. It is that spirit that we allude to. Similarly, one should not interpret the word "Revolution" in its literal sense. Various meanings and significances are attributed to this word, according to the interests of those who use or misuse it. For the established agencies of exploitation it conjures up a feeling of blood-stained horror. To the revolutionaries it is a sacred phrase. We tried to clear it in our statement before the Sessions Judge, Delhi, in our trial in the Assembly Bomb Case, what we mean by the word "Revolution".

We stated therein that Revolution did not necessarily involve sanguinary strife. It was not a cult of bomb and pistol. They may sometimes be the mere means for its achievement. Undoubtedly they play a prominent part in some movements, but they do not for that very reason become one and the same thing. A rebellion is not a revolution. It may ultimately lead to that end. The sense in which the word Revolution is used in that phrase, is the spirit, the longing for a change for the better. The people generally get accustomed to the established order of things and begin to tremble at the very idea of a change. It is this lethargic spirit that needs to be replaced by the revolutionary spirit. Otherwise degeneration gains the upper hand and the whole of humanity is led astray by the reactionary forces. Such a state of affairs leads to stagnation and paralysis in human progress. The spirit of revolution should always permeate the soul of humanity, so that the reactionary forces may not accumulate (strength) to check its eternal onward march. The old order should change, always and ever, yielding place to new, so that one "good" order may not corrupt the world. It is in this sense that we raise the shout "Long Live the Revolution".

Yours sincerely,
—Bhagat Singh

38

Why I Am An Atheist?

A new question has arisen. Is it due to vanity that I do not believe in the existence of an Omnipresent, Omniscient God? I have never imagined that I would ever had to confront such a question. But conversations with some friends had given me a hint that certain of friends—if I am not claiming too much in thinking them to be so—are inclined to conclude from the brief contact they had with me, that it was too much on my part to deny the existence of God and there was a certain amount of vanity that actuated my disbelief. Well, the problem is a serious one.

I do not boast of being above these human follies. I am, after all, a human being and nothing more. And no one can claim to be more than that. I have a weakness in my personality, for pride is one of the human traits that I possess. I am known as a dictator among my friends. Sometimes I am called a boaster. Some have always been complaining that I am bossy and I force others to accept my opinion. Yes, it is true to some extent. I do not deny this charge. We can use the word 'vainglory' for it. As far as the contemptible, obsolete, rotten values of our society are concerned, I am an extreme sceptic. But this question does not concern my person alone. It is being proud of my ideas, my thoughts. It cannot be called empty pride. Pride, or you may use the word, vanity, both mean an exaggerated assessment of one's personality. Is my atheism because of unnecessary pride, or have I ceased believing in God after thinking long and deep on the matter? I wish to put my ideas before you. First of all, let us differentiate between pride and vanity as these are two different things.

I have never been able to understand how unfounded, baseless pride or empty vanity can hinder a person from believing in God. I may refuse to acknowledge the greatness of a really great person only when I have got fame without making any serious efforts or when I lack the superior mental powers necessary to become great. It is easy to understand but how is it possible that a believer can turn into a non-believer because of his vanity? Only two things are possible: either a man deems himself to be in possession of godly qualities, or he goes a step further and declares himself to be a god. In both these states of mind he cannot be an atheist in the true sense of the word. In the first case, it is not an outright rejection of God's existence; in the other, he is affirming the existence of some kind of supernatural power responsible for the working of the Universe. It does not harm our argument whether he claims to be a god or considers God to be a reality in existence above his own being. The real point, however, is, that in both cases he is a theist, a believer. He is not an atheist. I want to bring home this point to you. I am not one of these two creeds. I totally reject the existence of an Omnipresent, all powerful, all knowing God. Why so? I will discuss it later in the essay. Here I wish to emphasise that I am not an atheist for the reason that I am arrogant or proud or vain; nor am I a demigod, nor a prophet; no, nor am I God myself. At least one thing is true that I have not evolved this thought because of vanity or pride.

In order to answer this question, I relate the truth. My friends say that after the Delhi bombing and the Lahore Conspiracy Case, I rocketed to fame and that this fact has turned my head. Let us discuss why this allegation is incorrect. I did not give up my belief in God after these incidents. I was an atheist even when I was an unknown figure. At least a college student cannot cherish any sort of exaggerated notion of himself that may lead him to atheism. It is true that I was a favourite with some college teachers, but others did not like me. I was never a hardworking or studious boy. I never got an opportunity to be proud. I was very careful in my behaviour and somewhat pessimistic about my future career. I was not completely atheistic in my beliefs. I was brought up under the care and protection of my father. He was a staunch Arya Samaji. An Arya Samaji can be anything but never an atheist. After my elementary education, I was sent to DAV College, Lahore. I lived in the boarding house for one year. Besides prayers early in the morning and at dusk, I sat for hours and chanted religious mantras. At that time, I was a staunch believer. Then I lived with my father. He was a tolerant man in his religious views. It is due to his teachings that I devoted my life for the cause of liberating my country. But he was not an atheist. His God was an all-pervading entity. He advised me to offer my prayers every day. In this way I was brought up. In the Non-Cooperation days, I got admission to the National College. During my stay in this college, I began thinking over all the religious polemics such that I grew sceptical about the existence of God. In spite of this fact I can say that my belief in God was firm and strong. I grew a beard and 'Kais' (long head hair as a Sikh religious custom). In spite of this, I could not convince myself of the efficacy of Sikhism or any religion at all, for that matter. But I had an unswerving, unwavering belief in God.

Then I joined the Revolutionary Party. The first leader I met did not have the courage to openly declare himself an atheist. He was unable to reach any conclusion on this point. Whenever I asked him about the existence of God, he gave me this reply: "You may believe in him when you feel like it." The second leader with whom I came in contact was a firm believer. I should mention his name. It was our respected Comrade Sachindra Nath Sanyal. He was sentenced to life imprisonment in connection with the Kakori Conspiracy Case. Right from the first page of his only book, *Bandi Jivan* (Imprisoned Life) he sings praises to the Glory of God. See the last page of the second part of this book and you find praises showered upon God in the way of a mystic. It is a clear reflection of his thoughts.

According to the prosecution, the 'Revolutionary Leaflet' which was distributed throughout India was the outcome of Sachindra Nath Sanyal's intellectual labour. So often it happens that in revolutionary activities a leader expresses his own ideas which may be very dear to him, but in spite of having differences, the other workers have to acquiesce in them.

In that leaflet, one full paragraph was devoted to the praises of

God and His doings which we, human beings, cannot understand. This is sheer mysticism. What I want to point out is that the idea of denying the existence of God did not even occur to the Revolutionary Party. The famous Kakori martyrs, all four of them, spent their last day in prayers. Ram Prasad Bismil was a staunch Arya Samaji. In spite of his extensive studies in Socialism and Communism, Rajan Lahiri could not suppress his desire to recite hymns from the *Upanishads* and *Gita*. There was only one person among them who did not indulge in such activities. He used to say, "Religion is the outcome of human weakness or the limitation of human knowledge." He is in prison for life. But he never dared to deny the existence of God.

Till that time I was only a romantic revolutionary, just a follower of our leaders. Then came the time to take the whole responsibility. For some time, a strong opposition put the very existence of the Party into danger. Many leaders as well as many enthusiastic comrades began to uphold the Party to ridicule. They jeered at us. I had an apprehension that some day I would also consider it a futile and hopeless task. It was a turning point in my revolutionary career. An incessant desire to study filled my heart. 'Study more and more', said I to myself so that I might be able to face the arguments of my opponents. 'Study' to support your point of view with convincing arguments. And I began to study in a serious manner. My previous beliefs and convictions underwent a radical change. The romance of militancy dominated our predecessors; now serious ideas ousted this way of thinking. No more mysticism. No more blind faith! Now realism was our mode of thinking. At times of terrible necessity, we can resort to extreme methods, but violence produces opposite results in mass movements. I have talked a great deal about our methods. The most important thing was a clear conception of our ideology for which we waged a long struggle. As there was no election activity going on, I got an ample opportunity to study various ideas propounded by various writers. I studied Bakunin, the anarchist leader. I read a few books by Marx, the father of Communism. I also read Lenin and Trotsky and many other writers who successfully carried out revolutions in their countries. All of them were atheists.

The ideas contained in Bakunin's *God and State* seem inconclusive, but it is an interesting book. After that I came across a book *Common Sense* by Nirlamba Swami. His point of view was a sort of mystical atheism. I developed more interest in this subject. By the end of 1926, I was convinced that the belief in an Almighty, Supreme Being who created, guided and controlled the universe had no sound foundations. I began discussions on this subject with my friends. I had openly declared myself an atheist. What it meant will be discussed in the following lines.

In May 1927, I was arrested in Lahore. This arrest came as a big surprise for me. I had not the least idea that I was wanted by the police. I was passing through a garden and suddenly the police surrounded me. To my own surprise, I was very calm at that time. I was in full control of myself. I was taken into police custody. The next day I was taken to the Railway Police lockup where I spent a whole month. After many days' conversation with police personnel, I guessed that they had some information about my connection with the Kakori Party. I felt they had some intelligence of my other activities in the revolutionary movement. They told me that I was in Lucknow during the Kakori Party Trial so that I might devise a scheme to rescue the culprits. They also said that after the plan had been approved, we procured some bombs and by way of test, one of those bombs was thrown into a crowd on the occasion of Dussehra in 1926. They offered to release me on condition that I gave a statement on the activities of the Revolutionary Party. In this way I would be set free and even rewarded and I would not be produced as an approver in the court. I could not help laughing at their proposals. It was all humbug. People who have ideas like ours, do not throw bombs at their own innocent people. One day, Mr. Newman, the then senior Superintendent of CID, came to me. After a long talk which was full of sympathetic words, he imparted to me what he considered to be sad news, that if I did not give any statement as demanded by them, they would be forced to send me up for trial for conspiracy to wage war in connection with the Kakori Case and also for brutal killings at the Dussehra gathering. After that he said that he had sufficient evidence to get me convicted and hanged.

I was completely innocent, but I believed that the police had sufficient power to do it if they desired it to be so. The same day some police officers persuaded me to offer my prayers to God twice regularly. I was an atheist. I thought that I would settle it to myself whether I could brag only in days of peace and happiness that I was an atheist, or in those hard times I could be steadfast in my convictions. After a long debate with myself, I reached the conclusion that I could not even pretend to be a believer nor could I offer my prayers to God. No, I never did it. It was the time of trial and I would come out of it successful. These were my thoughts. Never for a moment did I desire to save my life. So I was a true atheist then and I am an atheist now. It was not an easy task to face that ordeal. Beliefs make it easier to go through hardships, even make them pleasant. Man can find a strong support in God and an encouraging consolation in His Name. If you have no belief in Him, then there is no alternative but to depend upon yourself. It is not child's play to stand firm on your feet amid storms and strong winds. In difficult times, vanity, if it remains, evaporates and man cannot find the courage to defy beliefs held in common esteem by the people. If he really revolts against such beliefs, we must conclude that it is not sheer vanity; he has some kind of extraordinary strength. This is exactly the situation now. First of all we all know what the judgment will be? It is to be pronounced in a week or so. I am going to sacrifice my life for a cause. What more consolation can there be! A God-believing Hindu may expect to be reborn a king; a Muslim or a Christian might dream of the luxuries he hopes to enjoy in paradise as a reward for his sufferings and sacrifices. What hope should I entertain? I know that it will be the end when the rope is tightened round my neck and the rafters move from under my feet. To use more precise religious terminology, that will be the moment of utter annihilation. My soul will come to nothing. If I take the courage to take the matter in the light of 'Reward', I see that a short life of struggle with no such magnificent end shall itself be my 'Reward.' That is all. Without any selfish motive of getting any reward here or in the hereafter, quite disinterestedly have I devoted my life to the cause of freedom. I could not act otherwise. The day shall usher in a new era of liberty when many men and women, taking courage from the idea of serving humanity and liberating them from sufferings and distress, decide that there is no alternative before them except devoting their lives for this cause. They will wage a war against their oppressors, tyrants or exploiters, not to become kings, or to gain any reward here or in the next birth or after death in paradise; but to cast off the yoke of slavery, to establish liberty and peace they will tread this perilous, but glorious path. Can the pride they take in their noble cause be called vanity? Who is there rash enough to call it so? To him I say either he is foolish or wicked. Leave such a fellow alone for he cannot realise the depth, the emotions, the sentiment and the noble feelings that surge in that heart. His heart is dead, a mere lump of flesh, devoid of feelings. His convictions are infirm, his emotions feeble. His selfish interests have made him incapable of seeing the truth. The epithet 'vanity' is always hurled at the strength we get from our convictions.

You go against popular feelings; you criticise a hero, a great man who is generally believed to be above criticism. What happens? No one will answer your arguments in a rational way; rather you will be considered vainglorious. Its reason is mental insipidity. Merciless criticism and independent thinking are the two necessary traits of revolutionary thinking. As Mahatmaji is great, he is above criticism; as he has risen above, all that he says, in the field of politics, religion, ethics, is right. You agree or not, it is binding upon you to take it as truth. This is not constructive thinking. We do not take a leap forward; we go many steps back.

Our forefathers evolved faith in some kind of Supreme Being, therefore, one who ventures to challenge the validity of that faith or denies the existence of God, shall be called a Kafir (infidel), or a renegade, even if his arguments are so strong that it is impossible to refute them. If his spirit is so strong that he cannot be bowed down by the threats of misfortune that may befall him through the wrath of the Almighty, he shall be decried as vainglorious. Then why should we waste our time in such discussions? This question has come before the people for the first time, hence the necessity and usefulness of such long discussions.

As far as the first question is concerned, I think I have made it clear that I did not turn atheist because of vanity. Only my readers, not I, can decide whether my arguments carry weight. If I were a believer, I know in the present circumstances my life would have been easier; the burden lighter. My disbelief in God has turned all the circumstances too harsh and this situation can deteriorate further. Being somewhat mystical can give the circumstances a poetic turn. But I need no opiate to meet my end. I am a realistic man. I want to overpower this tendency in me with the help of Reason. I am not always successful in such attempts. But it is man's duty to try and make efforts. Success depends on chance and circumstances.

Now we come to the second question: if it is not vanity, there ought to be some sound reason for rejection of age-old belief in God. Yes, I come to this question. I think that any man who has some reasoning power always tries to understand the life and people around him with the help of this faculty. Where concrete proofs are lacking, [mystical] philosophy creeps in. As I have indicated, one of my revolutionary friends used to say that "philosophy is the outcome of human weakness." Our ancestors had the leisure to solve the mysteries of the world, its past, its present and its future, its whys and its wherefores, but having been terribly short of direct proofs, every one of them tried to solve the problem in his own way. Hence we find wide differences in the fundamentals of various religious creeds. Sometimes they take very antagonistic and conflicting forms. We find differences in Oriental and Occidental philosophies. There are differences even amongst various schools of thoughts in each hemisphere. In Asian religions, Islam is completely incompatible with the Hindu faith. In India itself, Buddhism and Jainism are sometimes quite separate from Brahmanism. Then in Brahmanism itself, we find two conflicting sects: Arya Samaj and Sanatan Dharam. Charwak is yet another independent thinker of the past ages. He challenged the Authority of God. All these faiths differ on many fundamental questions, but each of them claims to be the only true religion. This is the root of the evil. Instead of developing the ideas and experiments of ancient savants and thinkers as a basis for our future struggle against ignorance and to try to find a solution to this mysterious problem, we, lethargic as we have proved to be, raise a hue and cry of faith—unflinching and unwavering faith versions—and thus are guilty of stagnation in human progress.

It is necessary for every person, who stands for progresss, to criticise, disbelieve and challenge every tenet of old beliefs. Item by item, he has to reason out every nook and corner of the prevailing faith. He has to analyse and understand all the details. If after rigorous reasoning, one is led to believe in any theory or philosophy, his faith is appreciated. His reasoning may be mistaken and even fallacious. But there is a chance that he will be corrected because Reason is the guiding principle of his life. But belief, I should say, blind belief is disastrous. It deprives a man of his understanding power and makes him reactionary.

Any person who claims to be a realist has to challenge the truth of old beliefs. If faith cannot withstand the onslaught of reason, it collapses. After that his task should be to do the groundwork for new philosophy. This is the negative side. After that comes in the positive work in which some material of the olden times can be used to construct the pillars of new philosophy. As far as I am concerned, I admit that I lack sufficient study in this field. I had a great desire to study Oriental philosophy, but I could not get an ample opportunity or sufficient time to do so. But so far as I reject the old time beliefs, it is not a matter of countering belief with belief, rarher I can challenge the efficacy of old beliefs with sound arguments. We believe in nature and that human progress depends on the domination of man over nature. There is no conscious power behind it. This is our philosophy.

Being an atheist, I ask theists a few questions:

1. If, as you believe there is an Almighty, Omnipresent, Omniscient God, who created the earth or universe, please let me know, first of all, as to why he created this world? This world which

is full of woe and grief, and countless miseries, where not even one person lives in peace.

2. Pray, don't say it is His law. If He is bound by any law, He is not Omnipotent. Don't say it is His pleasure. Nero burnt one Rome. He killed a limited number of people. He caused only a few tragedies, all, for his morbid enjoyment. But what is his place in history? By what names do we remember him? All the disparaging epithets are hurled at him. Pages are blackened with invective diatribes condemning Nero: the tyrant, the heartless, the wicked. One Genghis Khan killed a few thousand people to seek pleasure in it and we hate the very name. Now, how will you justify your all powerful, eternal Nero, who every day, every moment continues his pastime of killing people?

How can you support his doings which surpass those of Genghis Khan in cruelty and in misery inflicted upon people? I ask why the Almighty created this world which is nothing but a living hell, a place of constant and bitter unrest. Why did he create man when he had the power not to do so? Have you any answer to these questions? You will say that it is to reward the sufferer and punish the evildoer in the hereafter. Well, how far will you justify a man who first of all inflicts injuries on your body and then applies soft and soothing ointment on them? How far were the supporters and organisers of Gladiator bouts justified in throwing men before half-starved lions, later to be cared for and looked after well if they escaped this horrible death? That is why I ask: Why did the Conscious Supreme Being create this world and man in it? Was the creation of man intended to derive this kind of pleasure? Where then is the difference between Him and Nero?

Open your eyes and see millions of people dying of hunger in slums and huts dirtier than the grim dungeons of prisons; just see the labourers patiently or say apathetically while the rich vampires suck their blood; bring to mind the wastage of human energy that will make a man with a little common sense shiver in horror. Just observe rich nations throwing their surplus produce into the sea instead of distributing it among the needy and deprived. There are palaces of kings built upon the foundations laid with human bones. Let them see all this and say "All is well in God's Kingdom." Why so? This is my question. You are silent. All right. I proceed to my next point.

You, the Hindus, would say: Whoever undergoes sufferings in this life, must have been a sinner in his previous birth. It is tantamount to saying that those who are oppressors now were godly people then, in their previous births. For this reason alone they hold power in their hands. Let me say it plainly that your ancestors were shrewd people. They were always in search of petty hoaxes to play upon people and snatch from them the power of Reason. Let us analyse how much this argument carries weight.

Those who are well versed in the philosophy of jurisprudence relate three or four justifications for the punishment that is to be inflicted upon a wrong-doer. These are: revenge, reform, and deterrence. The Retribution Theory is now condemned by all the thinkers. The deterrent theory is on the anvil for its flaws. The Reformative theory is now widely accepted and considered to be necessary for human progress. It aims at reforming the culprit and converting him into a peace-loving citizen.

But what in essence is God's Punishment even if it is inflicted on a person who has really done some harm? For the sake of argument we agree for a moment that a person committed some crime in his previous birth and God punished him by changing his shape into a cow, cat, tree, or any other animal. You may enumerate the number of these variations in Godly Punishment to be at least eighty-four lakhs. Tell me, has this tomfoolery, perpetrated in the name of punishment, any reformative effect on human man? How many of them have you met who were donkeys in their previous births for having committed any sin?

Absolutely no one of this sort! The so-called theory of *Puranas* (transmigration) is nothing but a fairy-tale. I do not have any intention to bring this unutterable trash under discussion. Do you really know the most cursed sin in this world is to be poor? Yes, poverty is a sin; it is a punishment! Cursed be the theoretician, jurist or legislator who proposes such measures as push man into the quagmire of more heinous sins. Did it not occur to your All Knowing God or he could learn the truth only after millions had undergone untold sufferings and hardships?

What, according to your theory, is the fate of a person who, by no sin of his own, has been born into a family of low caste people? He is poor so he cannot go to a school. It is his fate to be shunned and hated by those who are born into a high caste. His ignorance, his poverty, and the contempt he receives from others will harden his heart towards society. Supposing that he commits a sin, who will bear the consequences? God, or he, or the learned people of that society?

What is your view about those punishments inflicted on the people who were deliberately kept ignorant by selfish and proud Brahmins? If, by chance these poor creatures heard a few words of your sacred books, Vedas, these Brahmins poured melted lead into their ears. If they committed any sin, who was to be held responsible? Who was to bear the brunt?

My dear friends, these theories have been coined by the privileged classes. They try to justify the power they have usurped and the riches they have robbed with the help of such theories. Perhaps it was the writer Upton Sinclair who wrote somewhere "only make a man firm believer in the immortality of soul, then rob him of all that he possesses. He will willingly help you in the process." The dirty alliance between religious preachers and possessors of power brought the boon of prisons, gallows, knots and above all such theories for mankind.

I ask why your Omnipotent God does not hold a man back when he is about to commit a sin or offence. It is child's play for God. Why did He not kill war lords? Why did He not obliterate the fury of war from their minds? In this way He could have saved humanity of many great calamities and horrors. Why does He not infuse humanistic sentiments into the minds of the British so that they may willingly leave India? I ask why He does not fill the hearts of all capitalist classes with altruistic humanism that prompts them to give up personal possession of the means of production and this will free the whole labouring humanity from the shackles of misery. You want to argue the practicability of Socialist theory, I leave it to your Almighty God to enforce it.

Common people understand the merits of Socialist theory as far as general welfare is concerned but they oppose it under the pretext that it cannot be implemented. Let the Almighty step in and arrange things in a proper way. No more logic chopping! I tell you that the British rule is not there because God willed it but for the reason that we lack the will and courage to oppose it. Not that they are keeping us under subjugation with the consent of God, but it is with the force of guns and rifles, bombs and bullets, police and militia, and above all, because of our apathy that they are successfully committing the most deplorable sin, that is, the exploitation of one nation by another. Where is God? What is He doing? Is He getting a sadistic pleasure out of it? A Nero! A Genghis Khan! Down with Him!

Now another piece of manufactured logic! You ask me how I will explain the origin of this world and origin of man. Charles Darwin has tried to throw some light on this subject. Study his book. Also, have a look at Sohan Swami's *Commonsense*. You will get a satisfactory answer. This topic is concerned with Biology and Natural History which is a phenomenon of nature. The accidental mixture of different substances in the form of Nebulae gave birth to this earth. When? Study history to know this.

The same process caused the evolution of animals and in the long run that of man. Read Darwin's *Origin of Species.* All the later progress is due to man's constant conflict with nature and his efforts to use nature for his own benefit. This is the briefest sketch of this phenomenon. Your next question will be why a child is born blind or lame even if he was not a sinner in his previous birth. This problem has been explained in a satisfactory manner by biologists as a mere biological phenomenon. According to them the whole burden rests upon the shoulders of parents whose conscious or unconscious deeds caused the mutilation of the child prior to his birth.

You may thrust yet another question at me, though it is merely childish. The question is: If God does not really exist, why do people come to believe in Him? Brief and concise my answer will be. As they come to believe in ghosts, and evil spirits, so they also evolve a kind of belief in God: the only difference being that God is almost a universal phenomenon and well developed theological philosophy. However, I do disagree with radical philosophy.

It attributes His origin to the ingenuity of exploiters who wanted to keep the people under their subjugation by preaching the existence of a Supreme Being; thus claimed an authority and sanction from Him for their privileged position. I, however, do not differ on the essential point that all religions, faiths, theological philosophies, and religious creeds and all other such institutions in the long run become supporters of the tyrannical and exploiting institutions, men and classes. Rebellion against any king has always been a sin in every religion.

Regarding the origin of God, my thought is that man created God in his imagination when he realised his weaknesses, limitations and shortcomings. In this way he had the courage to face all the trying circumstances and to meet all dangers that might occur in his life and also to restrain his outbursts in prosperity and affluence. God, with his whimsical laws and parental generosity was painted with variegated colours of imagination. He was used as a deterrent factor when his fury and laws were repeatedly propagated so that man might not become a danger to society. He was the cry of the distressed soul for he was believed to stand as father and mother, sister and brother, brother and friend when in times of distress a man was left alone and helpless. He was Almighty and could do anything. The idea of God is helpful to a man in distress.

Society must fight against this belief in God as it fought against idol worship and other narrow conceptions of religion. In this way man will try to stand on his feet. Being realistic, he will have to cast his faith aside and face all adversaries with courage and valour. That is exactly my state of mind. My friends, it is not my vanity; it is my mode of thinking that has made me an atheist. I don't think that by strengthening my belief in God and by offering prayers to Him every day (this I consider to be the most degraded act on the part of man), neither these prayer can bring improvement in my situation, nor can they further deteriorate it. I have read of many atheists facing all troubles boldly, so I am trying to stand like a man with my head high and erect to the last; even on the gallows.

Let us see how steadfast I am. One of my friends asked me to pray. When informed of my atheism, he said, "When your last days come, you will begin to believe." I said, "No, dear sir, never will it happen. I consider it to be an act of degradation and demoralisation. For such petty selfish motives, I shall never pray." Reader and friends, is it vanity? If it is, I stand for it.

[Here a short note on ancient Indian philosophy on Atheism called 'Lokayata'/'Charvaka', is being given. Of course, it was not a part of Bhagat Singh's pamphlet titled, 'Why I Am An Atheist?'

Lokayata/Charvaka: Indian Materialism

In its most generic sense, "Indian Materialism" refers to the school of thought within Indian philosophy that rejects supernaturalism. It is regarded as the most radical of the Indian philosophical systems. It rejects the existence of other worldly entities such an immaterial soul or god and the after-life. Its primary philosophical import comes by way of a scientific and naturalistic approach to metaphysics. Thus, it rejects ethical systems that are grounded in supernaturalistic cosmologies. The good, for the Indian materialist, is strictly associated with pleasure and the only ethical obligation forwarded by the system is the maximisation of one's own pleasure.

The terms Lokayata and Charvaka have historically been used to denote the philosophical school of Indian Materialism. Literally, "Lokayata" means philosophy of the people. The term was first used by the ancient Buddhists until around 500 BCE to refer to both a common tribal philosophical view and a sort of this-worldly philosophy or nature lore. The term has evolved to signify a school of thought that has been scorned by religious leaders in India and remains on the periphery of Indian philosophical thought. After 500 BCE, the term acquired a more derogatory connotation and became synonymous with sophistry.

It was not until between the 6th and 8th centuries that the term "Lokayata" began to signify Materialist thought. Indian Materialism has also been named Charvaka after one of the two founders of the school. Charvaka and Ajita Kesakambalin are said to have established Indian Materialism as a formal philosophical system, but some still hold that Brahaspati was its original founder. Brahaspati allegedly authored the classic work on Indian Materialism, the Brahaspati Sutra. There are some conflicting accounts of Brahaspati's life, but, at the least, he is regarded as the mythical authority on Indian Materialism and at most the actual author of the since-perished Brahaspati Sutra. Indian Materialism has for this reason also been named "Brahaspatya."]

39

Musings of an Author

Grabbing a Slice of the Popularity of Bhagat Singh

Every year on March 23, the Publicity Wing of the government, used to take a Press Party to Hussainiwala, where on the banks of river Satluj the bodies of three martyrs—Bhagat Singh, Sukhdev and Rajguru, had been secretly cremated at the dead of night on March 23, 1931 by the British Government and where a memorial of them had been built. Some VIP, usually the Chief Minister, would pay his floral tributes and thereafter address a public meeting. The purpose of the whole exercise used to be to grab a slice of the immense popularity, the three noble sons of India enjoyed amongst the people thoughout the country.

The Press Party used to be headed by the head of the Department and the junior officers used to look after the convenience and comforts of the pressmen. Amongst the numerous senior Civil Service officers who came to serve the Department as its head, there were two who in a relaxed mood after office hours on a few occasions reposed their trust in one of his junior officers by sharing their innermost thoughts on the various socio-political issues facing the country. Their views used to be often contrary to what they articulated during the office hours. A quote from one of them was something like, "had I not been selected in the IAS, I would have joined Bhagat Singh's Party." As the junior officer could not comprehend what he meant, he would continue talking about Bhagat Singh and Che Guevera, stating such revolutionaries are no more alive, yet they are born in every generation. They keep fighting against oppression and injustice and are never afraid of laying down their lives and such talk would continue.

The other officer who had retired from a senior publicity job in the Government of India whom the same junior officer used to see in connection with his professional duties at New Delhi, would also sometimes talk similarly. He, even when in a meeting of the officials of his office, would welcome and make him sit on a chair along with himself while the meetings went on.

These noble officers are now up and above on the sky and would not be able to see this piece.

A Follower of Bhagat Singh

It was 5.30 pm. My wife and I had returned from their respective offices when a good looking well educated young man appeared at our doors and requested if he could share a cup of tea with us. We were in a relaxed mood and so welcomed him. My noble and grand old mother as usual brought three cups and he—the young man started talking on various socio-political issues facing the country. The talk went on and he, amazingly, a treasure of knowledge on Marxism-Leninism and Maoism that too from rural Punjab astonished us. We were so impressed that the talk continued till it was dinner time. We asked him to keep on and have dinner with us. Again, my noble mother having already prepared the dinner for all of us brought the same to the table. It was 11 pm and neither would he stop talking nor did we stop listening to him. At about 12 at night, he asked us if he could spend the night and how at that awkward time could we refuse. The next morning, after taking a cup of tea, he left us. While leaving he said he was Shaheed-e-Azam Bhagat Singh's follower who was his idol and like him he too would die young. And sadly after a few days we learnt he had died.

B.K. Dutt Was Treated Poorly in Independent India

Once in 1960, I saw B.K. Dutt, the revolutionary colleague of Bhagat Singh, sitting in one of the offices of a Government Department in the Secretariat. It was a pleasant surprise but also shocking. He was in a dejected and unhappy mood. It was learnt he had come to see the state's Chief Minister who was once upon a time, it was said, was his colleague in the now famous Naujawan Bharat Sabha. I did not expect him in such a state. I visualised him being accorded a VIP. treatment as a state guest lodged in Raj Bhawan and even being honoured at a grand public reception.

True and Fake Left Parties

"We Are Diplomats"

There was a women's conference at New Delhi affiliated to a Left Party. I just happened to see and talk to a well-educated senior woman leader at the venue. I, while talking asked her which, in her opinion, is the true left party from amongst a dozen operating in the country, each claiming to be the *'Asli'* [true] while debunking the others as *'Naqali'* [fake]; she replied. "It was Bhagat Singh's Party active in a new form and others were *'Naqali'* [fake]". I pointed out to her speech a short while ago claiming her Party the true great left party. "That was diplomacy", she replied. "There were many other comrades as well who share her views but would not say so as all of them are diplomats."

Plight of a Whistle-Blower

"You are my eyes and ears", declared the Chief Minister. He was addressing nearly 100 rural publicity workers of his State. "There will be now zero tolerance of corruption." "Anyone indulging in corrupt practices would be severely dealt with," the Chief continued. He asked the workers "to just drop a ten paisa postcard to his office about anyone found to be corrupt." The workers were former freedom fighters paid an honorarium of Rs. 100 every month. Their job was to publicise the government's policies and achievements and shower praises of the Chief Minister.

Those were early days of independence. At the next monthly meeting of the publicity workers of the district, a worker came forward with a letter addressed to the Chief Minister reporting against a police official harassing the poor peasants and demanding a bribe. He requested his officer to forward the same to the Chief Minister's office. The officer told him, "not to do so as that was not exactly their job and moreever it may be taken as a deficiency in their publicity work". The police officials should now be considered as the police of 'Azad Bharat' and not of the British Raj' as they used to be, the officer advised the publicity worker. "we are the Chief Minister's eyes and ears", replied the publicity worker and persisted in his resolve to forward his letter to the Chief Minister which the officer reluctantly did. After a month at the next district workers' meeting, he seemed to be in a dejected mood while talking to his officer saying that his letter had been received by the same corrupt police official for his comments, thereby, getting him exposed.

The Corrupt Will be Hanged From the First Lamp Post of the Town

During the pre-Independence years in the 1940s, Pt. Jawaharlal Nehru often visited Lahore where he would address public meetings. He would declare, "The corrupt would be hanged from the first lamp-post of the town after India gained independence and there used to be thunderous applause from the public. After independence, corruption continued to develop and flourish but one never again heard of "The corrupt would be hanged from the first lamp post" from Pt. Nehru and other leaders.

A Feudal Landlord Calls Himself 'A *Mazdoor*' (Labourer)

Nawab Iftikhar Hussain Khan of Mamdot, one of the biggest feudal landloards of the country used to be the President of the Punjab Province Muslim League. During the elections held in 1946, while addressing public meetings, he would begin his speech saying, "*Mein Bhi Mazdoor Hoon.*" [I am also a worker] People would laugh at him. But without bothering what people thought of him, at the next meetings again he would start his speech saying, "*Mein Bhi Mazdoor Hoon.*" And he became the first Chief Minister of the West Punjab Province after the Partition in 1947.

Revolution is Marching Ahead

Every year on the opening day of the Parliament Session in New

Delhi, a huge protest demonstration jointly sponsored by all the Left parties used to be held near the Parliament Complex. Once in the evening, I, while going towards the railway station after the demonstration, met two comrades, each holding a flag aloft. I asked them about the demonstration? "Highly successful" was their response. My next question was, "how far has the revolution been advanced?" They paused and looked sideways on the right and the left and whispered in my ears, "that is being done by Bhagat Singh and their revolutionary colleagues in Chhattisgarh." On being further asked, "why they were looking sideways and whispered, they replied, "sir, the walls have also ears."

To Foreign Investors: "We Love You, Sir"

A newspaper headline, 'Minimum Alternative Tax to be waived for foreign institutional investors', allowing foreign direct investment in various sectors of the economy. The Prime Minister and other ministers were visiting foreign countries with offers of lucrative sops and tax concessions to invest in India.

One was reminded of Nawab Siraj-ul-Daula of Bengal. He had refused to grant trading concessions to the officers of the British East India Company. The result was he not only lost his Kingdom but also his head in 1757. Had the Nawab gone to Lord Hastings with folded hands saying, "I love you Sir." The people of Bengal love you sir, "he would have saved not only his Kingdom but his life as well. And some ones of his descendants might be holding not only the title of "Nawab" but also occupying ministerial posts in Dacca, Kolkata, Islamabad and New Delhi.

Descendants of Bahadur Shah Zafar Have Claim Over the Red Fort

The descendants of all the Maharajas and Nawabs who had played a treacherous role by supporting the British with massive military and financial aid besides providing thousands of soldiers to fight against the freedom fighters during the country's First War of Independence in 1857, were now being allowed to own huge properties worth thousands of crores of rupees in New Delhi and elsewhere. The descendants of Bahadur Shah Zafar, the last Emperor of India who, like a true patriot, had led the war of independence against the British, on the other hand, were languishing in poverty selling tea on the roadsides somewhere in West Bengal or are working as peons in the offices of some corporates. Should they not be allowed to own the Red Fort in Delhi as the rightful owners in our and their independent India? The British used to reward the treacherous Maharajas and Nawabs (Kings) lavishly. Shouldn't independent India reward the patriots and their descendants such as those of Bahadur Shah Zafar and stop not only rewarding the descendants of the treacherous kings of former Indian states, but confiscate whatever had been rewarded in the past?

How Syed Sajjad Zaheer, General Secretary, Pakistan Communist Party Was Saved in the Rawalpindi Conspiracy Case

After the formation of Pakistan, Syed Sajjad Zaheer, an eminent writer and a prominent communist leader of UP was sent to Pakistan appointing him as the General Secretary of the Communist Party of Pakistan. Soon after his arrival there, he was arrested in the Rawalpindi Conspiracy Case, the consequence of which could have been either the life imprisonment or even the gallows. His brother Syed Ali Zaheer was a Minister in Pt. Jawaharlal Nehru's first Cabinet after the Partition in 1947. He requested Pt. Nehru to help his brother. Pt Nehru phoned Mr. Liaquat Ali Khan who was the Prime Minister of Pakistan. The result was Syed Ali Zaheer was not only released from prison but also returned as India's citizen.

An Opportunistic and Anti-Marxist Policy Decision of the Communists

In 1946, Mian Iftikharuddin, an eminent progressive and a highly respected Muslim politician was the President of the Punjab Provincial Congress Committee. He was also a close friend of Pt. Jawaharlal Nehru from his student days in England and Pt. Nehru would often stay with him while on a visit to Lahore. According to a policy decision of the Communist Party, Muslim communists were directed to join the Muslim League, obviously, with a view to transform the League into a progressive and a pro-Communist Party. Mian Iftikharuddin a pro-Communist Congressman, too decided to join the Muslim League but gave no hint of this.

One fine morning, suddenly and stunning the people and especially the Congress leadership, Mian Sahib was found to be sitting in the office of the Muslim League occupying the chair of its Provincial President. On the previous day, he was sitting on the chair of the President of the Provincial Congress Committee in the Bradlaugh Hall, Lahore. 'The Muslim League's influence in Punjab was negligible as the Unionist Party dominated by the Muslim, Hindu and Sikh landlords was very powerful and its President had always been the Chief Minister of the Province. With the defection of Mian Iftikharuddin to the Muslim League, its influence in the province spread like wild fire and the streets of Lahore were, like a tidal wave, filled with thousands of Muslim processionists chanting slogans such as '*Pakistan Le Ke Rahenge*' in support of the Muslim League.

A Hindi-Lover and '*Pracharak*' (Preacher) Minister

Dr. K.L. Shrimali was the Education Minister in one of Pt. Jawaharlal Nehru's Cabinets. He was a great lover of Hindi. At every public and official meeting whatever the occasion and wherever the venue, he would start talking about Hindi, exhorting all those present to think in Hindi, speak in Hindi and write in Hindi. He would get the circulars issued directing the officials to do their file work in Hindi.

One fine morning people were astounded when they read a box news on the front page in *The Tribune* stating that Dr. K.L. Shrimali had written a letter requesting the Principal of Sanawar Public School. Sanawar in Himachal Pradesh [an English medium school] to reserve a seat in the school for his grandson. The Principal had proudly related it in the annual report of his school.

A Declamation Contest

The Second World War was going on. All the essential articles of daily use were in short supply and the same could be only available either through a ration card at officially fixed rates or at the excessive rates in the black market. The word rationing was on the lips of everybody—rich and poor. The year was 1945. I was a college student at Lahore. There was a Declamation Contest in the college. The topic was; 'Liberty is precious, so precious that it should be rationed'. I decided to take part in the contest. The question before me was which side I should take. Whether I should speak in support of the subject matter or oppose it. I thought of consulting my tutor, Professor Tara Chand Gupta.

Professor Tara Chand Gupta was a highly educated person with a fairly good knowledge and command of the philosophy of Marxism-Leninism. He was not part of any job as it was not easy to get one. I had engaged him as my private tutor to teach me English for an hour after my college hours in my hostel. I paid him a sum of Rs. 30 considered to be a princely amount in those days. With a sum of Rs. 30, one was able to meet one's daily expenses for a month. I may here mention as well that Professor Tara Chand Gupta, after independence, taught the subjects of Journalism and Mass Communication at the Panjab University, Chandigarh as well as at the University at Rohtak. Some of his students are well known journalists and columnists such as Nirupama Dutt and some have also qualified in the Civil Services such as Somesh Goyal, the present Director General of Police of Himachal Pradesh, who has won many Medals for his distinguished services including the President's Police Medal. Professor Gupta also served *The Tribune* for some time as a senior journalist.

My Professor's advice was that the precious 'liberty' should be rationed in the case of the ruling British administrators—the 'toadies' but in the case of freedom-fighters, it should not be rationed and there should be no restriction for them to exercise the right of freedom of speech and liberty in expressing their views and thoughts.

I took part in the Declamation Contest taking the stand advised by Professor Tara Chand Gupta, my tutor and I stood first in the contest.

A Page of My Days at Lahore

During my college days at Lahore in the early 1940s, I used to take an interest in the students' politics and there was a students' organisation, namely, 'The Students Federation of India'. Its Lahore branch used to hold meetings which were primarily attended by the university and college students. The students were from all over Punjab which at the time meant the present day of West Punjab (Pakistan), which even at that time extended upto about Peshawar though Peshawar was the capital of a separate province called 'Northern Western Frontier Province' and many students used to come to study in Lahore from that province. The province of then Punjab included not only the area what is called West Punjab, now part of Pakistan, the present Punjab of India, Haryana and Himachal Pradesh and of course many princely states. At the meetings there used to be very lengthy and impressive speeches. A postgraduate student, namely, Balraj Mehta used to be its all powerful and learned General Secretary. His knowledgeable speeches would cast a spell on the students. There used to be slogans which included 'Inquilab Zindabad (Long Live the Revolution)' and 'Imperialism Murdabad (Down With Imperialism)'. There, however, used to be another type of slogan, whenever the CID people or policemen were seen near the gathering. The shout used to be "Toady Bacha Hai Hai" (Death to the Toadies). In political writings the Indian officers serving the British rulers in the government used to be called *'Macaulay Puttar'* (Children of Macaulay). These were phrases of denigration and vilification. Macaulay had strongly recommended to the then British government in India to introduce and teach the English language in India and also science as a subject in the educational institutions of the country. He was considered an Englishman of the imperialist category who served the British imperialist interests and was, therefore, hated and so were hated the Indian officers in the British Government both in the Police and in the Civil departments.

Till a few days back I knew of Macaulay whose actions in India were harmful to India's interests but the article, 'The Macaulay We Don't Know' written by Bibek Debroy and published in *The Indian Express* of December 9, 2017 had changed my views of him. It contains a few of his quotations and so something original and reliable about him. I now have a far better opinion about him and I feel he had done something good for the Indians.

Every day I happen to learn something or the other of life and this episode about Macaulay is just one example. The conclusion is that it is not advisable to form an opinion favaourable or unfavourable about anybody—big or small till we read about him or know about him from some first-hand reliable account. In this case the first-hand account was, his quotes in the article. The media, especially, the print media which is widely read by the people is owned by the corporates owning millions and billions of dollars and so able to afford run widely circulated newspapers and magazines which play a very important role in the formation of views and opinions of the people in general. These corporate-owned media tends to slant and form news and views expressed in the media which serve the interests of the corporate world. In ordinary language, they are also called the upper-dogs while 90 per cent of the population belong to the category of under-dogs or the hoi polloi. Such media is not worthy of reposing blind trust, especially in case of issues which affect the lives of ordinary people. One needs to look into something original.

"People's War Char Anna", "People's War Char Anna"

During the 1940s, the Second World War was going on. It started when Nazi Germany led by Adolf Hitler, attacked the countries of Western Europe including Great Britain, in 1939. It was a war by Germany leading the Axis Powers including Italy, Japan, etc. for the annexation of the colonies in the continents of Africa, Asia, etc. then in the possession of countries calling themselves Allied Powers led by Great Britain. It was thus a clash between the two Imperialist Power Blocs. The countries called the Axis Powers practised 'Fascism' as their ideology while England, France, Holland, Belgium supported by the United States of America, called the Allied Powers, claimed to practising Democracy though this was, in fact, a Bourgeois Democracy [Democracy by the capitalists, of the capitalists and for the capitalists]. It was, thus, a clash between the two Imperialist Power Blocs.

Later on, when Hitler attacked the Soviet Union in 1941, it turned into a war between Imperialism and Fascism on the one side and Scientific Socialism on the other side. The armed forces of Nazi Germany had made swift advances capturing large territories of the then Soviet Union and not before long were knocking at the doors of Leningrad, Moscow and Stalingrad. The Soviet people led by the great J.V. Stalin, were defending every inch of the sacred land of Scientific Socialism with all their might.

By 1945, the Patriotic War had reached the final stage. The German soldiers had entered Leningrad, Stalingrad and Moscow and were walking on the streets of these gallant cities, but only as war prisoners.

After the German attack on the Soviet Union in 1941, all the progressive, democratic and socialist-minded forces of the people of the world, had initiated a massive campaign in support of the Soviet Union. The Communist Party of India was leading the campaign in India. The name of its weekly journal, which was being published under the name, *New Age*, was changed to *People's War.*

I was a college student at Lahore and was one of the numerous students who used to sell *People's War*, the weekly publication of the Communist Party of India, sitting on the various corners of the roads of Lahore. Amongst those, selling the weekly along with me, calling the commuters "People's War Char Anna", "People's War Char Anna", used to be many sons and daughters of the senior officers of the British Indian Government.

"A Staunch Atheist"?

Shaheed-e-Azam Bhagat Singh was not a follower of any religion and did not believe in God. He was a staunch atheist and had written an impressive, persuasive and convincing pamphlet titled, 'Why I Am An Atheist'. I, being an admirer and follower of Bhagat Singh, also claimed to be a staunch atheist.

I was to undergo a serious surgery of my heart, called the 'triple bypass surgery' at the University Hospital of Philadelphia in the United States of America. I was on the operation table surrounded by my doctors and was about to be administered the General Anesthesia. My son, Shalley, was still holding the handles of my operation table. Addressing my doctors, I took the courage of telling them, "Sir, I do not believe in God". "I believe in Medical Science and in my medical doctors". My Cardiac Surgeon replied, "Sir, we believe in God, so that we perform our job well".

Navratras are observed and celebrated in India in the month of September every year when families prepare a variety of dishes—vegetables and sweets. Young girl children called 'Kanjkas' are invited, seating them on a mat on the floor of the kitchen. *Dongas* [plates] of all such dishes along with some cash are served to each of them, touching their feet with folded hands by the males of the house. Immediately after that two or three plate-like large *thaals*, full of vegetables and sweets as well as fruits and puris and some currency notes are taken to the nearby temple and presented to the priests bowing before them as well as before the stone and cloth idols of the many gods beautifully decorated in costly dresses embroidered with gold and silver threads. These delicious foods are, it is supposed, would be taken further by the Brahmin priests and served to the ancestors now residing in the heaven.

In our family, I used to practise all the rituals connected with the festival of 'Navratras', thus, paying my homage to my long departed parents, grandparents, forgetting my Atheism and thinking for a while, that the Brahmin priests would serve the delicious dishes to my ancestors.

40

A Valiant Spartacus

"The young man (Bhagat Singh) who was suspected to be the murderer of Saunders could have easily committed, had he wished, many such actions by remaining underground, beyond the reach of the authorities; and that could have caused a sort of terror in the hearts of the enemies of the country and given solace and strength to the sufferers at their hands. I don't know how far it was correct for such a young man to have got himself arrested for doing such a small job (throwing a bomb in the Assembly). But as far as I am concerned, I would not have been happy even seeing Bhagat Singh doing the former job, that is, leading a band of some 10 to 20 guerrillas and doing daring deeds (to frighten the rulers and encouraging his compatriots) for I have always visualised a different Bhagat Singh. He had infinite potential to be one who could, after receiving proper education in warfare, lead, at an appropriate moment, the armies for the liberation of India and be the arbiter to decide the fate of the battles fought for changing her history. That Bhagat Singh had capacity and capabilities to play such roles would not be known to those who are full of him only after seeing a small part played by him.

[Professor Jayachandra Vidyalankar in
Abhyudaya, May 8, 1931]